D1565213

CERTAIN SAINTHOOD

CERTAIN SAINTHOOD

CANONIZATION AND THE ORIGINS OF PAPAL INFALLIBILITY IN THE MEDIEVAL CHURCH

DONALD S. PRUDLO

CORNELL UNIVERSITY PRESS
Ithaca and London

First published 2015 by Cornell University Press

Printed in the United States of America

Library of Congress Cataloging-in-Publication Data

Prudlo, Donald, 1976– author.
   Certain sainthood : canonization and the origins of papal infallibility in the medieval church / Donald S. Prudlo.
        pages cm
   Includes bibliographical references and index.
   ISBN 978-0-8014-5403-5 (cloth : alk. paper)
   1. Canonization—History—To 1500.   2. Christian saints—Cult—History of doctrines—Middle Ages, 600–1500.   3. Popes—Infallibility—History of doctrines—Middle Ages, 600–1500.   4. Papacy—History—To 1309.   I. Title.
   BX2330.P78 2015
   235′.2409—dc23
                                                2015015955

Cornell University Press strives to use environmentally responsible suppliers and materials to the fullest extent possible in the publishing of its books. Such materials include vegetable-based, low-VOC inks and acid-free papers that are recycled, totally chlorine-free, or partly composed of nonwood fibers. For further information, visit our website at www.cornellpress.cornell.edu.

Cloth printing   10 9 8 7 6 5 4 3 2 1

❧ Contents

☙ Acknowledgments

      This project was long in germination and incurred many debts, ones that are a pleasure to recognize but are difficult to repay. I am grateful to my institution, Jacksonville State University, for its generous assistance and support in the composition of this work. I thank my long-suffering department chair, Gordon Harvey, for his indefatigable assistance and for graciously aiding me in a multitude of administrative ways. The sympathy of one's department head is a luxury in academia and one I do not take for granted. Once again I am indebted to Russel Lemmons for his friendship and collegiality and for his infinite patience in reading nearly everything I have written and commenting with perspicacity and the grammatical laser vision of a nineteenth-century German philologist (though of course any errors that remain are entirely my own).

Historians cannot do their work without the significant cooperation of those who are the keepers of the resources. My university's interlibrary loan service, particularly Debra Deering-Barrett, has been invaluable in acquiring rare and little-known sources, and for this I am quite thankful. I am also heavily indebted to various European archives and libraries, whose almost invariable kindness to a hapless foreigner continues to be much appreciated. In this regard I wish to mention the Biblioteca Apostolica Vaticana, the Biblioteca Nazionale Centrale Firenze, and the Bayerische Staatsbibliothek, as well as the libraries of the Graduate Theological Union at Berkeley and the University of Virginia and the marvelous jewel of a library at Christendom College. I also thank Liberty Fund, where as a postdoc I was able to plant the seeds of this project. Thanks are also due to the patience and dedication of Peter Potter at Cornell Press, who helped to shepherd this project to completion. I am also in debt to my careful anonymous readers, and to the production team at Cornell.

It would also be not out of place to thank my saints. One of the pleasures of hagiography is to work closely with those whom you are writing about, being able to see where they lived, worked, and died and to gauge their effects on the societies in which they lived, even long after their passing.

Dominic, Francis, Thomas Becket, Thomas Aquinas, Peter of Verona, Anthony of Padua, Clare, Elizabeth, and a host of others have been my constant companions in this journey, and I am grateful for their example and their activities.

To my long-suffering family, whom I repeatedly carted all over Europe, through musty churches and crypts with the only reward being pizza or gelato, I cannot say thank you enough. An academic spouse who appreciates the importance of a work that she has heard again and again is the greatest treasure that one can have. My wife, Therese, is thankfully also a medieval aficionado and a dauntless traveler, taking our children in and out of airports, hotels, apartments, and train stations. It is quite an adventure, and I would spend it with no one else.

This work itself is dedicated to my *Doktorvater*, Augustine Thompson, O.P. Fr. Augustine was my mentor at the University of Virginia, and his attention to detail, his care for the "ordinary" people of the medieval ages, his erudition, and his humor have been my constant inspirations. I have never met anyone who can incarnate "doctor" and "father" in the manner in which he does. I am immensely privileged to have studied with him, and my only hope is that this work may add some modest contribution to his well-deserved reputation.

✒ ABBREVIATIONS

AB	*Analecta Bollandiana*
AFP	*Archivum Fratrum Praedicatorum*
ALK	*Archiv für Literatur- und Kirchengeschichte des Mittelalters*
AS	*Acta Sanctorum quotquot Toto Orbe Coluntur vel a Catholicis Scriptoribus Celebrantur ex Latinis et Graecis Aliarumque Gentium Antiquis Monumentis Collecta, Digesta, Illustrata*, 2nd ed., ed. Godefridus Henschenius et al., 60 vols. in 70 (Paris: Palme, etc., 1867–1940)
BHL	Bibliotheca Hagiographica Latina (Brussels, 1898) and Bibliotheca Hagiographica Latina Novum Supplementum (Brussels, 1986)
BOP	*Bullarium Ordinis Fratrum Praedicatorum*, ed. Thomas Ripoll, 7 vols. (Rome: Ex Typographia Hieronymi Mainardi, 1759)
Döllinger	Ignaz von Döllinger, ed., *Beiträge zur Sektengeschichte des Mittelalters*, 2 vols. (1890; repr. New York: B. Franklin, 1970)
Fontanini	*Codex constitutionum quas summi pontifices ediderunt in solemni canonizatione sanctorum a Johanne XV. ad Benedictum XIII sive ab A.D. 993. ad A.D. 1729*, ed. Giusto Fontanini (Rome: Ex typographia Rev. Camerae Apostolicae, 1729)
HHMA	*Heresies of the High Middle Ages*, ed. Walter L. Wakefield and Austin P. Evans (1969; New York: Columbia University Press, 1991)
LA	Jacobus de Voragine, *The Golden Legend*, trans. Granger Ryan and Helmut Ripperger (New York: Arno, 1969)
Lambertini	Benedict XIV, "De Servorum Dei Beatificatione et Beatorum Canonizationis," in *Opera Omnia*, 7 vols. (Prati: Alberghetus, in Typographia Aldina, 1839–47)
Limborch	Philippus Limborch, *Historia inquisitionis cui subjungitur Liber sententiarum inquisitionis tholosanae* (Amsterdam: Henricus Wetstenius, 1692)

MGH   Monumenta Germaniae Historica
MOPH   Monumenta Ordinis Praedicatorum Historica
PL   Patrologia Latina
Potthast   *Regesta Pontificum Romanorum inde ab a. post Christum Natum MCXCVIII ad a. MCCCIV.* ed. Augustus Potthast (Berlin, 1875)
RLS   Johann Baptist Schneyer, *Repertorium der Lateinischen Sermones des Mittelalters*, 13 vols. (Munster-Westfalen: Aschendorffsche, 1969–90)
SOP   Thomas Kaeppeli, O.P., *Scriptores Ordinis Praedicatorum Medii Aevi*, 4 vols. (Rome, 1970)
VF   Gérard de Frachet, *Vitae Fratrum Ordinis Praedicatorum*, ed. Benedict Maria Reichert, O.P., Monumenta Ordinis Fratrum Praedicatorum Historica 1 (Leuven, 1896)
VSP   *Vita S[ancti]Petri Martyris Ordinis Praedicatorum*, ed. Ambrogio Taegio, O.P., Acta Sanctorum 12 (April 3), 686–719

Introduction

On July 31, 2002, Pope John Paul II solemnly canonized Juan Diego Cuauhtlatoatzin, the seer of Guadalupe. Before the ceremony, doubts arose as to whether Juan Diego actually existed—a sure barrier to canonization if ever there was one. In spite of some scholarly criticism, the ceremony went on, and the pope inserted Juan Diego into the catalogue of the saints. This act would not have stirred historians and theologians so much were it not for an old debate on the nature of papal infallibility. Over the course of centuries it has come to be the common theological opinion that the pope is infallible when solemnly canonizing saints. It became such a common teaching that few thinkers of stature denied the infallibility of the pope in these matters after the fourteenth century.[1] Indeed, no one had challenged this consensus for hundreds of years. Present theological discussion of canonization has become bound up with the definition of papal infallibility made at Vatican I in 1870. The responsible

---

1. The best theological work on infallibility in canonization identifies only four thinkers in this vein: Franciscus Veronius, S.J. (1578–1649) was concerned that canonization could not be the object of an infallible definition; Vincentius Baronius, O.P. (1604–74) agreed with Veronius; Natalis Alexander, O.P. (1639–1724) and Ludovico Muratori (1672–1750) opposed the doctrine on historical grounds. After these no Catholic thinker of stature until the Second Vatican Council admitted that the pope can err in solemn canonization. Schenk, *Die Unfehlbarkeit des Papstes*, 59–63. Since then some theologians have questioned ecclesial infallibility broadly considered (canonization is rarely mentioned), a debate beyond the subject of this book.

historian needs to avoid the polemics associated with this near-contemporary development and situate its evolution in context. The seemingly inexhaustible supply of candidates so honored by John Paul II and the rapidity of advancement advocated by Pope Francis for some recent figures have also stimulated current arguments. However, one must turn to the Middle Ages to trace the origins of this theological and historical debate both in order to better understand Christian sainthood and to have a more informed view of contemporary discussions on the subject. It is the development of the role of the pope in canonizing saints and its relation to infallibility that are the subject of the present work.

At the outset of any project, the definition of terms is critical. The doctrine of infallibility has a long pedigree in the Christian church but has left a particular legacy on the Roman Catholic communion. Infallibility means the inability to err particularly in the areas of faith and morals and can be applied to any one of several concepts in the tradition. Nearly all Christians ascribe levels of infallibility to the scriptures, though that is usually distinguished by the term "inerrancy." The term can also describe the infallibility of the church as a whole, whether found in the unanimous testimony of the fathers or in the united *sensus fidelium* (the "Sense of the Faithful") of all of its members. More particularly, infallibility can apply to the promulgation of particular teachings by the institutional church. Most widely recognized are the decisions reached by ecumenical councils, for example, the anathemas against Nestorius issued by the Council of Ephesus in 431. For mainline Christian denominations, especially the Catholic and Orthodox Churches, these decisions are infallible and irreformable. This means that the defined doctrines are an expression of the absolute truth of God's revelation and are guaranteed by him. Any dissent from them is de facto heresy. In addition, a special charism of fidelity was attributed to the Roman church during the first millennium and was one of the roots of the doctrine of papal primacy. After the split between east and west around the year 1000 and in light of the Gregorian reform, the west began to look more and more to the Roman bishop for leadership. This was especially true in cases of faith and morals. As time went on, the popes began to make definitive decisions in the absence of councils (though such meetings would continue to promulgate infallible doctrine themselves, as attested by Lateran IV, Trent, and Vatican I). Around the year 1250, the Catholic Church began to discern a special charism of the Roman bishop for a personal infallibility in his office. This dogma was itself infallibly defined at the First Vatican Council in 1870 and describes this special charism of the pope:

We teach and define that it is a dogma divinely revealed that the Roman Pontiff, when he speaks ex cathedra—that is when in discharge of the office of pastor and doctor of all Christians—by virtue of his supreme Apostolic authority, he defines a doctrine regarding faith or morals to be held by the universal Church, by the Divine assistance promised to him in Blessed Peter, he is possessed of that infallibility with which the Divine Redeemer willed that his Church should be endowed in defining doctrine regarding faith or morals, and that therefore such definitions of the Roman pontiff are—of themselves and not from the consent of the Church—irreformable.[2]

Much ink was spilled both before and after the council about the content and nature of this declaration, but it remains as a binding belief of Roman Catholics. While the language and doctrine of infallibility have their origins in the evolution of canonization, as I propose to show, their application to a broader world of faith and morals lies beyond the purpose of the book.

Canonization, too, requires some explanation. Since the veneration of saints is one of the oldest and most characteristic Christian practices, it did not take long for the official church to begin to establish oversight over such cults (with the simple meaning from the Latin *cultus*, public veneration or worship). By the fourth and fifth centuries, bishops had begun to exercise control over the recognition and worship accorded to various saints in their own territories. As time went on and as the prestige of the Roman church waxed, bishops would bring their saints to Rome to be recognized by the premier see. Around the turn of the millennium, we begin to see both the independent establishment of saints by the Roman bishop and the employment of the word "canonization," which means an enrolling into the list of men and women recognized in public liturgical worship as exemplars of Christ and intercessors in heaven. Into the Middle Ages the popes began to claim the exclusive right to authorize universal cults, though in practice local and episcopal recognition of saints continued into the seventeenth century. By the time of the Reformation, the consensus had emerged that the pope alone had the right of canonization. The word ceased to mean any local veneration or simply episcopal authorization and had come solely to signify solemn liturgical recognition and declaration by the pope himself, after a rigorous examination of the life and miracles of the person in question. At the same time, canonizations themselves came to be considered infallible acts. It is that unexpected and compelling crossover that I wish to trace.

---

2. *Dei Filius*, c. 4, First Vatican Council.

Previous studies on the history of canonization in the Middle Ages were deficient in several ways. Past writers on the broader institutional development of the papal monarchy, while generally thorough, almost universally ignored the deployment of canonization as a tool for the centralization and consolidation of the medieval papacy. Many authors ignore developments in the theory and practice of canonization in the western church, largely because that development was sporadic and unsystematic and was not cited as an area of concern by the Gregorian reformers.[3] Precisely because innovations in canonization were made before the Gregorian reform, scholars have not attached to it a critical importance in terms of the growth of the papal monarchy. A lull in saint-making settled over Rome in the late eleventh century, and the refinement of canonization sped up only after the Gregorians. Claims of infallibility do not appear until relatively late in the Middle Ages, usually after the "classical" period of the acquisition of papal hegemony over such cases. I will argue that the development of canonization and later ascriptions of infallibility were organic and, in a certain sense, accidental. It was not part of a concerted papal push to acquire authority by reserving saint creation to itself. That said, several excellent studies exist of the institutional and legal history of canonization, works that do trace the history of the practice.[4] Yet missing from these works is a broader approach from which to consider how the issue of saint veneration was lived out in the church-at-large. While these works accurately describe the development of the legal and institutional facets, lived religion and response are not present. How the laity and heretics interacted with the new developments emanating from theologians and the papal curia, as well as how papal canonization affected local sanctity, is a central concern of this book.

The transition from narrow institutional foci to broader social and cultural themes opened up new horizons for the study of saints and sainthood.[5] One should particularly mention André Vauchez's indispensable works on

---

3. Ullmann, *Growth of Papal Government*; Morris, *Papal Monarchy*. Both works gloss over or omit canonization entirely as a tool of papal policy. Robinson, *Papacy*, 110–13, briefly mentions canonization and forgoes analysis.

4. Kemp, *Canonization and Authority*. Kemp's foundational study on canonization in the western church was over sixty years old at the time of this writing. While it represents the very best scholarship then available and is still very useful, it shows its age. Biased toward institutional history, it makes several unwarranted assumptions and misses the larger picture. In spite of that, many of Kemp's arguments are good, and the first chapter of this book follows his general outline of the problem. For legal history, see Kuttner, "La réserve papale du droit de canonisation," 172–228. A legal study is Wetzstein's *Heilige vor Gericht*. Sieger offers an overview of the legal situation of canonization down to the twentieth century in *Die Heiligsprechung*.

5. A good overview of the revival of interest in hagiography and hagiographical sources is in Geary, "Saints, Scholars, and Society," 1–22.

saints in the western church and on lived religion.[6] He and subsequent scholars have made much progress in the analysis of the society-wide phenomenon of saints and their cults. Their works on the lived religion of medieval
European Catholics offer insights absent from the efforts of the previous generation of scholars on sainthood. In spite of these new vistas, many of these
recent histories neglect to connect themselves to previous achievements in
institutional and intellectual history. What they have failed to do is to follow
up these findings and apply them to developments in the structures of church
law and of theology. In this sense both approaches—the legal-institutional-
intellectual on one hand and the sociocultural on the other—have not interacted. This leaves the story half-told from either side and misses the
cross-fertilization and insights the distinct approaches can give when brought
together.

This study is an experiment in the interrelationship between lived religion and intellectual history. While I am well aware of the problems that
arise when attempting to connect intellectual work to lived reality, the
evidence in the medieval period invites the hypothesis of a symbiotic relationship. In this sense, some of what I propose is suggestive, rather than definitive. In accord with present scholarship, this study refuses to dichotomize
"elite" versus "popular" religiosity; rather, it suggests a dialogic interrelationship conducted on different levels of discourse.[7] Developments in papal
canonization and centralization in the control of the recognition of sanctity
led to reactions among those within and outside the bounds of church orthodoxy. In response to these challenges on the ground, the institutional
church reacted, refined, and modified where necessary. In the end new challenges led the Roman church to solidify a doctrine that was centuries in the
making and served as the basis of future inquiries into ecclesial infallibility.
While the extension of infallibility to cover further areas of faith and morals
by personal decisions of the Roman pontiff is beyond the purview of this
book, the tools, processes, and procedures that facilitated such a development are intrinsic to my arguments.

Some historians have sought to inquire into the historical origins of the
doctrine of infallibility, with mixed results. Brian Tierney's famous attempt
in the 1970s led to much scholarly challenge, a tradition that continues in

---

6. See esp. Vauchez, *Sainthood in the Later Middle Ages.* I am indebted to the studies of individual saints
and canonizations that have appeared since the 1980s. A representative example of such work is
Jansen, *Making of the Magdalen.*

7. In this I am especially influenced by Brown, *Cult of the Saints*; Thompson, *Cities of God*; and
Jansen, *Making of the Magdalen*, 6–8.

this work.[8] His otherwise well-researched and well-written work is marred by an omnipresent polemical edge and mocking tone conceived in the atmosphere of Catholic dissent following the Second Vatican Council, and his conclusions are, in places, subject to challenge. Despite his excellent and in-depth knowledge of the canonical tradition, his lack of appreciation for the interplay between theological and social dynamics leads him to have a restricted breadth of vision. Indeed, had he considered canonization at any length, he could have modified many of his conclusions, especially his contention that papal infallibility was forged in the conflict with the Spiritual Franciscans. In tying the origins of the infallibility conflict to the question of poverty, Tierney is followed by many eminent scholars.[9] Neither the early Canonists (who were dubious about the infallibility doctrine, particularly as it infringed on the prerogatives of the popes to determine discipline and doctrine) nor the late assertions of Peter John Olivi (1248–94) were instrumental in framing the terms of the debate. Rather, the questions faced by the church about infallibility were shaped by the close alliance between the popes and the first two generations of mendicants and their theologians. These were united in defense of their mendicant saints and the fight for the vindication of their mendicant rights. After laying out my case in the first several chapters, I reserve an extended discussion of Tierney's work to chapter 5.

Conversely, some modern writers have taken on the problem from the Catholic position. Unfortunately, these have predominately come from the direction of canonical or theological history, with little appreciation for the social or cultural meaning of saints and canonization, especially in the axial medieval period.[10] Intellectual historians have also occasionally taken aim at the problem, with the attendant advantages and disadvantages of that genre, not the least being a complete separation from either institutional or

---

8. Tierney, *Origins of Papal Infallibility*. See the exchanges between Tierney and Alfons Stickler in *Catholic Historical Review* 60 (1974): 427–41 and 61 (1975): 265–79.

9. See Horst, *Unfehlbarkeit und geschichte*, esp. the last chap. See also his *Dominicans and the Pope*, 23–41. Horst mentions the canonization debates and then dismisses them as bearing little relevance to the main questions. August Bernhard Hasler follows Tierney: see Hasler, *How the Pope Became Infallible*, esp. 31–50, though the discussion is cursory. I am more inclined to agree with Klaus Schatz, who sees the roots of this doctrine in various places and developing over a long period of time; see Schatz, *Papal Primacy*.

10. Francisco Spedalieri, S.J., undertook a study of the contemporary canonical problem of infal-libility in canonization in 1949, but his work was notable for its lack of historical perspective. Spedalieri, *De Ecclesia Infallibilitate*.

social history.[11] In spite of that limitation, these works are foundational for the present study. Their theological and institutional perspectives will frame my approach, which aims to integrate the cultural history of the period when papal centralization led to claims of infallibility in canonization. It is with the structures already created by these scholars that this book begins its work, in the hopes of providing a logical and careful analysis of the development of this significant area of church history. The present work traces various strands in the first three chapters, which only later came together in the thirteenth century. It proceeds in a chronological manner within separate thematic elements, until all of the threads are finally brought together in chapters 5 and 6.

After the medieval period, theologians and canonists generally agreed in assigning the prerogative of infallibility to the pope in canonizing for three reasons. First, in declaring canonizations, popes spoke solemnly and used the language of infallibility ("declare, pronounce, and define"), which for most thinkers put canonizations in the realm of an infallible decree. Chapter 1 of this work traces the deployment of the legal language and liturgical practices surrounding canonization that would later be marshaled for a comprehensive infallibility claim. Second, such thinkers stated that the popes intended to bind the whole church when they made their pronouncements. The transition from merely local relic translations to calls for worldwide veneration also forms a central component of chapter 1. Third, citing the protection of the Holy Spirit over such pronouncements, the popes made the assertion that such a declaration was not and could not have been liable to error. This was a later development which this work also examines. These three factors proved decisive in creating the general atmosphere of agreement among thinkers after the fourteenth century: that popes could not err in the solemn proclamation of saints.

More central to the purpose of this book is that the development of this doctrine did not take place in a vacuum. Infallibility of the pope in solemn canonization was not a teaching that simply arose in the rarefied halls of academic debate. I argue in chapter 2 that it was the result of a dynamic process. Different events and interests shaped and molded the controversy in the central medieval period. Subtle opposition to saints within the church forced clearer articulation of the nature and value of papal canonization, beginning

---

11. Schenk, *Die Unfehlbarkeit des Papstes*. While he provides a very useful overview, Schenk did not speculate as to the origin of this doctrine, the conditions under which it developed, or why it might have arisen at a particular time and place.

with the glorification of Thomas Becket in 1173, which is the focus of chapter 3. Though quiet opposition within the church to newly canonized saints grew throughout the 1200s, it was the alternate doctrinal systems ascribed to medieval heretics that led to open attacks on both saints and the papacy. When the mendicant orders began to receive the honors of canonization, this quiet opposition sometimes broke out into the open, the subject of chapter 4. These issues came to the fore between the late twelfth and the early fourteenth centuries—the axial age of papal centralization in canonizing.

In light of this developing tradition, theologians and canonists were concerned about the possible implications of such a teaching. Some of these issues involved the problem of the church defining an issue that was not to be found in the scriptures or was not clearly a statement about faith or morals. Foremost in their minds was the possibility of error as a result of false human testimony. This constantly checked the canonists and some theologians from assigning papal infallibility in canonization as a dogma of the faith, especially in the thirteenth century. The problem of canonizing unworthy or unhistorical figures came up repeatedly, causing the papacy to institute all manner of safeguards to ensure veracity and holiness, such as lengthy investigations of life and miracles. In addition to all of these, the possibility of human frailty remained very much in the forefront of theological writings. It was the central argument *against* the doctrine in the medieval period. How church thinkers overcame this conundrum is a central key to understanding the creation of general consensus. The reservations and solutions offered by thinkers in the thirteenth century form the bulk of chapter 5. It is in this chapter that I offer a counterargument to the views advanced by Brian Tierney.

The book then traces the development of several factors that intersected in the second half of the 1200s. The first was the papal reserve on canonizations, especially as it was being theoretically worked out in the period from 1170 to 1234. Since the papacy did not and could not monopolize canonizations—indeed, local ones continued with vigor—it began a process of centralization and redefinition that would take hundreds of years. This redefinition began qualitatively to reinterpret what papal canonization meant as opposed to local elevations. This book contends that the qualitative redefinition was far more significant than merely the papal attempts at legal centralization. The second factor was the exceptional number of mendicant saints proclaimed between the years 1228 and 1255. The new alliance between the papacy and the mendicant orders produced an interdependent bloc of interests, with each defending the other from attacks and with much of the cooperation focused on sainthood. The final and decisive aspect of the problem was the wholesale denial of the usefulness and efficacy of the communion of saints by some medieval heretics. Coupled with this was a non-heretical trend of lay piety that resented imposition of universal cults and the suppression of local ones. I contend that these factors met directly in the late thirteenth century and resulted in a decisive shift in theological opinion among church officials and thinkers. Such conflict intensified the battle against heresy and tipped the balance in favor of closer clerical supervision on the ground. What began as a general denial of the veneration of saints intersected dramatically with the cults of certain papally sponsored mendicant saints by the end of the period. I detail each stage separately and trace the outlines of the history in order to demonstrate how this shift came about and what its results were. The conflict resulted in a clearer articulation and genuine development in church teaching on the nature of canonization itself. A doctrine unheard of in 1150 became, by 1350, the common theological consensus of the Roman Catholic Church.

The central component, then, in understanding the revision of the concepts of sanctity and canonization in the Middle Ages is not canonical reservation, as many scholars of institutional and legal history have thought, but rather the description of a qualitative difference between papal and local canonizations articulated during this period. Given the antecedent and continued centrality of the saints to medieval Christian life and piety, this successful redefinition had stunning results for the enhancement of the authority of the papacy, for the confirmation of the significance of the mendicant orders in the church, and for the creation of the possibility to redefine and redirect patterns of holiness on a large scale.

Several problems are attendant on such a project. It is always difficult to connect intellectual history and lived religion. Rarely is there ever clear evidence that the scholastic thinkers were responding to actual events contemporary with their writings.[12] Thomas's *Summa* is replete with repeated references to and deep reflection on the goodness of creation, yet there is scant evidence that he was directly contending against the Cathar dualism against which his order was then fighting so strongly. In such a case, the historian can only assemble a preponderance of circumstantial and chronological evidence. I believe that I can demonstrate a related shift in both intellectual and social reality in this case. The outlines of the intellectual development of the doctrine are clear and traceable. The general evolution of heretical thought is also traceable, though this is not without its own interpretive issues. There are crucial and logical correlations between intellectual and social reality in this case. The cult of papally canonized mendicant saints is the

---

12. The mendicant controversy at the University of Paris is a salient exception.

key to unraveling the connections between the two perspectives that are so often dissociated.

A complication arises when attempting to speak about general beliefs of heretics or even those of the laity in the Middle Ages.[13] Belief and identity are fluid qualities. Rarely is there ever a particular brand of Catharism that the historian can find over and over. The belief systems of medieval heretics were dynamic, and they were liable to extensive conventionalization and contrast against Catholic tenets.[14] Further, there is the interpretive issue of discerning actual lived beliefs. In all but a few cases, reports of heresy come to us through the inquisition, creating a very difficult interpretive situation. The inquisition represented a fearsome power to frightened people, the application of remote powers directly in the lives of individuals. Depositions given in local dialects were translated into Latin and sometimes later polished by notaries. Inquisitors sought to systematize disparate and sometimes illogical systems and in doing so heaped their own interpretive categories on already heavily mediated inquisition proceedings.[15] Such a situation is not hopeless for the historian, however. Though mediated through several interpretive levels, inquisition records can sometimes be corroborated by other sources, even the few remaining heretical ones. In the present case, these issues are somewhat beside the point. My intention here is not to offer a systematic reconstruction of heretical belief, if such a project is even possible. It is to extract and trace the development of a certain strand of thinking and map its progress through the central and late medieval periods. In the case of saints, opposition was real, immediate, and concrete, as opposed to theoretical speculations regarding various shades of dualism. Certain assertions come up repeatedly in many different places and texts. Used judiciously, these can offer clues to the general direction of belief. Further, when the church responded to heretical beliefs regarding saints and sanctity, as I contend it began to do in the 1250s, it was responding precisely to those beliefs as reported by the inquisitors. If the inquisitors themselves began to discern a general pattern, then that was the picture sent to church thinkers and to the curia. The story

13. Mark Pegg has repeatedly argued that characterizations of Cathar belief are largely idealized and intellectualized. See his "On Cathars, Albigenses and Good Men," 181–95; in this he follows the outlines developed by R. I. Moore and reaffirmed in Moore's *War on Heresy*. This view is too extreme; Catharism was far more than a clerical invention. It may not have been as systematic as many churchmen thought. Nonetheless, it really existed. Lansing, *Power and Purity*, 82.

14. Lansing, *Power and Purity*, 83.

15. On the problems of interpretation inherent in inquisitional texts, see Given, *Inquisition and Medieval Society*; and Arnold, "Inquisition, Texts and Discourse," 63–80. Lucy Sackville offers a more balanced view of these texts, particularly inquisition manuals, in Sackville, *Heresy and Heretics in the Thirteenth Century*.

of this doctrine is the story of the church's response to the perception of a growing threat, whether or not that threat actually existed in any systematic manner. Few studies of heretical belief have focused on their doctrines of the communion of saints or of the veneration of saintly individuals.[16] I hope to remedy this absence.

Fundamental to this book are the mendicant orders, their saints, and their thinkers. Chapters 3, 4, and 5 detail the articulation of the doctrine of infallibility in the thirteenth century as a result of universalizing ambitions on the part of the orders and of the papacy. The mendicants gave the papacy a church-wide influence at a level that it had not had to that point. What occurred, especially in the mid-1200s, were mutual defense and reinforcement on the part of the orders and the papacy. While the papacy was proposing mendicant saints such as Francis (1181/2–1226) and Dominic (1170–1221), opponents of the orders were marshaling arguments against them. The saints of the orders provided a focus for opposition, though the disagreements ranged over broad areas of church life and practice. In the end the mendicant theologians provided stunningly new interpretations of papal authority that confirmed their own orders, defended their new saints, and enhanced the position of the papacy. The proposition of controversial saints by the church (particularly in the case of Peter of Verona [d. 1252], the martyred Dominican inquisitor) had the effect of throwing previously vague ruminations, both orthodox and heretical, into a new light. What before had been a slowly evolving practice of papal centralization and qualitative redefinition became focused into a question of papal authority touching the very fabric of the unity of faith. An ill-defined heretical uneasiness with the Christian preoccupation with the body, manifested in the pilgrimages and relics of the saints, became sharply defined when people were ordered to venerate a contemporary seen by many as an interloper at best and as a vicious persecutor at worst. When one considers the point to which the debate had come and the specific historical events that precipitated the new direction, the period between 1228 and 1260 is crucial. Chapter 6 discusses the resolution of the issue and investigates the response of various groups in the church, such as the Spiritual Franciscans, the Canonists, the theologians, and the curia—always, however, looking toward the laity.

In the end, the purpose of this book is to explore the articulation of a Christian doctrine and to situate it among the historical events that underlay its development. It is an exercise in dialogue between intellectual history

16. I heavily depend on d'Alatri's excellent "Culto dei santi ed eretici," 85–104, repr. with slight changes in id., *Eretici e inquisitori in Italia*, 1:23–43.

and lived religion. Its intention is to shift focus away from areas that in the past were unduly emphasized, to make clear understudied phenomena, and to present new evidence to build on recent scholarly work on sainthood, inquisition, heresy, and theology. The new work done in those fields is enlightening and bold, and my intention is to unite many of these innovative insights to paint a comprehensive picture of the problem in question. The solutions gradually arrived at by the 1300s were part of a long process of dialogue and challenge yet were at the same time startlingly original. They provided a new vocabulary and a new lexicon with which to carry on development of the infallibility discussion into the Counter-Reformation and beyond.

CHAPTER 1

"By the Authority of Blessed Peter"
Making Saint-Making

The cult of the saints is one of the oldest manifestations of orthodox Christianity. From the early days of the Christian martyrs to the transition to monastic confessors and then to the geographical extension of new cults in recently Christianized areas, sainthood was an essential correlative to the spread of the Gospel. Even today, in spite of grave challenges from the Protestant Reformation, it still plays a dominant role in the Christian churches most attached to their historical pedigrees: in Roman Catholicism and in Eastern Orthodoxy and, to a lesser extent, among certain high-church Protestants. Such practices had deep roots in popular consciousness and were ubiquitous in first-millennium Christianity.[1] So commonplace was this spontaneous cultic expression that few complaints were lodged against it in the whole of the patristic period, aside from a few sporadic cautions about excessive enthusiasm.[2] The church hierarchy failed to

---

1. For this phenomenon, see Brown, *Cult of the Saints*. See also Delehaye, *Legends of the Saints*; Bynum, *Resurrection of the Body*; and Wilken, *Spirit of Early Christian Thought*, 262–311.

2. The fathers are unanimous in their support of the cults of the saints, and many of them become cultic promoters themselves, or *impresarios*, to use Peter Brown's term. We can see enthusiasm for the saints as early as the letter of St. Ignatius of Antioch (ca. 110), the account of the Martyrdom of Polycarp (ca. 160), and the Passion of Perpetua and Felicity (ca. 200). Julian the Apostate in the 360s saw the cult of the saints as a salient mark of Christianity: "You keep adding many corpses newly dead to the corpse of Christ of long ago. You have filled the world with tombs and sepulchers."

make many inroads in regulating the cult of saints during that age and in many cases embraced popular cults simply because the laity would not have tolerated otherwise.[3] Though many church leaders attempted to manage existing cults or occasionally to foster new ones, sainthood remained largely an effect of the expression of popular sentiment.[4] The communal practice surrounding the veneration of holy men and women was nearly one thousand years old by the time two very different movements developed in the eleventh and twelfth centuries that would change the way sanctity was experienced in the western Christian world.

Around the year 1100 two streams of thought emerged that were to have profound implications for perceptions of sanctity in the Christian west. One of these came from above, and another came from below. Like many corollary phenomena, these developments in thinking about saints' cults were an aspect of the revival of Christian life during the Gregorian reform of the late eleventh century. Two separate groups began to conceptualize the nature of sanctity in the Christian life in novel ways. One was various factions of heterodox believers, who began to express increasing animosity toward saints and sainthood for a variety of reasons and who are the subject of chapter 2. The focus here is the second: the hierarchical church, particularly the bishop of Rome and the prelates immediately attached to the Roman curia. In the first millennium of Christianity, sainthood had been a local function of Christian piety, sometimes sanctioned by the local bishop by translation of a saint's body and sometimes not. Because of the changes that began in this period, the conception of local sanctity would change irrevocably.

During the period of the Gregorian reform, efforts at centralization around the Roman curia proceeded apace.[5] Gradually church leaders realized that the papacy could and should take a more direct role in the creation of saints.

Cited from Julian, *Contra Galilaeos*, 335c. Brown, *Cult of the Saints*, 7. When the doctrine was challenged, the orthodox response was swift. See St. Jerome's *Contra Vigilantium*, PL 23, 353–68.

3. See, for example, the tumults over the attempted suppression of cults in northern Italy in the latter thirteenth century in Thompson, *Cities of God*, 430–33.

4. See Brown, *Cult of the Saints*, chap. 3, for a discussion of the importation of the patron-client relationship into the spiritual lives of early Christians.

5. There are many studies of the Gregorian reform, but all of them ignore the place of canonization, largely because it was not a preoccupation of the period 1050–1150. See Blumenthal, *Investiture Controversy*; id., *Papal Reform and Canon Law*; Ullmann, *Growth of Papal Government*; Schimmelpfennig, *Papacy*; Morris, *Papal Monarchy*; and Robinson, *Papacy*. For a discussion that connects social and institutional history, see Moore, *Origins of European Dissent*. For correctives, see the essays in Frassetto, *Heresy and the Persecuting Society*, particularly essays by Edward Peters, 11–30, and Bernard Hamilton, 93–114. Scholars of canonization do observe the legal changes underlying canonization that took place while not generally connecting them to the growing qualitative difference that emerges. See Wetzstein, *Heilige vor Gericht*.

Several reasons for this were apparent. First, the papacy could propose and control models of holiness with the idea of directing and molding Christian piety. Second, the popes could nominate attractive individuals for the veneration of the whole church, inserting them in liturgical calendars and thus underpinning its accomplishments such as those achieved during the standardization of the liturgy during the Carolingian period. Finally, the popes, in the act of canonization, could manifest their authority and deepen the identification of their mission as keepers of the keys to the kingdom, creating a new locus for the public recognition of papal claims. All of these would serve to undergird papal authority and speed along the centralization of ecclesiastical authority.

This sounds rather like cold, political calculation on the part of the Roman church, but a broader interpretation is needed. First, the process whereby the popes acquired the practice of canonization and later claimed the sole right to canonize was much more organic and gradual than the preceding account suggests. This transition took place languidly over many centuries with remote origins in the patristic and Carolingian periods, reaching its culmination from the early 1100s through the 1300s and perhaps not fully completed until the final reservation of canonization by the papacy by Urban VIII in 1634.[6] It was conditioned by historical events and did not proceed in a direct course. Neither is there direct evidence of a process with internal logic that unfolded itself by means of a coherent trajectory. It is rather an uneven history of practical development, punctuated by many fits and starts.

Beyond the evolution of legal and institutional procedures and the evolution of narratives to explain them, good and sound religious reasons existed why papal canonization developed and gained acceptance. Medieval Christians saw Rome as the center of the church. To travel to Rome was to go *ad Urbem*, or to *The* City. Confirmation of a local cult by the chief bishop of Christendom was far more significant than a mere translation by the town ordinary.[7] In an age of increasing communication and travel, international recognition was something highly desirable for a locality and its saints. Rome guaranteed universality and orthodoxy, and holiness in that period was becoming closely linked with both of these notions. In general the medieval laity and clergy accepted the growing centralization of canonization; they

---

6. The definitive study from a Catholic and theological perspective is the magisterial work of Benedict XIV, *De Servorum Dei* (hereafter, Lambertini). Benedict's effort is stunning in its comprehensiveness and balance and, while dated, is still an essential reference text for this subject. Also good for institutional appraisals are Kemp, *Canonization and Authority*; and Kuttner, "La réserve papale du droit de canonisation," 172–228.

7. For episcopal canonizations, see the study by Amore, "La canonizazzione vescovile."

embraced it even though they did not give up on local sanctity. A broadening of the holy was a welcome development to all. People from every corner of Christendom began to be presented to the papacy for recognition spontaneously, speeding the process of centralization from the grass roots. One could say that this was a popular centralization.

The outline of this organic development unfolds in this manner. In the first place the immemorial practice of the church was the spontaneous local recognition of sanctity, a process that extended back into the dim past. This long-established practice resulted in the ongoing recognition of new saints. Leaders of the church began to realize that not all of these saints were worthy of the title, for various reasons. In some cases the clergy desired a more refined view of Christian holiness, while in others it deplored an excess of popular credulity or found problems in the saint's life or cult that generated suspicion. Note that this does not imply a dichotomy, for clergy and laity were unanimous in their devotion to the cult of saints. They just began to diverge in their approaches. Local bishops had exercised (or tried to exercise) a supervisory role at least as far back as the fourth century. As the church became more international in the early-to-central Middle Ages, this supervisory role shifted to local synods and eventually to the Roman pontiff himself. In some cases the popes restricted unsuitable cults. In turn this created a new type of demand: local churches slowly began to clamor for a papal *nihil obstat* regarding their saints.[8] The desire of the papacy and the episcopacy to suppress unsuitable candidates morphed into a truly pan-European desire to see the recognition of saints on a church-wide level. Popularity drove centralization, and the papacy began to marshal its resources to create institutional processes that could handle such requests (remember that the speedy development of the papal chancery as the court of appeal for Christendom was contemporary with these phenomena). In creating this system, the papacy began to present saints for universal liturgical and paraliturgical veneration. What previously had been a hazy and local concern now became a matter of universal import touching both the nature of Christian holiness and the office of the pope. As a result of this increased precision and presentation, for the first time challenges arose against individual holy men and women, stemming from a broader assault on the communion of saints and the goodness of the material world. This resulted in increasing canonical and theological defenses of the new processes and ended with a new articulation of both sanctity and papal authority that would reverberate through the centuries.

---

8. This demand can first be discerned in the papal canonization of Ulrich in 993 and developed slowly after that.

For its part, the Roman church made no special effort during the eleventh or twelfth century to demand the presentation of candidates for judgment by the curia. Though later the popes felt the need to recognize sanctity and present it to the Christian world, no systematic evidence exists of a single concerted model of holiness proposed by the church in the Middle Ages (though the period of concentrated mendicant canonizations 1228–55 may be an exception). Medievals, like their Christian forebears of the first millennium, believed in the efficacy of saints, a fact testified to by hundreds of sanctoral sermon collections, miracle compilations, and pilgrimage routes. For the clergy of the church as well as the laity, recognition of those glorified by God in turn brought that glory back down to earth, with promises of help and grace from above with it. The unfolding of this process then was propelled by a combination of political and religious motivations, moderated by the contingent historical events during which it transpired.

☛ The Development of Papal Canonization

In order to appreciate the development of canonization, especially as it applies to the qualitative theological difference it begins to acquire in the thirteenth century, one needs to review the content, purposes, and evolution of papal elevation of saints. Studying canonizations from the papal perspective might seem like an outdated exercise in institutional history, but it tells the story of the canonical and theological appropriation of saints and sainthood by the highest levels of the church. It also anticipates the dialogue between official church practices and lived religion in the subsequent periods of transition. In tracing this process one can lay out the pieces that will come together in the late twelfth century to form the basis for central medieval and early modern conceptions of saintly elevation. In addition, when compared with the history of sainthood on the ground as well as the response of groups opposed (or coming gradually to oppose) saints in the church, it delineates the cultural nexus in which church policy came into conflict with lived religion in the middle of the thirteenth century.

This chapter follows much of the work done by Eric Kemp in the 1940s in his institutional analysis of the development of canonization. Here the focus is on the developments that led to a qualitative differentiation between papal, episcopal, and popular canonizations. While Kemp is a useful starting point, his scope was limited. First, his definition of canonization is too strict and confining, ignoring popular canonizations altogether and gradually marginalizing episcopal translations. This is because he follows a strictly legal analysis assuming, for instance, that papal reservation of canonization was an accomplished fact simply because Alexander III's letter *Audivimus* was included in the Decretals of 1234.[9] Kemp's penetrating analysis of canonizations ends at this year, for he assumed the reservation was accepted universally. His study of canonizations after this date is cursory, yet I contend that canonizations done after this date are axial for understanding that the reservation had a qualitative meaning beyond mere acquisition of a hegemonic authority over saint creation—if such a thing existed at all at that date.[10] Further, though he attempts to avoid anachronism, at several points Kemp attempted to place the late medieval–early modern distinction between beatification and canonization in the late 1100s or early 1200s. In this he followed the thorough but dated work of Benedict XIV (r. 1740–58), who, though an excellent scholar himself, had a tendency to read back later practices into early history—understandable in a book that was primarily theological. Finally Kemp devoted some eighteen pages to infallibility in canonization—a substantial number for a then-little-studied subject—yet he made the mistake of isolating it within legal and theological discussions while missing the broad social and political realities that gave birth to that doctrine. This is not to take away from Bishop Kemp's accomplishment. Any work that begins as a BA thesis and is still a *locus classicus* nearly seventy years later is a significant—nay, extraordinary—achievement. My criticisms are somewhat unfair in that much of the later social and cultural scholarship simply was not there when Kemp undertook his study in the midst of World War II. That I follow his lead in this chapter, though making significant adjustments, is a testimony to the durability of his scholarship.

While the evidence is plentiful for early popular canonizations, and even for episcopal and synodal translations, the first extant record of papal association with canonization came from a council convened in Rome in 993.[11] At the synod the bishop of Augsburg read out an account of the life and miracles of Bishop Ulrich (d. 973), which the members of the synod received with approbation, and at once they acclaimed the deceased to be a

---

9. See later in this chapter for a detailed analysis of *Audivimus*.

10. Working with the limitations imposed by World War II, one should not fault Kemp for overly relying on the Acta Sanctorum and the Patrologia Latina, two sources that would have been readily available to him. The Patrologia ends at the pontificate of Innocent III, the point at which Kemp's work becomes far less useful.

11. Benedict XIV alleges that the translation of St. Landoald was authorized by the pope sometime between 980 and 982 and as such is an early example of papal canonization; however, Kemp, usually content to follow Benedict's lead, is doubtful: Kemp, *Canonization and Authority*, 50. Benedict sees traces of papal intervention in saints' cults very early, but the evidence is scattered, incidental, or anachronistic; see Lambertini, 1:38–46.

saint. It had become standard, if not universal, practice since the late seventh century to reserve some canonizations to a local synod, and so this Roman synod was merely following established custom.[12] This itself is evidence of the increasing desire for a more universal sanction in an age that was moving quickly from localism to a more cosmopolitan outlook. Pope John XV (r. 985–96) issued a document confirming this decision backed up by the assertion that he did this "by the authority of Blessed Peter prince of the Apostles" and threatened anathema against all those who refused to obey.[13] All of the members of the synod signed the document, and John addressed it to the entire higher clergy of Germany. Several things were significant about this act. First, it was collegial in nature, and the language associated with that collegiality would continue throughout the entire medieval period, even after the custom of canonization within a synod passed into desuetude.[14] Second, it was the first recorded international canonization accomplished by the bishop of Rome. The pope conducted this elevation of a transalpine saint, rather than merely approving a local Roman or Italian figure, in the presence of Germanic bishops. Finally, and perhaps most notably, it cited miracles and holiness of life as evidence for Ulrich's sanctity, the two things that would develop as the *sine quibus non* of canonization. In this document of recognition, much of what was later identified as the essential qualities of papal canonization were present before the turn of the year 1000: collegiality, universality, and testimony of evidence of virtues and wonders.

Nevertheless, the "canonization" of Ulrich was not unusual, nor was it an innovation. Various quasi-official mechanisms for the glorification of saints had been in place for nearly five hundred years, in one form or another. It is possible that there were earlier papal canonizations, but given the paucity

---

12. Lambertini, 1:34–38. Some authors, after Benedict, have tried to advance other candidates as the first to receive papal approbation, such as St. Kilian or St. Swibert, but the evidence is just too thin.

13. "[To those who transgress] . . . sciat, se auctoritate beati Petri Princeps Apostolorum, cujus vel immeriti vices agimus, anathematis vinculo innodatum." John XV, "Cum conventus esset" [Canonization of Udalric of Augsburg, 993], *Codex constitutionum quas summi*, ed. Fontanini, 1–3. Hereafter Fontanini. Also PL 137, 845. For Ulrich, see the essays in Weitlauff, *Bischof Ulrich von Augsburg, 890–973*. For a thorough introduction to the legal and institutional approaches of the papacy toward canonization in this period, see Krafft, *Papsturkunde und Heiligsprechung*. Krafft is useful for locating publication histories and recent editions of all the bulls enumerated in the text.

14. Subsequent papal pronouncements always make a nod to consultation with "prelates residing at the Apostolic See." One can still see this tradition today in the presentation of those to be beatified or canonized in the context of a consistory of cardinals. This tradition of synodal glorification was resumed with the beatification of Charbel Mahklouf by Paul VI during the Second Vatican Council in 1965. Robinson discusses the synodal aspects of twelfth-century canonization in Robinson, *Papacy*, 110–13, but overemphasizes what had become a mere formality by the end of the period in question.

of documentation, Ulrich is the first one known. I think that the dearth of early bulls or other official written materials is likely, because the canonization of a saint was a primarily *liturgical* event and not initially a *juridical* one. Because of this, the thesis of continuity has much more support given the traditional nature of the Catholic liturgy. There was no written record, because the liturgical act itself was so normative. The innovation of the use of the term "canonize" itself derives from the insertion of the saint's name into the Eucharistic Canon. Indeed, to be a saint was to be *embedded liturgically* in the community. There is then a deep connection between liturgy and sanctity, and they developed in tandem.[15] As further evidence, no attempt was made at this time to create a systematic mechanism for the elevation of saints. The document reads as if it were a onetime event: an extraordinary recognition of holiness spontaneously orchestrated by the bishop of Augsburg in honor of one of his predecessors. While this was the case in 993, later thinkers, including popes, theologians, and canonists, would use this and subsequent canonization documents from the eleventh century as models for the articulation of what it meant to be a saint and what it meant to canonize. Clearly John XV and the bishops of the Roman synod of 993 were not aware that they were radical innovators. The extraordinarily early nature of the document itself belies the rather workaday theology behind it. Holiness and miracles had been the signs of sanctity in the Christian church since time immemorial. Calling attention to them in an official document after collegial recognition was not that strange.[16]

Two more "canonizations" occurred during the first half of the eleventh century, a period of pervasive uncertainty and disorder in the Roman church. Benedict VIII (r. 1012–24) received a petition for translation for Simeon of Padolirone sometime after the recluse's death in 1016.[17] Simeon was an Armenian gyrovague (a type of wandering monk, whose lives were castigated by St. Benedict in his rule). He had acquired a reputation for sanctity and had died in the vicinity of Padua.[18] Though some saw the document as the fastest canonization in history (an interval of only four months elapsed be-

---

15. See Bredero, *Christendom and Christianity*, 160.

16. For an early history of the sporadic development of ecclesiastical oversight of cults, see Brown, *Cult of the Saints*; Kemp, *Canonization and Authority*, 3–55.

17. "Translation" signifies the disinterment, recognition, elevation, and relocation of a saint's body as part of a liturgical ceremony that marked the celebration of holy men and women in the first thousand years of Christianity. Today it plays a smaller but still necessary step in the canonization of saints.

18. Benedict VIII, "Requisistis judicium nostrum" [Response to petition for translation of Simeon of Padolirone, ca. 1016–1024], ibid., 3. Both Fontanini and Broderick assume that the canonization took place in 1016, but without proof. There is no internal evidence of any date in the very short

tween death and authorization of cult if one accepts the 1016 dating), in reality Benedict only authorized the local ordinary to translate the body.[19] This accorded with immemorial Christian practice, which granted the right of translation to the local bishop. The real novelty was the request for permission from the papacy. Significantly it was an answer to a question concerning whether one with a reputation for sanctity ought to be accorded veneration. Benedict answered positively but made the decision contingent on the reliability of the miracle witnesses, a concern that would continue to be raised in the discussion over the possibility of infallibility in the future.[20] John XIX (r. 1024–32) permitted the translation of three saints (Bononius of Vercelli, Adalhard of Corbie, and Romuald), but none of those decrees are extant.[21] In spite of that, contemporary accounts of the case of St. Adalhard indicate that John assumed a general right to approve the translations of saints.[22]

In 1041 or 1042, Benedict IX (r. 1032–45) elevated another Simeon, this one of Syracuse. This decree hews more closely to the modern idea of papal canonization than what had come before. Simeon was another wandering monk who had died near Trier with a reputation for sanctity. Archbishop Poppo of the same town requested a determination of the question of Simeon's holiness, which is significant because in the future the developed canonization process would require such a petition from an ecclesial authority appealing to Rome.[23] In the document of canonization, Benedict is very

---

letter to Marquis Boniface of Mantua (who himself ruled until 1052). No recent scholarly work on St. Simeon has been done.

19. Broderick, "Census of the Saints," 87–115, considers this the fastest canonization, but his notion of papal canonization is far too broad. The document contains no formal declaration on life and miracles, reference to an investigation, or appeal to collegiality. Benedict XIV considers this the equivalent of a beatification. Kemp is also too fast and loose with the term "canonization" in this instance; Kemp, *Canonization and Authority*, 58. A later date, perhaps 1020, seems warranted.

20. Based on the letters of subsequent popes, it appears that the church in Mantua was in no hurry to translate the body, as it seems his relics were untranslated as late as the 1070s. Kemp, 58.

21. Ibid., 59.

22. "Unde missis legatis accipere benedictionem a Joanne papa, qui tunc temporis vicarius sancti Petri habeatur Romae pontificali hierarchia, non solum est permissus, sed etiam apostolica jussione jussus, quod libenter fecisset et injussus." Abbot Richard of Corbie; cited from Kemp, *Canonization and Authority*, 59. Lambertini, 1:47–48. Predictably Benedict sees this as a given, and Kemp sees it as an innovation. John does seem to assume that this is a natural right of the pope, and while perhaps this was a novelty to the rest of the church, John's language implies that Rome had been thinking along these lines for a while.

23. One should note the petition of Emperor Henry III to Pope Clement II in 1047 for the canonization of St. Wiborada. This shows that petitioning the papacy was becoming a more normative process. AS, May vol. 1, "Vita S. Wiboradae Virg. Mart.," 283, sec. A. Cf. Toynbee, *Saint Louis of Toulouse*, 136; Kemp, *Canonization and Authority*, 61.

clear and uses commanding language ("Statueremus et decerneremus" "We establish and decree") in virtue of his "apostolic authority." There is no evasiveness there; it is certain and invested with confidence. Further, for the first time a pope addressed all the Christian clergy and people, though he qualifies it with "especially in the German kingdom."[24] This document, rather than the earlier synodal confirmations or permissions for translation, should mark the beginning of papal canonization as such. This is because it was done under the aegis of papal prerogatives and does not directly involve a synod or council, nor is it concerned solely with translation of relics.

Benedict here was not simply authorizing but was commanding observance of a yearly feast; he was not granting permission to translate but was in fact demanding universal veneration. This is a significant departure. Though earlier documents concerned the elevation of saints, this is the first discrete, personal, and universal papal canonization. In a period when papal power and authority were flagging, at least two possibilities exist. On the one hand, this document may have been a desperate attempt to cling to the tattered remnants of papal primacy. Benedict was a notoriously dissolute and venal pope. It was during his reign that the papal name was struck off the diptychs in Constantinople, after a century of papal weakness.[25] Such elevated and formal language as this in a period of the papal nadir should give one pause. The exalted tone of the document leads to the second possibility: that this act of Benedict IX is merely the expression of papal custom long since established. Kemp notes the extraordinary solemnity of the text, canonizing a saint in far-off Trier, but then wholly leaves the subject without analysis.[26] Given the increasing circumstantial evidence that begins to appear in the eighth century, the more likely interpretation is not a weak pope desperately clamoring for the tattered remains of his authority, but the simple exercise of custom that found no opposition and was considered natural by the people and archbishop of Trier, not to say the whole church.

---

24. "Salubri definitione nostrae Apostolicae auctoritatis statueremus atque decerneremus; omnis, quos in salutatione praenotavimus, notum in his literis facimus, quid ex ea re consuerimus . . . concordi deliberatione determinavimus, et alta sententiae radice fundavimus, eumdem virum Dei Simeonem . . . ab omnibus populis, tribubus, et linguis Sanctum procul dubio esse nominandum, ejusque natalem singulis annis recurentem passim solemniter observandum." Benedict IX, "Divinae maiestatis inenarrabilis" [Decree on the Sanctity of Simeon of Trier, 1042], Fontanini, 4–5. For this saint, see Heintz, "Der Heilige Simeon von Trier," 163–73.

25. Benedict's successor, Victor III (r. 1086–87), wrote, "After his assumption of the priesthood, how dishonest, how loathsome, how foul, and how execrable has been his life, I shudder to relate." *Libelli de lite (Dialogi de miraculis Sancti Benedicti Liber Tertius auctore Desiderio abbate Casinensis ed.)*, MGH, Scriptores 30.2, 141.

26. Kemp, *Canonization and Authority*, 61.

☛ Gregorian Continuity

It is significant that these early examples of papal involvement transpired long before Leo IX (r. 1049–54) arrived in Rome to begin the process that would lead to the Gregorian reform. If one considers this, the reservation and exaltation of papal canonization were not an invention of the centralizing and resurgent clergy of the period. They existed in embryonic but rapidly developing form long before the restoration of the papacy. The reformers merely refined and enhanced already existing procedures. They knew that the Christian world was beginning to look to Rome for confirmation not because of a perceived qualitative difference (yet) but in order to give more honor and glory to their saints. The Gregorians saw the opportunities latent in such a move, and they embraced it with alacrity, though development continued well after them into the thirteenth century. Even so, the Gregorians did not make arrogating the power to canonize a priority, though it could have been a major ally in their efforts to reestablish the prestige and primacy of the Roman see. Few canonizations occurred during the hundred years from 1050 to 1150, and in some cases decades elapsed between each one. When the Gregorians did canonize, they did so using the language and assumptions developed over the previous 150 years. That the beginning of papal centralization occurred before the Gregorians while the golden age of papal canonization happened long after is quite shocking and too little noticed. One would have expected the Gregorians to focus on canonization and use it to innovate along with the variety of other tools they honed to streamline papal government. It could have been especially useful for their own political purposes, but surprisingly this did not happen. The development then was something far more organic, an evolution that supports the thesis of "popular centralization" as described earlier in this chapter and that complicates the view of those who attribute power as the sole motive of the popes of the Reform period.

Leo IX, the vanguard figure of the reform, canonized only two individuals: Deodatus in 1049 (whose bull is missing, if it ever existed) and Gerard of Toul in 1050. In this latter case Leo accomplished several things significant for the history of papal canonization. He asserted that the decree of glorification did nothing more than recognize publicly that which God had already done for his saints.[27] For Leo, God made known his

---

27. Western ideas of canonization really do parallel Eastern Orthodox doctrines of glorification. The canonization is not so much an act of the church on earth as recognition of an act realized by God in the saint.

predestined sons by the testimony of miracles, while reliable witnesses could attest to holiness of life. Taken together, these provided irrefutable evidence that "those (like Gerard) ought to be honored on earth by men, who are honored in heaven before God and the army of angels."[28] Further, this canonization accomplished by Leo continued the tradition of collegiality in recognition of holiness.[29] After hearing the testimony of the witnesses, a monk present at the Roman synod claimed to have had a vision of Gerard. Spontaneously, so the document goes, the assembly hailed Gerard a saint by acclamation. This included both clergy and laity, unanimity theoretically required for recognition of holiness or any definition of doctrine. Like Ulrich's document, this one included the signatures of the bishops present for the canonization. Leo averred to neither the authority of Peter the Apostle nor his own. Rather this canonization seems to be rooted in the universal acclamation of the assembled faithful.[30] Finally, Leo addressed the letter "To all sons of the Catholic Church," marking for the first time the realization that if Gerard was really a saint, he ought to be honored everywhere and by all.[31] In this document one can trace the essential elements of future canonization bulls. A thorough study of the language of these papal documents aids the researcher in ascertaining the chronology of developments in the theology of canonization. Though many of the basic building blocks of papal canonization were present in seed by this time, documents emanating from the Roman curia were few and far between (only four canonization bulls exist for the entire eleventh century). This was an extraordinary process, usually accomplished only in the context of a general synod as a result of exceptional requests accompanied by witnesses and sometimes wonders. One cannot yet make a general assessment of the theology behind these papal actions, but the roots of future rationales are already present.

Significantly, Leo personally translated Gerard's body *after* the decree of canonization. Prior to this, translations were simply done as the equivalent of a canonization or after receipt of permission, but here is the first explicit

---

28. "Eos honerari in terris ab hominibus, qui honerantur in coelis ante Deum ab Angelorum agminibus." Leo IX, "Virtus divinae operationis" [Canonization of Gerard of Toul, 1050], Fontanini, 6–9.

29. Deodatus's canonization had been in the context of a Roman synod as well. Glorification of saints demanded collegiality during this period.

30. Perhaps a foreshadowing of the Gregorian realization that the lay people were more allies of the papacy and of orthodoxy than the princes of the church, e.g., the anti-clerical Patarene movement in Milan in the 1070s that found a ready ally in the papacy.

31. "Cunctis catholicae Ecclesiae filiis . . . ," Fontanini, 6.

evidence of formal canonization language before translation.[32] In later centuries it would become more common for a saint to be translated only after a papal canonization. Perhaps the idea of translation was beginning to lose its luster among the upper levels of the Roman curia, or maybe the idea began to grow that because of the increasing number of appeals to Rome for permission to translate, perhaps it also belonged to the see of Rome to make a declaration on holiness rather than simply relying on local officials. Such a move would increase the prestige of Rome and allow it more control over models of Christian holiness. Even if that were the fact, though, episcopal translations continued until well into the early modern period. To emphasize this distinction further, Leo himself did authorize three more traditional translations during his pontificate. Yet the canonization of Gerard was different and presaged an increasing disparity that would grow between formal papal canonizations and the mere extension of permissions to translate locally.

Alexander II (r. 1061–73) authorized the cults of two individuals: Theobald of Vicenza and Robert of Chaise-Dieu. Neither of these was accomplished in the full form given to Simeon of Syracuse or Gerard of Toul.[33] This is somewhat startling given that the Gregorian reformers could have advanced the reservation of canonization as a potent assertion of papal centralization. In spite of aggressive political centralization in regard to Roman synods, canon law, papal legates, the rapidly developing curia, and many other innovative consolidations, the reformers did not use canonization in this way. Increasing papal oversight of the recognition of holiness in the Catholic Church was not a result of Gregorian predilections; indeed only two further canonizations took place during the eleventh century.[34] Urban II (r. 1088–99), riding on a wave of popularity at the success of the First Crusade, enrolled Nicholas the Pilgrim of Trani in the "catalogue of the saints." This is the first reference to this catalogue among the papal

---

32. Only in the early modern period will church thinkers apply the term "Equipollent Canonization" to the phenomenon of translation. See Urban VIII, "Caelestis Hierusalem Cives," July 5, 1634, sec. 4. Cited from Kemp, *Canonization and Authority*, 145. Here it merely means that it took the place of what would later be the ceremony of canonization.

33. Robert's bull has been lost, but Theobald's is in Alexander II, "Multa praeclara" [Canonization of Theobald of Vicenza, 1073], Fontanini, 23. There was a disagreement about whether Alexander II or Alexander III canonized this saint, but internal evidence and the arguments by the Bollandists and Kemp in favor of an earlier dating are convincing; Kemp, *Canonization and Authority*, 64–65.

34. Notably there is no record of Gregory VII canonizing *anyone*. He did appear to sanction two cults (Erlembald of Milan and Cencius the Roman prefect) in the Roman synod of 1078, but this appears to be only his recognition of the validity of their miracles, not a formal canonization; Robinson, *Papacy*, 110.

documents.[35] This terminology would continue throughout the medieval period, as subsequent popes would order the inscription of new holy men and women on the roll of the saints. The universalizing language of Leo IX's decrees did not make its way into this canonization, as Urban particularly addressed it to the clergy and people of Trani, indicating that adding a saint was not yet always considered a matter of primary concern to the universal church. Rather, the local church was still regarded as the locus of devotion for a new saint. The bull was also extremely short, not approaching the length of Gerard's letter of canonization, nor did it detail, even briefly, the life and miracles of the saint. One thing Urban did do differently from Leo was to order the elevation of Nicholas by his own authority, eschewing the collegiality exhibited in the canonizations of Ulrich and Gerard at least in reference to the final determination.[36] This is surprising because Urban himself had addressed a letter to the abbot of Quimperlé after 1088 asserting the necessity of the consensus of a plenary council in the glorification of a saint.[37] References to collegial decision making would become more and more attenuated as time went on, but they would never wholly disappear.[38] In a similar manner it appears that Urban authorized the celebration of the feast of the empress Adelaide, but this document has not survived. More significant is that Emperor Henry II recognized that her cult could not be publicly celebrated without the consent of the Apostolic See, a remarkably early testament to papal authority over these matters.[39]

---

35. Urban II, "Cum largiente Domino" [Canonization of Nicholas of Trani, 1094], Fontanini, 9. This usage probably came from the consideration of the Martyrology as a list or "Catalogue" of the saints, to which new saints were added—as was the wording in Benedict IX's canonization of Simeon of Trier. The term came to feature regularly in decrees of papal canonization.

36. "Auctoritate nostra," ibid.

37. This letter was preserved in a fragmentary form in the cartulary of Sainte Croix at Quimperlé, in reference to the possible canonization of St. Urloux, so it never became part of any collection of papal decretals. "Non enim Sanctorum quisque debet canonibus admisceri, nisi testes adsint, qui eius miracula visa suis oculis attestantur et plenarie synodi firmetur assensu." Ibid. Notice also the increasing demand for reputable eyewitnesses.

38. This is continued in the practice of the canonization consistories and still recorded in bulls of canonization immediately before the canonization formula, e.g., "ac de plurimorum Fratrum Nostrorum consilio." See Robinson, *Papacy*, 110–13. Interestingly this formula later became bound up in the problems of conciliarism, and some have gone so far as to suggest that such an arrangement was nascent parliamentarianism, with the King-in-Parliament being similar to the pope-and-cardinals. See, e.g., Alberigo, *Cardinalato e collegialità*. This is too much of a stretch for a statement that merely expressed the existence of a consultative consistory or even a simple verbal formula contained in the canonization texts.

39. In a life of Adelaide by St. Odilo of Cluny from the 1050s, Odilo stated that Henry II was prevented from the panoply of a full public cult for Adelaide because "sine apostolici decreto clerici consensu celebrari non licuit." MGH, Scriptores 4, 644. Kemp, usually circumspect in such early

After this, a nearly fifty-year period elapsed during which there were no formal, solemn papal canonizations, merely confirmations of cult or permissions to translate, thus reinforcing the perception that solemn canonization was still an uncommon practice.

From the study of canonizations in the first four decades of the 1100s, one gains the impression that very little changed. Three saints were honored by a form of canonization between 1109 and 1134. Paschal II (r. 1099–1118) recognized Peter of Anagni in 1109 in a document that bore substantial resemblance to previous decrees. Much occupied in the Investiture conflict, Paschal had little time to recognize multiple cults, and the one he did was a local one from just outside Rome (over which he had ordinary authority as the local bishop). One small innovation concerned the conclusion of the letter of elevation: a call for prayers and intercession from the new saint.[40] Most of the decrees drafted after this would include some appeal to the new saint. This was perhaps to act as an internal guarantee against hypocrisy: a demonstration that the canonizing pope actually believed in what he was doing. Innocent II (r. 1130–43) canonized three individuals, though reigning for a shorter time (perhaps because of the increased atmosphere of security for the church after the Concordat of Worms). Neither of the documents of canonization for either Godehard of Hildesheim (canonized 1131) or Hugh of Grandmont (canonized 1134) gives evidence for any substantial development in the thought about papal canonization.[41] This would not be the case with the third saint. In 1139, at the Second Council of the Lateran, Innocent II canonized his last saint: Sturm of Fulda.[42] The difference with this elevation was that Sturm had died in the eighth century, and his cult was now only encouraged in the mid-twelfth century. Innocent II chose to recognize Sturm, already the subject of a local cult at Fulda, at this ecumenical synod, perhaps recalling that the bishop in life had been a dauntless partisan

---

cases, remarks, "It is very remarkable to find such a clear statement of papal rights as early as this"; cited from Kemp, *Canonization and Authority*, 69.

40. "Et in futurum, opitulante divina clementia, piis eius intercessionibus, mereamur gloriam sempiternam." Paschal II, "Dominum excelsum habentes" [Canonization of Peter of Anagni, 1109], Fontanini, 10. Paschal apparently also authorized the cult of St. Canute of Denmark but long after Canute's remains had been translated and his feast celebrated among the Danes. Kemp, *Canonization and Authority*, 69–70.

41. Interestingly, though, we do have the first solid evidence of increased liturgical solemnity. When St. Godehard was canonized, the church's thanksgiving song of praise, the *Te Deum*, was sung. See Klauser, "Die Liturgie der Heiligsprechung," 230n21; also Frutaz, "Auctoritate beatorum apostolorum Petri et Pauli," 439n2.

42. Innocent II, "Dignum valde est" [Canonization of Sturm of Fulda at Lateran II, 1139], Fontanini, 13.

of the pope against episcopal and political opponents in Germany. Sturm's canonization seems to usher in the age in which the popes began to make political statements in canonization, a phenomenon ably studied by Michael Goodich, at least concerning the thirteenth century.[43] In any case, Innocent's recognition of Sturm opened a new chapter in this story: the acceleration of theoretical papal centralization in canonization. For the first time, it seemed that members of the curia knew that canonization could be used *for* some determinate end.

Given all of the foregoing material, it helps to take stock at this point of what canonization was and was not during this period and to ask the question of whether one can speak of papal canonization in a formal sense yet. Ever since the seventh century, canonization by synod—at first local, then Roman—was a normal but not exclusive path to the honors of the altar. In fact, the vast majority of canonizations were still by spontaneous local recognition.[44] The development of synodal canonization came about because of worry about unworthy candidates as well as a desire to honor the saint with recognition by an esteemed assemblage.[45] The initial Roman canonizations looked this way as well. The fact that Rome was at the center of the church and drew ecclesiastics from around Europe meant that eventually non-Roman and non-Italian saints were among those who began to be recognized. Canonization was not (in spite of Leo IX's universalizing language) intended to be a herald of a universal cult. Over the first four decades of the twelfth century, several more canonizations occurred that were limited in scope and addressed to local churches or provinces rather than to the universal church. This informs us of two things. First, the elements that would later be employed in the reservation of papal canonization and the articulation of its superiority over other forms were already present, many of them explicit, others in seed. Second, it was not the Gregorian reform that took the lead in this movement. Arguments about the qualitative superiority of papal canonization date from the late twelfth and early thirteenth centuries and not from the period in question.

Even so, Roman canonization was on the cusp of achieving the qualitative breakthrough that it would achieve in the thirteenth century, yet its mechanism still needed assembling. The popes backed up their decrees with

43. See Goodich, "Politics of Canonization"; id., *Vita Perfecta*.

44. This development is traced with economy in Kemp, *Canonization and Authority*, 34–36; also in Vauchez, *Sainthood*, 14–32.

45. Besides the recognized solicitude of the early Roman church for its martyrs, the earliest conciliar legislation regulating cults came as early as the Council of Carthage in 401.

language redolent of papal supremacy and primacy in the church, investing their decisions with the authority of Peter and Paul, something that local bishops and synods could not do.[46] The increasing coalescence of accomplished jurists and canonists around the court of Rome during and after the Gregorian reform meant that the theology and the process were undergoing transition to a more standardized procedure. In short, canonization was in flux at this point. On one hand, it accurately reflected the tradition of episcopal confirmation and oversight over cults that had its roots in the fourth and fifth centuries.[47] On the other, the novelty of confirmation by someone in the increasingly prestigious see of Peter opened a widening horizon over which the sun was just beginning to break in the twelfth century. The popular sentiment that motivated spontaneous recognition of holiness eventually rechanneled itself into seeking the exciting and newly universal confirmation that was offered by the bishop of Rome.

⌁ The Axial Age of Papal Centralization: Innovation in Continuity

By the mid-twelfth century several significant streams had come together that encouraged the articulation of a new theory of papal canonization. The Gregorian reform had been generally successful, and this served to purify the church and make the hierarchy focus more on spiritual goods than it had in the past. This reformation of the papal curia allowed churchmen to take inventory of the possibilities inherent in papal governance of the church. The second was the conclusion of the Investiture conflict. This led to a lull in the conflicts between church and state, and though more struggles were in store for the future, the solution reached in the Concordat of Worms provided new principles for the papacy and the church to resolve those conflicts. This interval allowed for new and innovative approaches to the machinery of the papal curia. The third fundamental factor was the rediscovery of Roman law, the foundation of the University of Bologna, and the work of Gratian and the Decretists who turned church law into a scientific discipline. With such tools, the canonists were in a prime position to articulate more fully the implications of papal history and policy. Finally, the church

---

46. On this formula, see Frutaz, "Auctoritate beatorum apostolorum Petri et Pauli," 435–501. A very useful article, but he is mostly concerned about the development of the canonization language rather than the canonical or theological issues.

47. For this phenomenon, see Brown, *Cult of the Saints*, esp. 52–58.

had lived through the age of St. Bernard (1090–1153), who provided new impetus for the continuation and consolidation of all of the movements mentioned above. His Cistercian reform laid the groundwork for new and purified orders and gave the medieval church an example of monasticism not seen since the glory days of Cluny. The model of holiness provided by Cîteaux, as well as by the preachers of the new apostolic poverty movement, propelled the recognition of sanctity in the 1100s. It was no coincidence that these streams began to merge when Bernard's protégé Eugenius III (r. 1145–53) was elected to the Chair of Peter and canonized Henry II, the former German emperor. He did this by his own authority, outside of the customary conciliar atmosphere. In place of a general council, he asserted that he consulted with the prelates residing at the Apostolic See, which would come to be the common phrase used in future bulls of canonization.[48]

In the meantime, the 1140s saw Gratian and the lawyers of the school at Bologna lay the groundwork for the creation of a stable body of universal canon law. The first product of this movement was Gratian's Decretum, a readily accessible and rational compilation of the decrees of church councils, popes, bishops, and church fathers.[49] Contained in the Decretum was a summary of liturgical law called by its title: *De Consecratione*. Though scholars debate whether *De Consecratione* formed a part of the primitive first edition of Gratian's work, the Italian Decretist commentators recognized and commented on it by the early 1150s.[50] Gratian's work evinces a very high theory of the papal monarchy through the employment of texts, both authentic and otherwise, from the Christian tradition. While no direct allusion to the papal reservation or to canonization itself is to be found, *De Consecratione* does obliquely refer to canonization in Distinction 1, in canons 36 and 37, when discussing the burial place of the saints. Contrary to the rest of Distinction 1, the emphasis on the transfer and custody of saints' bodies is made dependent not on the pope but rather on the local bishop in canon 36 and on a synod of bishops in canon 37.[51] Nor is this an innovation by the author of *De Consecratione*, for the early compilers Burchard of Worms (ca. 965–1025) and Ivo of Chartres (1040–1115) included both of these can-

---

48. Eugenius III, "Sicut per litteras" [Canonization of Henry II, 1146], ibid., 14–15.

49. For a good introduction to medieval canon law, see Brundage, *Medieval Canon Law*. Particularly useful for is period is Gilchrist, *Canon Law in the Age of Reform*.

50. For this debate, see Van Engen, "Observations on *De Consecratione*," 309–20; and Winroth, *Making of Gratian's* Decretum. *Pace* Winroth and his discoveries, it seems that *De Consecratione* was an integral part of the canonical tradition from a very early date, even if it was not in the First Recension.

51. *De Cons.* D. 1, c. 36 & 37, in *Decretum Magistri Gratiani*, ed. Friedberg.

ons.[52] Episcopal translation was still the norm for local saints in practice as well as in law, though as legal thought developed after Gratian, lawyers and the papacy both concurred in reserving more power to the Roman see. In any case, like the Gregorians, the early Decretists seem content to recognize the traditional power of the local ordinaries in the translation of saints' remains. The canonists would remain strikingly traditional in this respect, with most of the innovation coming from the papacy and the theologians, yet the tools for such development were beginning to appear. In spite of this traditionalism, one of the most masterful Decretists did note a development. The accomplished commentator Huguccio (d. 1210) noted in his comments on the canon regarding the translation of saints' bodies that they "were not to be transferred without the consent of the pope or the bishops."[53] Nor were relics of the canonized person (here an early canonical use of the term) to be venerated without such approbation.[54] Though he couched his comments in traditional language, the preeminent Decretist was bearing witness to both changing terminology and practice.

The long and troubled (but ultimately successful) papacy of Alexander III (r. 1159–81) is correctly seen as fundamental to the Roman centralization of canonization.[55] Yet this view lacks sufficient scope, for while it is true that during this pontificate the principles of canonization were formally established and promulgated, further considerations need to be taken into account. During this period, the possibilities and promise of papal canonization for the Roman see finally became apparent. Alexander and other thinkers finally realized that in drawing on already established tradition, they had all the tools at hand to turn papal canonization into a means for centralizing control of the recognition of holiness and for presenting desirable models to the church. They also confronted the possibility that canonization could readily and usefully be applied to political issues, thereby advancing the cultural and political purposes of the Roman see. Combining these two issues, they realized that here was an already existing process whose purpose could be reimagined and reoriented to provide a tool for universalizing the agenda,

52. Kemp, *Canonization and Authority*, 42.

53. For an introduction to this crucial, but unedited, Decretist, see Müller, *Huguccio*.

54. "Corpora sanctorum . . . a nullo esset transferrenda. sine consensu papae vel episcoporum . . . ostendit corpora canonizata et alicui ecclesia sua auctoritate deputata non dicit quod reliquie alique non possunt concedi sine consensu papae vel episcopi. sed si corpus alicuius sancti iacet in aliqua ecclesia canonizatum non debet inde feri ad alium locum sine consensu talis persone." Huguccio of Pisa, *Summa*, Vatican: Biblioteca Apostolica, MS. Borgh. 272, 187vb.

55. See the essays in Clarke and Duggan, *Pope Alexander III* particularly Duggan's two essays, "*Alexander ille meus*: The Papacy of Alexander III," 13–50 and "Master of the Decretals: A Reassessment of Alexander III's Contribution to Canon Law," 363–418.

both religious and otherwise, of the bishop of Rome and his curia. When considered in the context of other innovations designed to standardize church practice and extend the authority of Rome developed at this time—legatine commissions, canon law, Councils of the Lateran, and (later) the mendicant orders—canonization fits in as an apt instrument with which to extend the influence of the Roman church. Really the only astonishing thing is that the Gregorians did not make it part of their strategy for papal reform.

In terms of canonization, the development was twofold. First was centralization by legal reservation. By this time it had become accepted custom that the popes had to be consulted before a translation of a prominent saint. Increasingly popes had also undertaken more and more developed investigations of proposed candidates, aided by the rise in legal professionalism at the curia over the twelfth century. What remained was to assert a right over the recognition of holiness itself, an audacious move but one whose principles already existed in seed over the previous two centuries. The second avenue of development was the determination of the qualitative difference between papal and local canonizations. While previous historians have accurately represented the first as fixed in this period by Alexander's own decretals, they have neglected to see that the development of differing levels of canonization was beginning here as well. Notice that I do not mean the root of a separate conception of beatification and canonization. All too often have earlier historians, starting with Benedict XIV, attempted to project that very late medieval or early modern disjunction onto canonization proceedings during this period. To argue that church thinkers began to see a difference between the two, with canonization representing papal activity and beatification a local one, is clearly an anachronism. The qualitative difference I am speaking of is the growing realization (and conscious advancement of the idea) that papal canonization is superior to local, spontaneous, episcopal, or conciliar canonization. This superiority would be realized by any number of strategies: increased prestige from papal approval, universality of the appeal of papal saints, approval by recognized and respected authorities, and last and perhaps most essentially, the idea that papal canonization gave one *certitude* over the results. If the Roman church confirmed a cult, the last court of appeal had been reached: *Roma locuta est, causa finita est* ("*Rome has spoken, the case is closed*"). As the thirteenth century progressed, this type of thinking would spill over into nascent debates over the possibility of infallibility in canonization, the greatest conceivable qualitative difference compared to local canonizations. The fact of a papal desire for reservation is not terribly significant. It is a legal quibble and was irrelevant at the grassroots level, since local canonizations continued apace throughout the medieval period. The claims of qualitative difference did matter: to popes, to the church at large, and to opponents of orthodox Christianity in the Middle Ages. The claims of qualitative difference in canonization framed the controversy over many issues, including mendicant poverty, and in so doing laid the groundwork for the infallibility debates of the early modern, modern, and contemporary Christian world.

A series of events transpired during Alexander III's reign that shaped the future direction of papal canonization. To earlier legal and institutional historians, the fundamentally significant moment was in either 1171 or 1172 when Alexander issued a letter to a "King K" of Sweden, probably Kol.[56] The letter includes all manner of instructions on Christian living, and appended to it is a condemnation of the cult of a man killed in a drunken stupor. Scholarly consensus, following Sven Tunberg's research, concludes that the unnamed saint is St. Eric of Sweden, whose dynasty Kol was opposing. Alexander was very clear in declaring that "it is not permitted for you to venerate him publicly as a saint without the authorization of the Roman Church."[57] This was the first distinct papal message that the approval of the public veneration of saints was the sole prerogative of the Roman church. Before this letter (and in practice, long after), the custom of locally recognizing saints and sainthood was the normal way of proceeding, but there had been a shift at the top. In Alexander's mind, unless the Roman church had control over public cults, aberrations like the one described in the letter might occur, to the grave detriment of the church and the faithful.

The fact nonetheless remains that the letter was directed to one individual and not to the whole church. The question of the binding force of the decretal came up in the 1930s and 1940s in a debate between Kemp and Stephan Kuttner. Kuttner argued that the letter was essentially private and had no ramifications in the larger Christian world until its incorporation in the definitive decretal collection called the *Liber Extra* in 1234.[58] Kuttner's argument is convincing, because he traced the delay in incorporating the letter into generally circulated law books, thereby showing the gradual and haphazard deployment of the decree. He is on shakier ground in trying to prove that Alexander was not trying to articulate a general legal doctrine but was only attempting to legislate on a particular case. Kemp has shown

---

56. For the debate on who is the mysterious "K. King of Sweden," see Tunberg, "[Commentary]," AB 273.

57. "Non liceret vobis pro sancto absque auctoritate Romanae Ecclesiae eum publice venerari." Alexander III, "[Letter to the King of Sweden]," PL 200, p. 629, col. 1259.

58. Kuttner, "La réserve papale du droit de canonisation," 172–228.

definitively that the idea of the papal reserve was being spoken of from the 1170s and later.[59] From the actions of the papal curia, it is clear that some idea of a papal reserve was developing (notably in England, where the decree first found its way into legal collections). Kuttner is right in saying that the law did not have universal binding force, but conversely Kemp is right in seeing growing consensus among church leaders for the sentiment expressed in the letter. Indeed, the delay in appropriating the letter may be precisely because this oversight had become generally accepted over the course of the previous centuries, a possibility Kuttner did not examine. Alexander himself speaks in the letter in a manner that makes one assume he is articulating a legal principle and not a one-off declaration (it may not be too far a reach to suggest that he is stating a relatively self-evident proposition by that time). Is one to assume only those presumed saints killed in a state of sinfulness are to be referred to the Roman see? This seems farfetched. In any case, all legal disagreement ended in 1234 with the inclusion of part of the letter in the *Liber Extra* of Gregory IX, edited by Raymond of Peñafort. The part of the letter relating to papal reserve over saints became known by its first word, *Audivimus*, and formed the key legal proof text for the centralization of papal canonizations in the centuries to come.[60] Whatever the original intention of the lawgiver, the particular had become the universal.

A problem arises from both of these scholarly analyses. Kemp was an institutional and intellectual historian, whereas Kuttner was a legal historian. The binding force of *Audivimus* is tempered by a very real circumstance that neither of the two considered: after 1234 it was rarely followed save by the pope and the canonists who considered it to be binding law. All through the Middle Ages the immemorial practice of local canonization continued. Local people continued to venerate new local saints. Bishops continued the ancient practice of translation. Cults sprung up that had no relationship to saints proposed by Rome. A huge disconnect then came to exist between the official line of church law and the lived experience of the Catholic Church. Canonists, for whom custom was always supposed to be the best interpreter of law, seem to have been strangely blind in this case. One after the other insisted on the absolute right of the Roman pontiff alone to create saints, even given the evidence of strong and enduring cults throughout Europe at the local level.

---

59. Kemp, *Canonization and Authority*, 96–105.

60. Alexander III, "Audivimus," in *Corpus Iuris Canonici* II, ed. Friedberg, X 3.45.1. Also see Wetzstein, "Audivimus (X 3.45.1)."

Recently historians interested in the social aspects of lived religion have made this disconnect readily apparent. It seems that local sanctity continued unabated, with people not really interested in confirmation of a cult from Rome unless they had a candidate who was sufficiently attractive to the curia and if they had enough money to prosecute the case. Many who might have been happy to have Roman recognition simply were content with traditional local veneration. Though popes claimed the sole right to canonize, they too tolerated the continuing practice of local canonization.[61] While eager to centralize, the papacy knew that it would be very difficult, if not impossible, to forbid local canonizations. Thus instead of banning local elevations and translations, the popes followed the canonists and theologians who tried to make papal canonization qualitatively different. This is the critical point. The papal reserve was not, as historians in the past have suggested, the central method by which the papacy began to consolidate the cult of saints. Such a move would have been impossible to make on practical grounds. Instead, the curia, canonists, and theologians set about articulating a new vision of canonization, one that demanded the pope's unique participation and set papally created saints far above those who were merely the subject of unconfirmed popular veneration. This development in the idea of papal canonizations also reveals itself in the increasing popularity of papal saints in the thirteenth century and conversely hints about why opposition to such saints mounted exponentially at that time. In order to see how all this progressed, one needs to look back at Alexander III's canonization practice.

Alexander's letter was clearly not the driving force behind his policy on saint creation. Had Alexander's policy in this letter simply remained in effect, canonization could have been locally delegated to papal legates, as happened in several instances. This would have achieved the same purpose of papal centralization, since the solicitation of the approval of the papal representative would have been seen as equivalent to canonization by the pope himself.[62] This would not, in the end, qualitatively differentiate papal canonization. Many saints were raised to the honors of the altar in one way

---

61. Many local canonizations carried out in the period before the renaissance gradually won acceptance by the Roman church, with certain restrictions. They remained local, the saints were usually only accorded the title of "Blessed," and most significantly infallibility was not brought to bear in these Roman "confirmations." This was an early modern distinction, though. This method of promotion became known as "Equipollent" Canonization; see Lambertini, 2:49–120.

62. Kemp points to several instances of legatine deputation for canonization, notably the case of St. Anselm, delegated to Archbishop Becket in 1163, and the canonization of St. Rosendo by Cardinal Deacon Hyacinth (later Celestine III) in 1172; see Kemp, *Canonization and Authority,* 83, 89–90. Again, Benedict's denominating these canonizations as "legatine beatifications" is anachronistic,

or another by Alexander or his delegates. Alexander evinced political acumen in the canonization of Edward the Confessor in 1161, since in this action he recognized the growing influence of the English crown by rewarding a king who stood with him against Frederick Barbarossa. In this instance Alexander continued Eugenius III's practice of proceeding immediately to canonization outside of a council yet retaining the saving clause about consulting the prelates in residence at the Holy See.[63] In addition Alexander ordered the first recorded curial celebration of a new saint's Mass after this canonization, though he delegated it to a cardinal.[64] The growing importance of political pressure is betrayed in Barbarossa's attempt to have his antipope Paschal III canonize Charlemagne in 1166.[65] Not only political capital was to be gained from the canonization of the first Holy Roman emperor, for Barbarossa's appeal to the antipope illustrates that recognition of holiness, to be deployed properly, had to achieve acknowledgment at the highest level, which only the pope could provide by this time.

More than Alexander's particular practices in canonizing, or the unique letter *Audivimus* that would later be incorporated into canon law, it was the canonization of Thomas Becket that proved to be a watershed moment for papal canonization. The brutal murder of Thomas Becket occurred in Canterbury Cathedral in the winter of 1170.[66] News of the crime spread quickly throughout Europe, followed by a genuine and transnational *cultus* of the martyred archbishop. At the same time, in spite of the spontaneous outpouring of devotion, there was reticence to honor the saint before the correct time. The erudite John of Salisbury chafes at the delay in waiting for formal papal approval yet shows no indication of endorsing public veneration until the decision of Rome.[67] William of Canterbury, one of the compilers of Becket's miracle collections reported an incident where a priest had a vision. The priest dreamed he was singing the divine office. Two monks in the

though it is interesting that Pope Benedict XVI resumed the practice of legatine beatifications in the present day.

63. Alexander III, "Illius devotionis constantiam" [Canonization of Edward the Confessor, 1161], Fontanini, 15–16. For this canonization, see Scholz, "Canonization of Edward the Confessor," 38–60.

64. Schlafke, *De competentia in causis sanctorum*, 33.

65. See Folz, *Le Souvenir et la légende de Charlemagne*, 203–37, esp. 209–10. In recognition of the action of the antipope and as a result of the small cult engendered by his actions, the papacy later permitted a very restricted cult of Charlemagne, allowing public devotions to him only in Aachen. This underscored the qualitative difference between formal canonization and equipollent canonization.

66. For Thomas's life, see Barlow, *Thomas Becket*; and Knowles, *Thomas Becket*.

67. John of Salisbury writing to French bishops, PL 199, cols. 359, 362; cf. Kemp, *Canonization and Authority*, 88.

vision disagreed whether Thomas, not yet canonized, ought to be venerated in the commemoration of the saints. One monk said it was not right since he had not yet been canonized by apostolic authority.[68] They split the difference and sang a song in English to honor the martyr. Such musings were in the air: a difference existed between local saints and those who had received the ultimate sanction of Rome.

The much-harried Alexander III, to whose court Thomas had once presented himself, wasted no time in inscribing Becket's name in the calendar of saints. In 1173, for the first time in the history of papal canonizations, Alexander III addressed the bull "Redolet Anglia" not just locally but "to the prelates of the whole Church."[69] It was the first time such language was employed in the proclamation of a saint. Until that time papal bulls of canonization had been addressed to prelates and churches that were local to the place where the newly canonized was from.[70] Alexander himself, only twelve years before, had addressed Edward's bull of canonization solely to the English church. Thomas's canonization set a new pattern for the popes. Previously they had communicated to local churches and had permitted the celebration of the new saint's feasts in those places. It was probably understood that other churches could also now begin to celebrate the saint's day, but it was not made clear until "Redolet Anglia." Alexander underscores the celebration of the new saint's day in no uncertain terms. Speaking to the prelates of the whole church, he said, "We warn you and the whole Church, that by the authority that we discharge, we strictly command that you solemnly celebrate the feast of the said glorious Martyr annually on the

---

68. "Non eam authenticam esse; nondum enim ex apostolica auctoritate catalogo martyrum martyr ascriptus est," from William of Canterbury's miraculary, in *Materials for the History of Archbishop Thomas Becket*, 1:150; cf. Kemp, *Canonization and Authority*, 88.

69. Alexander III, "Redolet Anglia" [Canonization of Thomas Becket, March 12, 1173], in Fontanini, *Codex Constitutionum*, 17. Even this was only after Alexander had communicated the traditional local bull to the church of Canterbury. Eric Kemp says that there were two copies of "Redolet Anglia," one addressed to the clergy and people of England, and one to the combined prelates of England; see id., *Canonization and Authority*, 87. However, the text used by Fontantini simply says, "Ad omnes prelatos Ecclesie." The letters received in England bore the title "Ad omnis prelatis Anglie," probably since they were sent to England directly. Given that Alexander's registers are missing, we are reliant mostly on recipients' records. Fontanini cites Baronius, working from Roman curial documents, as giving the above reading. Many historians, working from only the English exemplars, seem to have missed this point.

70. The single exception is the bull announcing the canonization of St. Gerard of Toul in 1050 by Pope Leo IX, which is addressed to all "sons of the Catholic Church." This canonization was a synodal act, subscribed to by all the prelates currently in Rome. Leo IX speaks of the canonization as the unanimous decision of the whole synod, even of the laity present. Leo IX, "Virtus divinae operationis" [April 23, 1050], in Fontanini, 5–7.

anniversary of his death."[71] Alexander was doing something new. On his own
authority he was communicating the creation of a new saint to the whole
church and commanding the observance of his feast. Were it not for the up-
surge of devotion to Thomas, it would have been very difficult for the pope
to make this kind of assertion. As it was, Alexander capitalized on Thomas's
popularity by beginning in earnest the papal reservation of canonization. It
is not unthinkable that this worked merely in one direction. Thomas's cult
was the first truly universal, popular cult of the Middle Ages.[72] It is quite
possible that the papal sanction added significant luster to an already burgeoning veneration for Thomas. Here one can see a significant symbiosis
between lived religion and papal policy. Alexander then used the canonization to sanction the already existing universal cult, situating the papacy as
the primary patron and moving force. As if to underscore his liturgical intention, Alexander immediately sang Mass in honor of Thomas.[73] It is from
this date that papal bulls presume that the honor paid to their new saints
would be universal. Though this veneration sometimes did not materialize,
papal canonization was assumed to create a universal cult ipso facto. In any
case, *Audivimus* should be read in the context of Alexander's canonizations
(something that Kuttner and Kemp really do not consider, being mostly
concerned with legal and institutional history). As Cardinal Boso stated in
his history of the Barbarossa schism, Alexander "canonized the Martyr by
his Apostolic authority."[74] By the time of St. Bernard of Clairvaux's canonization (1174), the pope made this personally clear. After the elevation,
Alexander immediately said Mass in the new saint's honor.[75] The pope's
mind on this issue, circa 1171–74, was clear. The popes had the power and
authority to authorize universal cults by the authority that they enjoyed.
Alexander seems to have assumed this position as normative.

Subsequent occupants of the Chair of Peter proceeded with increasing
circumspection in the face of a rising tide of petitions for canonization. These
came from all over Christendom, indicating the increasing desirability of Roman sanction of local saints. They may have done this for a variety of reasons, but one fact is unmistakable: a rising tide of supplicants asked the Holy

71. "Universitatem itaque vestrum monemus, et auctoritate qua fungimur, disctricte precipimus, ut natalem predicti gloriosi Martyris diem passionis suae solemniter annis singulis celebretis." Alexander III, "Redolet Anglia" [March 12, 1173], in ibid., 17.

72. See Foreville, "La diffusion du culte de Thomas Becket," 347–68; and my analysis of the spread of Thomas's miracles in Prudlo, "Martyrs on the Move." See also Koopmans, *Wonderful to Relate*.

73. Boso, *Boso's Life of Alexander III*, 86.

74. Ibid.

75. See the letter of Abbot Tromond on the canonization, PL 185, 626–27.

See for recognition. So many of these arrived at the curia that the popes of the late twelfth century considered it necessary to delegate investigations and sometimes canonizations to local bishops or papal legates. While this may have been a sensible solution to increased petitioning from areas with which the pope was unfamiliar, such practices would later lead to problems in the articulation of a theory of canonization. An early example was in 1173 when Cardinal Deacon Hyacinth (later Celestine III, r. 1187–91) canonized St. Rosendo in Spain.[76] When elected pope, Hyacinth apparently had misgivings about the legitimacy of his legatine act and solemnly confirmed the cult of Rosendo with full apostolic authority.[77] Celestine III realized that if papal canonization was truly to be something different it could not, in the end, be delegated. Another decision concerned cases where the papacy considered that it did not have the time to do justice to a proper examination of the life and virtues of a candidate. In this case the cause was often referred back to the local episcopate with the stipulation that should they find in favor of the candidate, they could consider him canonized by apostolic authority and were thus entitled to publish the fact. This happened in the cause of St. Anselm in 1163, when the canonization was referred back to Archbishop Thomas Becket, and again in the case of St. Ketill, remanded to the bishops of the province of Lund in Sweden in 1188.[78] Even in these cases, the pope made sure to be clear that the local bishops proceeded with apostolic authority in these issues.

> When you [Thomas Becket] were in our presence, you humbly and devotedly petitioned us to canonize Anselm of holy memory . . . whose life and miracles you presented to us. Since there were many others urgently seeking the same thing on behalf of other holy men, we thought fit to defer your request. . . . Now we entrust the matter to your care and discretion and command you by apostolic letter to summon into

---

76. See Smith, "Saint Rosendo," 53–67, who follows García y García, "La canonización de San Rosendo," 157–72. The article gives an overview of the glorification. For Celestine's canonizations in general, see Goodich, "Canonization Policy of Celestine III," 305–17.

77. AS, October 13, 290–92. Benedict XIV considers this to be a legatine beatification, which is how the church would view it today, but such a view is anachronistic. One could describe it as "local canonization" or the glorification of one with limited cult. Celestine was troubled enough to renew the canonization when he became pope. Lambertini, 1:9.7 and 1:11.4.

78. Kemp, *Canonization and Authority*, 83, 95. Even then, St. Anselm's cult was reaffirmed by a papal bull in 1494. Similar implied confirmations happened around the margins of Europe. Before 1200, two saints were proclaimed by the Icelandic bishops at the Althing: Sts. Jón Ögmundarson and Þorlák Þórhallsson. Karlsson, *History of Iceland*, 39. For Iceland, see Cormack, *Saints in Iceland*. The effort to "regularize" such canonizations is still evident in the contemporary church: John Paul II canonized St. Þorlákr again in 1984 on a visit to Iceland.

your presence our brothers, you suffragan bishops . . . and, after solemnly
reading the life of that holy man . . . you may proceed with the support
of our authority to carry out the findings of the council in respect of his
canonization. . . . We shall, by the Lord's will, ratify and confirm whatever you and the fore-named brethren decide in this matter.[79]

Later popes would realize that this "passing the buck" was damaging to papal claims, though one can understand the motivation of transferring com-
petence in light of the overburdened calendar of the curia. Another approach
was tried with Anno of Cologne, who after many travails was canonized by
legates in Germany in 1183. These had relied on false information about their
delegated authority, so their actions were technically illegal. This gave rise
to a small-scale schism when news of the lack of papal authorization arrived.
Part of the Cologne church celebrated Anno's feast day, while the other part
sang requiems for his soul. This dispute is significant. It demonstrates a change
in clerical sentiment, probably supported by popular feeling, that the authorization of Rome was both needed and desired for a correct celebration of
a saint's feast.[80] The story of the monks who disputed about whether to chant
an office for Thomas Becket before his canonization is similar; one can see
that the theory propounded by Alexander III in *Audivimus* was beginning to
echo throughout Christendom.

    In smaller ways popes were also making adjustments that would lead to
the articulation of a qualitative difference. Sometimes they authorized local
cults with implicit or explicit permission. This happened in the late 1170s,
when Alexander permitted the local veneration of William of Malavale with
the command to use the Office of Confessors on his feast while asking petitioners to wait for a more opportune time to press the case at the curia.[81]
Future popes would increasingly emphasize the distinction between local
cults, which continued to flourish, and the universal cults that could be authorized only by the Roman see. To bolster their claims, the popes began to
demand better documentation both of vitae and of miracles. Lucius III
(r. 1181–85) remanded the cause of Peter of Tarentaise, rebuking the peti-

79. Alexander III, "Dum in celebratione" [June 9, 1163], in Thomas Becket, *Correspondence of Thomas Becket*, 1:27–29. For Anselm's canonization, see id., 2: app. 1. For more on Anselm's cult, see Urry, *Saint Anselm*.

80. For the complicated history of this legatine canonization, see Brackmann, "Zur Kanonisation des Erzbischofs Anno von Köln," 157–70. This article is summarized in Kemp, *Canonization and Authority*, 91–93.

81. Kemp, *Canonization and Authority*, 91.

tioners for failing to provide any written evidence.[82] The charismatic age of spontaneous saintly acclaim was drawing to a close, with the initial move coming from the very top of the church. Similar rejections of causes increased in frequency over the next several hundred years and were one of the most common reasons for the refusal to canonize.

Where the papacy earlier had merely authorized cults or confirmed petitions from local churches, it now requested causes be presented to it. Little opposition confronted such requests. Combining the growing power of Rome with the proposition of universal cults, the popes were charting new territory. Using papal authority to promote a cult where none had existed was very new. Sometimes it worked; sometimes it did not. Over the course of centuries, successful attempts at papal centralization at least assured the universal presence of these saints, if not their veneration. These new acts created a situation in which people could ignore a specific papal directive (which occurred increasingly in the thirteenth century). Even worse, they presented an occasion whereby people could begin to dissent openly from the papal admonition to venerate a particular saint. When political or religious issues made a certain saint distasteful, in the past people were free simply to refuse homage. When his or her veneration became tied to a specific papal command, though, and when seen as part of the papacy's attempts to acquire hegemony over liturgical and spiritual presentations of holiness, an explosive combination could result. Little opposition to saints and sainthood had occurred throughout Christian history up to this point, mostly because recognition of sanctity was spontaneous, local, and spread organically. Now a top-down method of promotion and mediation began to lead to friction. When confronted, the papacy and church thinkers pushed back. When rebuffed by sections of the church, the curia refined its thinking, codified its processes, and advanced new ideas. It was not only an exalted idea of papal prerogatives that drove the development; impetus came from much broader sources: on the one hand, the negative indifference of sections of the Christian faithful to papally proposed saints and on the other, the spread of heretical ideas, one of which was the denunciation of the power and efficacy of the communion of saints itself.

---

82. AS, May 2, 322–47.

CHAPTER 2

"They Trust not in the Suffrages of the Saints"

Saintly Skirmishes

From the papal perspective, the early 1170s saw two significant events in the history of Christian sainthood. The murder of Thomas Becket at Canterbury and the papal repudiation of the cult of St. Eric in Sweden served to reorient the debate significantly. While these events transpired on the fringes of Europe, they were to have stunning consequences for the development of canonization. They set in motion the centralization and solemnization of canonizations in the hands of the papacy, a long and arduous process that would not be completed for almost five hundred years. In addition, new developments manifested themselves on the margins of Christian orthodoxy. Various heterodox factions began to appear throughout southern Europe, most of which directly challenged the efficacy and usefulness of the cult of the saints. Some of these groups were critical of the wealth of the church, particularly—almost aggressively—on display in the shrines of the saints. Others were critical of lay piety and devotion toward holy men and women. Still more attacked the communion of saints wholesale, as part of a comprehensive assault on the Christian worldview, for in their critique of the saints they were fundamentally fixated on undermining the Christian teachings of the goodness of the material world and the reality of the Incarnation of Christ.

✒ Smacking of Heresy?

The history of medieval heresy is currently a topic of intense study. Historians throughout the last half century have detailed, outlined, and questioned the multifaceted components of medieval heretical belief systems.[1] Since then, the attention of scholars has turned to the social and cultural contexts of heresy. This has led to a challenge voiced in some works to the presumed unity of belief among medieval heretics. Some authors have contended that Catharism was largely a myth, a construct of systematizing Dominican inquisitors.[2] Some scholars claim that the church outright invented heresy in order to aggrandize its power over society. This approach, using the hermeneutic of power relations, certainly has something to offer, but it remains one-sided. It undermines the real and genuine religious concerns of premodern people. An inability to comprehend the idea that religion was axial in medieval society or even could be the singularly highest criterion for living one's life is a handicap in approaching the lived reality of the Middle Ages. Those whom the church termed heretics were not simply envious of the church's dominating role in society; they did not want simply to arrogate power to themselves. They thought the church was wrong and that it was sending souls to hell. The orthodox church taught and thought conversely. The struggle between the established church and heretics in the Middle Ages was, above all, a spiritual struggle rooted in religious realities. Souls and eternal salvation were at stake, not merely the church's power to determine

---

1. Here is not the place for a comprehensive bibliographical overview, but some of the key standards for the study of heresy in the past half century are Dondaine, "La hierarchie Cathare in Italie," 280–312; id., "Le Manual de l'Inquisiteur," 85–194; Borst, *Die Katharer*; Manselli, *Studi sulle eresi del secolo XII*; Wakefield, *Heresy, Crusade, and Inquisition*; the essays in *Concept of Heresy*; and Lambert, *Cathars*. Many medieval texts and sources have also been edited, and I will note those where they occur. Some medieval material has been collected in Wakefield and Evans, *Heresies of the High Middle Ages*. Some early works on the inquisition are also still useful, e.g., Giraud, *Histoire de l'inquisition au moyen âge*; and Lea, *History of the Inquisition*.

2. See Pegg, "On Cathars, Albigenses and Good Men," 181–95. He lays out this nominalist program in the preface to his work *Most Holy War*. This approach is directly traceable both to postmodernist thought and to the rise of the analysis of medieval heresy in terms of power relations such as can be found in Moore, *War on Heresy*, and in his earlier *Formation of a Persecuting Society*. One must explore how heresy moved a whole civilization to violent action and toward development in doctrine. Catharism was a genuine strain of thought. Cathars lived and preached, had real dissenting theologies, debated with Catholics, and, more tellingly, held debates with other heretics (the Waldensians) and disagreed among themselves about the nature of Cathar doctrine. Some of their works remain. The church responded to them with the intellectual tools at its disposal, in reasoned refutations and in thousands of sermons and preaching campaigns. Many died, on both sides, for the confession of their beliefs. At stake for these men and women was eternal salvation itself.

behavior or to collect tithes.[3] From the Catholic perspective, heresy was real. It was a threat to the established order, and more specifically it was a contest for souls with eternal consequences. In the church's view, heretics erred about the underlying principle of all Christian truth: the Incarnation of the Son of God. If one fails to comprehend that reality, seeing instead only through the anachronistic lens of power relations, one apprehends only a portion of the story and misses essential components of the medieval order.

That said, using some of the insights gained from the analysis of power relations can help to challenge and question the elaborate reconstructions of Cathar hierarchies and sects favored by Dominican historians of the middle of the twentieth century.[4] It is certainly possible that systematizing Dominican inquisitors and theologians may have presumed organization and coherence where there was none, and they may have imported labels from the fathers (particularly Augustine) in order to explain the realities they actually encountered.[5] This does not mean they did not accurately ascertain and analyze the beliefs of the heretics. Like the faith of individual heretics themselves, the value of the church writers' descriptions of belief fall on a continuum. Cathar hearers (Cathar sympathizers who were not perfected believers or 'perfects') found many ways to conventionalize their religion in order that they could live side-by-side with Catholics, and since the 1990s scholarship has emphasized the extreme fluidity of religious identities in medieval Italy.[6] Research also suggests the relative scarcity of actual Cathars, maintaining that perhaps as few as 750 avowed heretics (i.e., perfects) lived

---

3. For a corrective to this view, see Lansing, *Power and Purity*, which recognizes the fluidity of Cathar identity while admitting its existence. See also Ames, *Righteous Persecution*. Gregory, *Salvation at Stake*, also supplies a useful frame for the question, particularly in his introduction.

4. See Dondaine, "La hierarchie Cathare en Italie," 280–312; followed by Lambert, *Cathars*. Many of their data were taken from the *Summa* of the ex-Cathar inquisitor Rainerio Sacconi in Dondaine, "Le Manual de l'Inquisiteur," 85–194. A newer edition is Raynerius Sacconi, O.P., 31–60; *SOP* 3.3430. Parts of Sacconi's *Summa* were translated in *HHMA*, 329–45. I am particularly inclined to give precedence to such works as Sacconi, Andreas Florentinus, Bonacorso of Milan, and the summa attributed to Peter of Verona, as they aver having direct contact with medieval heretics. A hermeneutic of suspicion is useful; a hermeneutic of dismissal is not.

5. For instance, the troping of medieval dualists as *Manichaeans* is drawn largely from Augustine's *Confessions*. From a very early date, though, churchmen began productively to analyze the issue at hand. See esp. Sackville, *Heresy and Heretics*, which analyzes the ways in which churchmen wrote in response to heresy, grew more sophisticated, and matured in their interpretations.

6. Lansing, *Power and Purity*, 82–83. More pervasive than outright heresy at the time were different levels of indifference to the church in general and to popular piety (especially in Italy); see Murray, "Piety and Impiety," 83–106. For indifference, see Tanner and Watson, "Least of the Laity," 395–423.

in northern Italy during the period from 1260 to 1308.[7] In spite of this evidence, heresy was considered a grave threat by the church and the state, which both strove to uproot it. Though it is true that church intellectuals labored intensely to systematize a sometimes incoherent body of heretical beliefs, it remains that some truly held those beliefs, albeit with differing levels of commitment. Many of the extant sources are problematic—especially inquisitorial and hagiographical texts—yet even in those one can glimpse lived religion and attempt a reconstruction or at least retrieve an echo of the worldview of the medieval layperson or heretic. The preceding considerations notwithstanding, the key to the present work is precisely the way in which churchmen understood and responded to heretical belief as they saw it. For the response of the church in the development of the theology of papal canonization, the key is not what the heretics or laity actually thought but how that thought was understood by Catholic intellectuals responding to perceptions of lay or heretical thoughts and deeds.

Several facets of heretical thought repeated themselves throughout the medieval period often enough that church officials came to recognize them as central tenets. Among these strands was the condemnation of the idea of a communion of saints. Inquisitorial records and manuals, chronicles, and sermons all actively discussed this belief and imputed it to Cathar heretics. This doctrine manifested itself early in the history of medieval heresy and reappeared throughout the medieval period. Nor was the dissention limited to Cathars. Denigration of the veneration of saints was also a characteristic of the Waldensian heresy. Though Catharism and Waldensianism opposed each other in terms of their overall belief structure, they shared this doctrine, which the church discerned to be a growing threat. This general antisainthood tenet later became more complicated by the curious fact that it came to be particularized. By 1300 Cathars and later heretics began to set up a parallel communion of *heretical* saints and directly opposed them to particular Catholic saints—a clear example of what Carol Lansing calls the conventionalization

---

7. Zanella, "Malessere ereticale," 47–49. Zanella is writing about the period after the reaction of the church following the murder of Peter of Verona and the promulgation of "Ad extirpanda," Innocent IV's 1252 bull systematizing the papal inquisitions. In the early 1200s there were certainly many more Cathars, a result of the migration of Cathar perfects after the Albigensian Crusade and their expulsion from French-speaking territories. There was a serious decline in their numbers after the reaction to the martyrdom of Peter of Verona, particularly in Italy. See Prudlo, *Martyred Inquisitor*, 74–76. Rainerio Sacconi estimated that there were fewer than four thousand perfected Cathars in the whole of Christendom at the time he was writing, *HHMA*, 337; Zanella is of the opinion that the number was much smaller after 1260, which is very likely true. Catharism in Italy was on the road to extinction. The Cathars' theological significance was out of proportion to their numbers.

of heresy into the dominant forms of lived religion. To begin, one must investigate the origins of these convictions.

Some accounts of early medieval heresy note opposition to the veneration of saints as part of a laundry list of Catholic doctrines rejected by heretics.[8] Though these appear mostly as topoi of what an idealized "heretic" would reject, these narratives underscored that saints and sainthood were to be real and specific targets of the actual heretics who came later.[9] From late antiquity the cult of the saints had developed apace: a defining aspect of both eastern and western Christendom with very few voices raised against it. The cult of the saints, of very early Christian origin, developed quickly, marked by relics, altars, feast, vigils, and pilgrimages, and quickly came to dominate the Christian world.[10] The cult of the saints continued to flourish—perhaps the most prodigious indicator of lay religiosity in the early medieval world. But all was not well. In 970 the priest Cosmas preached a sermon about a group known as the Bogomils. He denounced them for their renunciation of icons and their rejection of the relics of the saints.[11] Similar sentiments began to appear in the west, too. Around the 1020s the French monk Adémar of Chabannes warned of the precursors of antichrist in his Aquitanian chronicle. In it he particularly cautioned about those who denied the intercession of the saints, for they were the forerunners of the antichrist who would seduce the Lord's flock.[12] One can sense his disquiet: those who would challenge such an immemorial and intrinsic part of Christianity must necessarily presage the end times.

Around the turn of the millenium various reports regarding heterodox groups began to appear in the west. This was uncommon. For long centuries the western half of Christianity had been seemingly immune from heterodox movements. From the narratives that have survived about these new groups, one discerns some unifying themes. Many clearly exhibited

---

8. See the account of the 1022 heresy outbreak in Orléans, where the heretics were accused of holding: "Sanctos martyres atque confessores implorare pro nichilo ducebant." "Codex Diplomaticus," ed. Guérard, 111; cited from *HHMA*, 20–21.

9. The best work done on this topic, though strikingly brief, is by d'Alatri. See his "Culto dei santi," 85–104, which is a bit expanded in his *Eretici e inquisitori in Italia*, 1:23–43. D'Alatri collected some of the scattered work on the subject by previous authors: Borst, *Die Katharer*, esp. 213–20, and Manselli, "Per la storia dell'eresia," 210–34.

10. "Late-antique Christianity, as it impinged on the outside world, *was* shrines and relics" (italics his), Brown, *Cult of the Saints*, 12 and passim; and Brown, *Society and the Holy*.

11. "He who does not honor all the saints and does not revere their relics with love, cursed be he!" Sermon by Cosmas the Priest, AD 970, edited in Peters, *Heresy and Authority in Medieval Europe*, 117. I make no claim here about the transmission of Bogomil theology to the west.

12. Adémar of Chabannes, *Chronique*; cited from Taylor, "Letter of Héribert of Périgord," 332.

distaste for institutional Christianity, accompanied by rejection of the external forms of Christian worship. This rejection involved not only saints and their images but also the sacraments and priestly ministry themselves. This may perhaps be related to a rising Donatist thread in the eleventh century: laity seeking out a purified Christianity and equating sin with a sort of ritual impurity that rendered the sacraments themselves null when performed unworthily. While this would later manifest itself positively in the Gregorian reform, in the first part of the eleventh century it was a troublesome indicator tied to a rejection of what some saw as impure, visible Christianity. This is not the only possibility. It is conceivable that a latent natural dualism had begun to appear, one that has sprung up in many times and cultures (for example, Zoroastrianism, Daoism, or various Hindu systems). Christianity had confronted this antimaterialism from the very beginnings, starting with Docetism and Gnosticism and continuing into fourth-century Manicheanism. Bolstered by its strong belief in the goodness of creation and its radically unique doctrine of the Incarnation, the church was long familiar with having to defend goodness of the visible created order. Indeed, the church positively reveled in the material world, with its valorization of water, oil, bread, wine, procreation, and such in its sacraments and tenets. The Christian church was a force against the popular tendencies to antimaterialism, while at the same time it similarly rejected a rarefied Platonism that saw the body as an unnecessary instrument. Such positions had generated strong reactions in the past, and the church was about to confront these familiar issues again.

✒ Heresy on the Ground

The first two reports of western medieval heresy come from France, one in Orléans in 1022 and one in Arras in 1025. While these two groups may be unrelated, they share some characteristics. The Orléans outbreak, as reported by the monk Paul of Chartres, embraced a docetistic Christ, ghostly and immaterial, who eschewed all of the bodiliness of orthodox Christianity, including Incarnation, death, and Resurrection. Flowing from this conviction, the Orléans heretics denied the visibility of the church, from the baptism of water to the consecration of bread and wine, and finally the invocation of martyrs and confessors.[13] Such antimaterialism was going to be at the heart

---

13. From *Vetus Avignon* 6.3, ed. Benjamin-Edmé-Charles Guérard, in "Cartulaire de l'abbaye de Saint-Père de Chartres," *Collection des cartulaires de France* 1, in Collection de documents inédits sur

of most medieval heresies. The denial of the Incarnation and the church's defense of the goodness of the material world would be the spiritual battleground of the Middle Ages. The heretics at Arras in 1025 sounded much the same; they denied baptism, the Mass, and marriage. They differed from the Orléanists in one interesting detail, though. They refused veneration to saintly confessors (people such as St. Martin or St. Augustine), though they admitted that apostles and martyrs were to be honored. One could speculate that the rejection of such specific episcopal saints could be a generalized antiauthoritarian reaction. This also may reflect a growing insistence on the necessity of hewing to early Christianity, especially to practices sanctioned by the New Testament. It may also be an early expression of the idea that true Christianity had been lost at the age of the closing of the Great Persecutions.[14] Desire for a purified Christianity, free of the corruption of the early eleventh-century church, began to mix with a spiritualist and idealist vision for the Christian faith. The inability to combine creatively the ideas of purity and materiality—which had always been a part of orthodox Christianity—led some in the Middle Ages to seek antimaterial answers and to sunder the connection between the material world and the idea of the good. Such concepts fed into reform movements on one hand—which resulted in the purification of church life without rejection of the material—and heretical groups on the other, who sought to make the divorce between goodness and materiality final, a position that left them diametrically opposed to historical Christianity. In the end, it is very difficult to discern more than furtive glances from eleventh-century sources, for the real story of medieval heresy begins in the twelfth century.[15]

In the 1140s there was an outbreak of heresy in central France, which placed the movement directly in the path of St. Bernard at the height of his influence.[16] Around 1144 Eberwin, the Norbertine prior of Steinfeld, wrote to St. Bernard to ask his advice on a group of heretics that had been uncovered in Cologne. Eberwin identifies what may be an early precursor to Cathar beliefs in the antimaterialism and Donatism of the group. Their emphasis on purity meant that the group rejected the external church and in-

---

l'histoire de France, ser. 1: Histoire politique (Paris: 1840), 1:111–12. See above, n8, cited from *HHMA*, 78.

14. *Acta synodi Atrebatensi*, 1:3, cited from *HHMA*, 83.

15. For a summary of the long debate about the significance of eleventh-century heresy, see Siegel, "Italian Society," 43–72, particularly 44n3.

16. For Bernard, see Bredero, *Bernard of Clairvaux*. One should also see the extensive work of Jean Leclercq, including his last, *Second Look at Bernard of Clairvaux*, the fruit of a lifetime of consideration of Bernard, the Cistercians, and the religious world of the twelfth century.

stead focused on their perception of an unadulterated New Testament Christianity. In light of this they declared that one called on the saints to no avail, and they condemned any observances not clearly instituted by Christ or the apostles.[17] A radicalized emphasis on purity led them from a mere rejection of institutional Christianity to antimaterial doctrines. So far, saints and sainthood were rejected only insofar as they pertained to the repudiation of the externals of the Catholic Church, a rejection of post-apostolic practices, or to corruption. There seems to be no direct attack on saints or sainthood yet. Such a tack continues throughout the eleventh century. In an instance in Rheims in the 1170s, two heretical women—I will not wade here into the debate about their supposed witchcraft—profess their disdain for begging the intercession of the saints. As was common in other instances, this was related to the doctrine of purgatory and for prayers offered for the dead.[18] Both of these instances seem to relate to popular discontent (though not, by implication, widespread), and it seems that such ideas found popularity in urban environments among the lower classes. In many of these movements there was a decidedly anticlerical spin, but by no means was dissent relegated just to the poor and unlettered.

Two movements arose around the late 1100s that came from learned quarters. The small movement begun by the Piacenza jurist Hugo Speroni was one of these. Not especially concerned with antimaterial doctrines, he was beset by a virulent hostility to the institutional church, perhaps born of frustrated litigation. This anticlerical hatred, not necessarily heretical in itself, began to veer in that direction as he began to embrace Donatist-type positions around 1177. Master Vacarius, in a letter confronting the errors of his onetime friend, details Hugo's position on saints' days. Speroni had denied that saints' days were to be days of rest and feasting, and Vacarius corrected him.[19] In this case there appears to be no organic connection to antimaterialism, but rather a serious grudge against the church, exemplified in a strong emphasis on predestinarianism and the rejection of good works (many of which in the Middle Ages involved devotion to saints' cults). Speroni's heresy is interesting because he underlines the disconnect generated when two attitudes common among the medieval laity came into contact:

---

17. "In suffragiis sanctorum non confidunt . . . caeterasque observantias in Ecclesia quas Christus et apostoli ipso discedentes non condiderunt, vocant superstitiones." *Letter of Eberwin of Steinfeld to Bernard*, PL 182, col. 679.

18. "Non credunt ignem purgatorium restare post mortem, sed statim animam a corpore solutam vel ad requiem transire, vel ad damnationem." Ralph of Coggeshale, *Chronicon Anglicanum*, 124, cited from *HHMA*, 253.

19. Da Milano, *L'Eresia di Ugo Speroni*, 480–81, cited from *HHMA*, 157.

anticlericalism and ardent veneration of the saints.[20] Many laypeople could be, and regularly were, critical of the clergy, yet their devotion to the saints was unbounded. This anticlericalism worked itself out in any number of efforts to circumvent the established church, most of them nonheretical. The apostolic poverty and preaching movement was born of such a tension, as well as the call for increased clerical purity. The turn to new religious and monastic orders, the founding of lay confraternities, and the increasing lay patronage of saints' cults were all conditioned to some extent by anticlericalism. Coming from the wealthier classes of the city, it was all well and good for Hugo to be anticlerical—there were sympathetic enough ears for that—but to demand work on feast days is probably what led to his heretical group being small and short-lived. A generalized anticlericalism was accepted, but when it began to impinge on other treasured areas of medieval Christianity, people rejected such a movement out of hand. Medieval laypeople, mostly content to mock the clergy over their wine cups, were reluctant to bend on a doctrine that not only was dear to their piety but also guaranteed so many of the benefits of living in medieval society.

A second source of learned opposition came from the circle surrounding the arts master Amalric of Bena at the University of Paris. Caesarius of Heisterbach, the Cistercian chronicler, described the condemnation of his group of followers in 1210. In it one can detect a trace of disparagement of unlearned lay religiosity among Amalric's followers: "They said to erect altars to the saints and to use incense before sacred images was idolatry. They mocked persons who kissed the bones of martyrs."[21] This heresy seems to stem from theological speculation and had no popular support whatsoever. One can infer a tone of academic contempt and superiority regarding normative lay practices. It is interesting, though, that opposition to saints' cults cut across social and educational boundaries, however weak and sporadic that opposition might have been. Clearly there was something in the church's embrace of the cult of the saints that made it a lightning rod for criticism. It was the most external and visible manifestation of incarnational faith among clergy and laity. The cult of the saints—in addition to the doctrine of the

---

20. The profusion of scholarship on saints' cults demonstrates this enduring lay preoccupation with sainthood. For an overall introduction, see Vauchez, *Sainthood*; id., *Laity*. The studies on individual saints, too numerous to mention, underscore this point. Anticlericalism was a constant leitmotif in the Christian societies of the period, most often not indicating heretical sentiment. Anticlericalism certainly played a decisive role in both the early reform movements and the nascent heretical groups.

21. "Altaria sanctis statui, et sacras imagines thurificare, idolatriam esse dicebant; eos qui ossa martyrum deosculabantur, subsannabant." Caesarius of Heisterbach, *Caesarii Heisterbacensis*, 1:304, trans. in *HHMA*, 259.

sacraments—came under grave attack. In being so intimately associated with lived Christianity, those who embraced heterodox opinions concentrated much of their attack on the two aspects of the faith that most demonstrated an incarnational worldview: saints and sacraments. Public, visible manifestations of the Catholic commitment to the goodness of the material world made easy targets for learned and unlearned alike. Spurred on by theological criticisms, the battle over lay religiosity and heresy would center on those two central aspects of medieval Christianity.

Up to this point we possess only a series of short narratives, stretching over a period of one hundred years. These are impressionistic and far from comprehensive or coherent. They offer glimpses of a world in which saint veneration was ubiquitous but was nevertheless seen as a target for criticism in many parts of Christendom and from various levels of society. Indeed, opposition to the cult of the saints in some form crossed various doctrinal and geographical boundaries. In the foregoing examples, one can see a pattern developing in which objection to saint's cults in some form is characteristic of medieval heresies, to the extent of its being a salient doctrinal deviation that should fix our attention by its ubiquity. One should investigate how and why this came to pass. In the first place, medieval Christians, clergy and laity alike, embraced saints' cults, most especially their local and traditional ones. Besides the sacraments, which were occasional highlights in a person's life during this period, the interaction with saintly patronage dominated medieval conceptions of Christianity. Indeed, as Peter Brown shows, such devotion most clearly demonstrates the artificial distinction between lay and elite religiosity. Simply, the laity and the clergy together loved the saints, prayed to them, endowed their shrines and altars, made arduous pilgrimages to come into physical contact with their earthly remains, and expected no less than miracles.[22] While there were other factors in play—economics, politics, and a premodern conception of patron-client relationships—the fundamental factor here is religious. Some of these activities may have been about power, but such an explanation is anachronistic and alien to premodern minds. Above all, the response to saints was devotional, born of the incarnational character of orthodox Christianity. It would be most unfair, then, to characterize the scattered opposition to saints and sainthood as anything less than a properly religious response. The key question is, what sort of contrary religious response would occasion a rejection of one of

---

22. A vast literature exists on medieval hagiography. I proceed from the assumptions of Peter Brown, in his *Cult of the Saints*. See also Bynum, *Resurrection of the Body*; Freeman, *Holy Bones, Holy Dust*; and Vauchez's corpus, esp. *Sainthood*. For a particularly insightful recent effort into the cult of a single saint and her place in medieval Europe, see Jansen, *Making of the Magdalen*.

the most indigenously Christian practices that bound society together across time, geography, and social category?

At this juncture, one could make several tentative speculations. Given the popularity of saints' cults, it may be possible to infer from the frequency of miracle stories—thousands of which remain from the period—that some felt frustrated and excluded by the inability of a patron to come to their assistance. This is a possible reason, but solid evidence is lacking. I merely suggest it as plausible given the popularity of saints' cults paired with the possibility of marginalization or alienation because of the perceived ineffectiveness of the patron. The mental condition of one who has made an arduous journey seeking healing and has come away uncured can certainly be plagued with discouragement, even when buoyed by faith. In spite of this, little recorded evidence of embittered clients of saints exists. The usual reaction was merely to select a more productive patron.[23] A position with more support in the sources is that the rising tide of Donatistic ideas and everpresent anticlericalism led some to rebel against the apparatus of medieval sainthood because of its too-close connection with the institutional church.[24] One sees this in the repeated references to perceived early Christian or New Testament observances being the sole criteria for valid Christian practice (a contention that will survive into the Reformation era). Given the absence of a clearly manifested cult of the saints in primitive Christianity, heretics called for a purification that would kill two birds with one stone: excessive clericalization as well as unbiblical practices relating to the cults of saints. Along these lines, perhaps heretics rebelled against the cult of saints because they were a means of clerical social control. I think that this approach is quite wrongheaded, since scattered opposition to saints existed long before the church began to implement procedures for the selection of those to be canonized or the standardization of church doctrine on this matter.[25] It was really the reverse, for it was precisely heretical opposition that drove institutional change and refinement of doctrine. Related to this was perhaps a

---

23. A position that might be termed *Kathenodulia* (with credit to Max Müller's concept of *Kathenotheism*). It would be an interesting study to map out medieval Christians' strategies of invocation.

24. Part of the genius of orthodox Christianity had been to see the popularity of saints and their cults from almost the beginning and to create a system of oversight of such lived piety, making it almost impossible to disentangle "clerical" or "institutional" Christianity from the cults themselves. One thinks of Peter Brown's memorable image of Paulinus of Nola and Ambrose as *impresarios*, working to manage local cults and through them marshaling support for orthodoxy. Brown, *Cult of the Saints*, 30–38, 49, 63–67, 90. Similar to this is the case of Athanasius and his patronage of the cult of Antony of the Desert.

25. In the heresies of the eleventh century, not to mention the difficulties posed by the priest Vigilantius to St. Jerome, ca. 400 AD.

growing individualism. Exclusion, self-imposed or otherwise, from one of the primary communitarian practices of the age may have reinforced the idea of the individual.[26] Freed from the social ritual of procession, feast, fast, and pilgrimage, one was able to manifest independence from social convention, an experience simultaneously liberating and alienating. In the end most of these antihagiological tendencies worked themselves out into the radical spiritualist puritanism of antimaterialism. Sainthood, like the rest of the ceremonies of Catholicism, is immersed in materiality. Robert Wilken has commented, "Christianity is an affair of things."[27] The sacraments are intimately related to the material world and so came under attack. Likewise, sainthood, from the perspective of its devotees, was all about bodiliness. Veneration of relics, shrines, physical presence, posture, visible ceremony—all of these are integral components of the cult of saints. They are a material manifestation of spiritual realities. That Christianity recognized this is what separated it from all other religious worldviews: matter itself was salvific. In the hands of nascent dualists, such things above all else had to go. Instead of scattered instances of clumsy attacks on Church power, one can attribute a staggering unity and consistency to such rebellion: it assailed the church in these externals because it was going ultimately after the Incarnation.[28]

➷ The Rise of the Cathars

As one can discern in the report about the proto-Cathars at Cologne, heresy was moving from Donatistic versions of purifying the church into an antimaterialism that would eventually morph into outright dualism. Earlier, it could be said that the denial of saints' cults was a stereotyped charge leveled against earlier heretics, a trope used by writers as shorthand to indicate heterodox people. As time went on, this commonplace view began to transition into more sophisticated theological claims. Mariano d'Alatri traced the development from topos to lived denial of the communion of saints in his work. It began not as attack on the saints as such but rather as an affirmation

---

26. See Morris's interesting but problematic *Discovery of the Individual*.

27. Wilken, *Spirit of Early Christian Thought*, 261. He goes on, "At the center of Christian worship is a material, palpable thing, the consecrated bread and wine, through water one is joined to the church, and through things, the Holy Cross, the rock of Calvary, the sacred tomb, God accomplished the salvation on the world."

28. Andreas Florentinus clearly makes this connection. Himself a heretic for fourteen years, he identifies their central error not as dualism, but as denial of the incarnation, which then leads to errors about everything else, like creation and marriage. Andreas Florentinus, *Summa contra hereticos*, 39.

of the equality of believers and of an exclusive salvation doctrine.[29] He tracks Cathar denial of this belief first to their idea of a total equality of reward in heaven and punishment in hell.[30] This led them to claim that the saints were no more exalted in heaven than anyone else. Inquisitors would challenge them in this belief by asking "whether the Blessed Virgin Mary and Blessed Agnes had greater merits than any sinner newly consoled."[31] Later, Rainerio Sacconi, a Cathar-turned-Dominican-inquisitor, contended that his former coreligionists in Lombardy maintained that no saints were in heaven until the final judgment. Moneta of Cremona and Anselm of Alexandria concurred that the Cathars held these beliefs.[32] Rainerio, though, was the most direct and the most compelling. Citing the personal evidence of seventeen years among them, he marveled that the Cathars never prayed in private, invoked the intercession of the saints, or used the sign of the cross.[33] In this Rainerio touched on something of lay piety. Laypeople knew exactly who the heretics were: they did not behave ritually or cultically as Catholics. For everyday medieval men and women it had nothing to do with orthodoxy or belief but rather whether their neighbors did Catholic things.[34] This would lead to a disjunction in the late 1200s between lay emphasis on orthopraxis and clerical insistence on orthodoxy.

Perhaps most distressing to any further formalization of the theory of canonization was the growing perception of Cathar insistence on exclusive salvation. The clerical sources all agree that for a person to go to heaven, Cathars demanded that a person be consoled. For them the *consolamentum* was the sine qua non of membership in the true church and admission into paradise. This had an array of theological implications (and could certainly be seen as a response to exclusivist Catholic belief). In one fell swoop, this Cathar belief eliminated the need to appeal to the external instruments of salvation: good works, pilgrimage, almsgiving, saints' cults, and most particularly the sacraments mediated through the church. Baptism of material water could

---

29. D'Alatri, "Culto dei santi," 86–87.

30. See, e.g., *Beiträge zur Sektengeschichte des Mittelalters*, ed. Döllinger, 2:66, "quod culpae et gratiae non sunt aequales, nec poenae nec proemia, et quod aliqui aunt nunc in paradiso"; also, from Bonacorso of Milan's anti-Cathar tract (ca. 1170), "Omnes erunt equales tam in gloria quam in pena, sicut ipsi credunt, exceptis albanensibus," discussed in d'Alatri, *Eretici e inquisitori*, 25.

31. Dollinger, 2:325; cited from d'Alatri, *Eretici e inquisitori*, 1:25. "Si beata Maria virgo et b. Agnes sunt majoris meriti quam aliqua peccatrix noviter consolata."

32. D'Alatri, *Eretici e inquisitori*, 1:26; for Anselm, see *HHMA*, 362–63; for Moneta, see ibid., 309–29.

33. "Nunquam etiam implorant auxilium vel patrocinium angelorum, seu beate Virginis, vel sanctorum, neque muniunt se signo crucis." Raynerius Sacconi, *Summa de Catharis*, 45.

34. For this, see Thompson, *Cities of God*, particularly the epilogue.

not gain one salvation; neither could communion of material bread or the veneration of a material relic. This heretical doctrine clearly has political as well as religious overtones, breaking down social boundaries and emphasizing an ultimate equality, much as later *danse macabre* images would emphasize the universal destination of rich and poor alike. Salvation had been brought by Christ, who was no "respecter of persons."[35] Through Cathar consolation, of course, one could achieve the perfect equality of heavenly bliss denied by the vagaries of material reality and accidental social condition. Further, not only was salvation equally *possible*, but the bliss of the spiritual homeland was itself *equal* in all the elect.[36] Contrary to the Catholic belief of perfect bliss for all, while maintaining different degrees of happiness according to merit, this was equality absolutized, in every area of human existence, earthly and paradisal. Its implications reached to the roots of human anthropology and changed the entire received basis of soteriology. Ironically, of course this perfect equality of access gave birth to a spiritual elite: the consoled themselves. One spiritual elite of Catholic saints was merely replaced by another of consoled perfects.

In this sense, the church itself was but an accidental enemy, a foe that had merely embraced materialist practices antithetical to true religion. The real enemies were the material world itself and the "Prince of this world," who exercised his dominion though materiality.[37] A dualist theology of history arose from this position. All of salvation history could be neatly divided into two easily separated classes. The first was shot through with the many who defended materiality with its attendant violence, coercion, wealth, social distinctions, and the various institutions that defended these things, including such social essentials as marriage, seen as the root perpetuator of materialism, the enemy of the spirit. Ranged on the other side was the much smaller number of those who knew the true and straight path, who saw through the manifold temptations of the material world to the true nature of reality. These saw Christ as a mystical teacher of spiritual truths. Material appearances such as birth, death, and resurrection were utterly tangential to what Christ had really come to accomplish. What was necessary was the aural communication of the spiritual truths about the evil of the material world. Hearing and accepting this message was salvation. Rejecting it and fighting against it

---

35. Acts 10:34.

36. Peter of Verona's *Summa* (ca. 1235) explicitly attacks this doctrine of the equality of punishment and merit; Perugia: *Biblioteca Comunale*, MS 1065, f. 80va–82rb.

37. This view is not only found in the clerical antiheretical literature but also on full display in the Cathar *Book of Two Principles*, less an anti-Christian book than a full dualist apologia. *HHMA*, 511–92.

enlisted one among the defenders of false, materialist Christianity joined in a diabolical alliance with the state, which together strove to defend the status quo that perpetuated the subjection of those enslaved to matter. In this cosmic struggle it was vital to identify the protagonists, to name those who stood on either side. The heroes of "materialism" had to become villains, and so as the 1100s ended and the 1200s began, the theological implications of equality in salvation and exclusivity began to reveal themselves in confrontation with the saints of the Catholic Church.

For the purposes of this study, the central result of these claims was the elaboration of persons whom Cathars emphatically considered *not* to be in heaven. Bonacorso of Milan, writing as an early convert from Catharism sometime between 1176 and 1190, is an extremely valuable early witness.[38] His work represents the earliest anti-Cathar text from someone who claimed inside knowledge of the groups. The overall impression one gets is that the Cathars of Italy were at that time quite advanced in their theological speculations and had begun sophisticated biblical exegesis using their speculative dualism. Their first target was the Old Testament. While there had always been some discomfort in the Christian tradition with certain episodes from the Old Covenant, orthodox theology had been able to offer defenses of questionable practices. The problem was that these did require some theological sophistication to grasp.[39] When one heard stories about God's command for Abraham to sacrifice Isaac, his order for the spoliation of the Egyptians, or his call for the prophet Hosea to take to himself a "wife of fornications," it could be easy to jump to the conclusion that the God of the Old Testament was a demon. Ever since the heresy of Marcion in the second century, the church had ceaselessly proclaimed the goodness and necessity of the Old Testament, but Catharism provided an exceptionally easy way to explain these texts to people.[40] Simply put, the "God" of the Old Testament was Satan.[41] This had a marked effect on their exegesis. Bonacorso

---

38. Bonacorso of Milan, *Vita haereticorum*, PL 204, 775–91, partially translated in *HHMA*, 171–73. Studies include Ilarino da Milano, "La 'Manifestatio heresis catarorum,'" *Aevum* 12 (1938): 281–333; and Manselli, "Per la storia dell'eresia," 189–211.

39. Practical dualism offered simple explanations of hard texts. Speculative monotheism, on the other hand, involved the three monotheistic religions in deep and exceptionally difficult theodicies about the place of evil in the providential design of an omnipotent God.

40. Foreshadowings of the repudiation of a Docetistic-Gnostic dualism can be seen in the Gospel of John itself.

41. This position is outlined in the *Summa* by Praepositinus of Cremona around 1200, where he writes against "Opinio hereticorum qui dicunt legem et vetus testamentum a diabolo datam et nullum ante Christum salvum fuisse." Praepositinus of Cremona, *Summa contra Catharos*, Vat. Lat. 1291, f. 179ʳ.

says that the Cathars, not content simply to attribute demonic influence, declared the patriarchs themselves to be demons.[42] They say similar things of other figures such as Moses, David, and Elijah, though Bonacorso asserts that the heretics were split about the prophets.[43] Such examples demonstrate the perennial appeal of dualism. It becomes terribly easy to explain away unclear, troubling, or seemingly evil actions, those attributed both to God and to the protagonists of the Old Testament stories. Such a tactic was useful in highlighting the apparent chasm that lay between the Hebrew God and the person of Christ, but for the Cathars one could not stop there, for the New Testament needed aggressive pruning as well.

A lightning rod for Cathar criticism and a common test case for Cathar belief was John the Baptist, whom early Cathars often condemned.[44] Execration of John the Baptist assumed the status of a common theme in many Cathar texts. For them he became a sort of summation of the materialist message of the satanic God of the Old Testament and a foil to Christ, the prophet of the spirit of God. John then became the axial transition figure, who recapitulated all of the materialist evil of the Old Testament and who marked the beginning of their efforts to reimagine the New. Neither was this excoriation simply a predilection of the northern Italian Cathars described by Bonacorso. Such beliefs were common to French heretics as well. Peter of Vaux-de-Cernay, writing during the Albigensian Crusade in 1213, describes the beliefs of Cathars there. He depicts them, after declaring the God of the Old Testament to be a liar and a murderer, as saying "all the patriarchs of the Old Testament were damned, and declared that St. John the Baptist was one of the greatest devils."[45] While some development in heretical approaches to John occurs later, this theme continues to be operative.

---

42. "Iterum asserunt, quaecunque sunt facta vel dicta Abrahae, Isaac, et Jacob, a daemone dicta et facta esse." Bonacorso, *Vita haereticorum*, PL 204, 776. One should note that the patriarchs, prophets, and other figures of the Old Testament are considered to be saints in heaven in the orthodox Christian tradition.

43. "De dictis sanctorum prophetarum dicunt quaedam esse revelata a Spiritu Dei, quaedam a spiritu maligno." Ibid., 777. Such sentiments continue throughout the thirteenth century; see the *Summa* of Rainerio Sacconi, *HHMA*, 344; and Peter of Verona spends significant time defending the church's Old Testament beliefs in *Summa*, 38va–48vb.

44. "Ipsum quoque Joannem, quo nemo major est, testanto Domino, damnant: Quare? Quia Dominus dicit in Evangelio: 'Quo minor est in regno coelorum, major est in illo.' Et quia dubitavit de Christo, cum dixit 'Tu es qui venturus es, an alium exspectamus?'" Bonacorso claims that Cathars condemn John the Baptist for his doubt, and take the "none born of woman" comment of Christ as an antimaterial irony. Around the 1240s Cathars began to reappraise John the Baptist, but by then condemnation of other particular saints became a point of focus. *HHMA*, 592.

45. "Omnes Veteris Testamenti Patres, damnatos affirmabant; Johannem Baptistam unum esse de majoribus daemonibus asserebant." Peter of Vaux-de-Cernay, *Hystoria albigensis*, PL 213, 546.

A Franciscan summula on heresy from the 1250s still sees Cathars describing John as an "evil angel." While the author notes disagreement among various sects, the belief in the malicious nature of John seems to be common.[46] Later, Andreas Florentinus (ca. 1270) spends time defending against heretics who say that John "is not good and is deprived of eternal life."[47] John confronted the Cathars as a difficult figure, although his asceticism seemed germane to their purposes, his water baptisms and place as the final prophet of the Jewish law, in the end, sealed his fate.

By the 1200s the issue had come to be a defining feature in the conflict. In an anonymous manual from between 1225 and 1250, preachers are directed to give sermons explicitly defending the goodness of the Old Testament. The bulk of the preaching manual is given over to defenses of individuals and stories from the Old Testament. One had particularly to defend the conclusion that "John the Baptist was holy and just."[48] Clearly the Old Testament and its transition to the New were a conspicuous battleground in this fight. This novel theology of the ancient covenant helped to hone Cathar approaches to those called holy in the New Dispensation. It became easy for heretics, having easily dismissed some of the most venerated biblical saints of the Middle Ages, to deny the sainthood of any particular individual in the calendar. This tendency unfolded in many different ways.

☙ Waldensianism: A Different Path to the Same Destination

Waldo of Lyons, a merchant, was the founder of the Waldensian movement. Gradually developing guilt about his material wealth, he began a career as a medieval penitent in the 1170s. He attracted followers who were drawn to his penitential preaching. However, they found themselves shunned by the church at the Third Lateran Council (1179) as uneducated and backward.[49] Rejection by the institutional church led the group more and more into increasingly sophisticated theological critiques of the political and material power of the Catholics. By the late 1180s and 1190s they had clearly sepa-

---

46. *Brevis Summula contra herrores notatos hereticorum*, ed. Douais, 125.

47. Andreas Florentinus, *Summa contra hereticos*, 22.

48. *HHMA*, 299.

49. For Waldensianism as a movement, see Merlo, *Valdesi e valdismi medievali*; Audisio, *Waldensian Dissent*; and Cameron, *Waldensees*.

rated themselves from Catholic unity and had created a parallel system of church governance that, while small in overall numbers, would survive into the Reformation and modern world as the oldest western non-Catholic ecclesiastical group. The Poor of Lyons, as they came to be called, opposed the Cathars and their dualism; indeed, their debates with the Cathars are one of the most striking proofs of the presence of lived Cathar doctrine in the Middle Ages. This controversy helped to prevent the antiwealth musings of the Waldensians from becoming a full-blown theology that rejected the goodness of the material world. In terms of the Incarnation, the Waldensians held to an orthodox line. In order to underscore their opposition to the power and wealth of the church, the Poor of Lyons began to find targets that would focus their abstract theological opinions into more concrete language and to personalize it. To that end, just as the Cathars focused on John the Baptist, the Waldensians trained their sights on early Christianity, trying to pinpoint just where the church went wrong in the search for a purified form of Christianity.

Waldensians, with their interest in Gospel poverty, homed in on the sanctity of Pope St. Sylvester (r. 314–35), who had in their view brought wealth and political preferment to the church. The recipient of the supposed Donation of Constantine (the alleged conferral of political authority on Sylvester by the emperor) became the locus of hatred for those who derided the power and riches of medieval Catholicism.[50] The hatred focused on Sylvester would be instrumental in articulating later heretical challenges to newer, papally canonized saints. The vitriol against him was the first to be consciously directed at a particular postapostolic saint, putting a face on more generalized anticultic sentiment. The irony of the successor of Sylvester canonizing wildly antiheretical saints would not be lost on the heretics. Though this criticism was directed against church wealth, nevertheless it opened a wedge in their theology of sanctity. If the sanctity of one post-apostolic saint could be derided, then no one thought to be in the Church Triumphant was safe. To Sylvester the Waldensians later added St. Laurence, though he was famous for protecting the poor. They doubtlessly cited him as a standard-bearer for the Roman church; one can see that many in the orthodox church considered Laurence to be an especial defender of Roman primacy.[51]

---

50. Cathars concurred in this assessment: "They assert that the Blessed Sylvester was the Antichrist . . . the Son of Perdition." Bonacorso, 1170, in *HHMA*, 173. The amount of vitriol against Sylvester is exceeded only by the paucity of actual historical information about this "silent" pope. Such is an excellent recipe for the development of polemical legends.

51. "In hoc concordant pauperes de Lugduno cum pauperibus lonbardis contra ecclesiam, scilicet quod papa Silvester et Laurentius martyr non sunt sancti." From Anselm of Alexandria, *Tractatus de*

The Waldensians represented a more sober and less esoteric critique of the communion of the saints. Their rejection of Sylvester and Laurence in particular led to their denial of veneration to any nonscriptural saint. Interestingly the theological development here seems nearly opposite to the Cathars. Cathar theology regarding the saints seemed to progress from general theological ideas surrounding the equality of merit and the exclusivity of Cathar salvation to the lived denial of certain biblical and (later) postbiblical saints. The Waldensians, on the other hand, coming out of a lived and contextual critique of church practice, seem to have progressed from the denial of particular saints to more generalized criticisms of the theology of sainthood. In the end, both approaches would equip these groups for a confrontation with the developing situation regarding papal canonization in the middle of the thirteenth century.

Several different sources exist concerning more generalized Waldensian beliefs. Stephen of Bourbon, an inquisitor in France from 1232 to 1249, was informed that the Waldensians, with their emphasis on literal observation of the Gospels, found ecclesial observances such as fasts, feasts, and processions "worthy of derision." Anyone who observed saints' days was, in Stephen's words, a "laughingstock."[52] Again, the Waldensian critique grew from lived experience and the practical outworking of their version of a New Testament–inspired Christianity. This led them to an extreme simplicity that discounted veneration of images or relics (though the Poor of Lyons were not antimaterial). In spite of this, some of them still observed the feast days of Mary and of the apostles.[53] Their beliefs were likely unpopular, since Bernard Gui in the early fourteenth century alleged that the Waldensians kept three convictions very private: disbelief in miracles, refusal to invoke saints' aid, and a denial of the observance of holy days.[54] Such provocative beliefs would

---

hereticis, cf. d'Alatri, *Culto dei santi,* 34n49. Laurence was seen as an especially "Roman" saint in the Middle Ages; witness the numerous churches dedicated to him in Rome and his inclusion in the canon of the Mass. Jacobus of Voragine was typical when he pointed to Laurence as the epitome of a martyr "for the Roman Church" in his sermon on Peter of Verona's feast: "Si quis vult venire post me," in Paris: Bibliothèque Nationale MS Lat. 3285A, fol. 248ʳ, *RLS* 3, 255n430.

52. "Ipsi irrident eos qui luminaria offerunt sanctis ad illimuminandas ecclesias. . . . Item dicunt nullam esse sanctitatem nisi in bono homine vel muliere." Stephen of Bourbon, O.P., *Traité sur les sept dons du Saint Esprit,* 298.

53. Some Waldensian sanctoral calendars exist, though they are predictably sparse, e.g., Dublin: Trinity College, MS 267. That at least German Waldensians continued to venerate Mary while rejecting the saints, see Kurze, *Quellen,* 124, 145, 159, 178, 226–27.

54. "The heretics refuse to accept the reality of miracles within the Church because of the merits and prayers of the saint who, they maintain, have never intervened in any way. In the same way, they insinuate among themselves that the saints in heaven do not listen to prayers and pay no attention to the homages we on earth pay to them; the saints do not pray for us, it is therefore useless to

have been entirely at odds with the orthopraxis of much of the orthodox laity.

Some may allege that in citing the preceding examples I am hewing too closely to the systematic beliefs imputed to heretics by the inquisitors who attempted to describe these heresies. Certainly these systematic presentations leave out the fluidity of personal belief and the ability of people to conventionalize esoteric creeds. Yet this very conventionalization sometimes became a locus for opposition to the church in the period from 1250 to 1325. Further, when the church reacted to heretical belief in any systematic way (such as I argue in this case), the reaction was in light of the stereotyped descriptions of heresy made by the inquisitors. I contend that in terms of the issue under consideration, actual heretical belief in the earlier period is not as crucial as what the church *thought* the heretics believed. If the church considered that a pervasive, widespread opposition to the cult of the saints existed, then it would act on that belief, as the Roman church proceeded to do in the case of the theology of canonization. During this period such beliefs were still only generalized among a host of other heterodox opinions. As yet heretics did not seem particularly to deny the powers of the church to canonize. It would only be when they came into direct opposition with nascent papal claims that the particularization of their heterodoxy would become a central axis of conflict. What began as indifference to saints in general would change to positive contempt at the same time the church began to expand its claims over saints' cults. The intersection of these trends would be explosive.

---

entreat their suffrage. Consequently the Waldensians hold in contempt the solemnities which we celebrate in honor of the saints, as well as other signs of veneration and homage, and on saints' days, if they can do so without too great a risk, they work." Bernard Gui on the Waldensian heresy: *HHMA*, 391. On this conventionalization, see Kurze, *Quellen*, 172–73.

CHAPTER 3

"That the Perversity of Heretics Might Be Confounded"

From Practice to Theory

While heretical musings continued to develop, papal canonizations proceeded apace, and theories elucidating them began to coalesce in the thirteenth century. Up to this point we have traced two disparate threads. One was the slow but steady innovation in the machinery and language of papal canonizations, and the other outlined the evolution of the theologies of various heterodox movements. In the period leading up to the year 1200, the two had been disconnected. After that time, though, they would collide with remarkable results. From the side of the church, thoughts about canonization unfolded over the course of centuries in the context of the practice of canonization. Here the popes innovated in continuity with tradition, sometimes changing words or ceremonies ever so slightly. Only after the appearance of the many customs that came to be associated with saintly glorification, coupled with increasingly heterodox opinions regarding the saints, did churchmen slowly begin to undertake a systematic examination of the nature and purpose of papal canonization. Connected with this was the question of how papal glorification could be distinguished from other types of saintly recognition. As described in chapter 1, it was in the canonization of Thomas Becket, rather than the obscure letter to "King K," that Alexander III truly innovated in the practice and possibilities of canonization.[1] In this action he combined the innovations of previous years into one forceful document, "Redolet Anglia." Included among these were such revolutionary aspects as the recognition of an international cult, vigorous promotion of that cult by papal decree, addressing the whole of the Catholic Church at once, and aligning the papacy itself as the *impresario* of Thomas's immense public *cultus*. Other popes would build mightily upon the strong foundations laid down by Alexander III.

The pontificate of Innocent III (r. 1198–1216) is axial for the medieval papacy, an aspect of which are his innovative policies on canonization.[2] Innocent drew together in harmonious union many threads that had been quite disparate. He laid down the pattern that would be critical for the elucidation of the qualitative difference in papal canonizations that would arise after his death. He was the one who gathered together legal expertise, examination of well-founded biography, solid testimony of miracles, and the considerable application of papal authority, all of which would provide the foundation for the growth of a theory of infallibility. His work in gathering all these different pieces together to make a coherent whole was critical to the process. One sees this in his first canonization, that of the layman Homobonus (Omobono) of Cremona.[3]

Innocent glorified the merchant-saint following a petition from Homobonus's hometown in 1199. His canonization bull "Quia pietas" is the longest document of that genre to that date, already indicating something different in Innocent's style. "Quia pietas" may be one of the most significant in terms of reorienting the canonization process from the papal perspective. In the first paragraph Innocent unites three topics that will become paramount for the future evolution of the doctrine. First, he discusses the necessity of signs and wonders as a signal precondition for sainthood, along with the testimony of a life lived according to the virtues. This recipe became the standard for canonizations right up to the present day: a heroically lived life that is recognized by God after death by the operation of miraculous signs. Both are essential to the ecclesiastical recognition of sainthood. "Two things are necessary for one who is publically venerated as a saint in the Church militant: virtuous morals, and the power of signs, namely works

---

1. *Pace* both Kemp and Kuttner.

2. For institutional assessments, see Tillman, *Pope Innocent III*, with correctives in Moore and Bolton, *Pope Innocent III and His World*; for canonization, see esp. Goodich, "Vision, Dream, and Canonization Policy"; and Paciocco, "'Virtus morum' e 'virtus signorum,'" 597–610.

3. For Omobono, see Vauchez, *Omobono di Cremona*.

of piety in life and the sign of miracles after death."[4] While Innocent avers that only final perseverance is absolutely necessary for sainthood simply considered, he maintains that the public veneration of such a person requires signal divine testimonies. Both are required for public sanctity, "for neither are works sufficient by themselves, nor signs alone."[5] This is because some seek glory by their good deeds, thereby vitiating their virtue. So virtues are necessary, since even demons can work miracles. The question then is this: who is authorized to discern whether a life was truly well lived or whether miracles were actually from God? Innocent points to Mark 16:20, whereby the preaching of the apostles was confirmed by their miraculous deeds. When holiness of life is accompanied by signs, then one can have certitude concerning divine origin. Innocent is convinced that only the papacy has both the means to carry out such an investigation and the divinely appointed authority to make a declaration. In order to establish his point, Innocent included a saintly biography and a brief list of wonders performed by the new saint. Many scholars have correctly noted this as a turning point in papal theories of canonization, with the deliberate linking of life to miracles, with the assumption of clear and detailed investigation.[6] Vauchez notes that while this was innovative in terms of elevating holiness of life to equal the importance of supernatural wonders, at the same time it deferred to the ancient notion that there must be a public cult, manifested in the reception of miracles. The pope cannot canonize at will, but canonizations must be referred to him.[7] It was a balanced and well-rooted decision in terms of theology, as well as in the lived experience of the church.

One should ask why, in this particular context, Innocent would be so clear in uniting life and miracles. I would propose that it was the examples offered by the evangelical and Cathar heretics then flourishing in southern Europe.[8] On one hand, these unorthodox preachers demonstrated to the faithful lives of apostolic simplicity, which was especially clear in contrast to some con-

---

4. "Duo tamen, virtus videlicet morum, & virtus signorum, opera scilicet pietatis in vita, & miraculorum signa post mortem, ut qui reputetur Sanctas in militatni Ecclesia requiruntur." Innocent III, "Quia pietas" [Canonization of Homobonus of Cremona], January 12, 1199, in Fontanini, 34–36; Potthast, n573.

5. "Nec opera sufficiunt sola, nec signa." Fontanini, 34–35.

6. Kemp noted this in *Canonization and Authority*, 104, but the most significant work on the subject is Paciocco's "'Virtus morum' e 'virtus signorum.'" Another of Paciocco's books is also exceptionally useful for the 1200s, as he picks up where Kemp leaves off; see Paciocco, *Canonizzazioni e culto dei santi*. Paciocco is mostly concerned with legal history, especially the incorporation of miracle stories in canonization dossiers.

7. Vauchez, *Sainthood*, 38–39.

8. Paciocco comes to a similar conclusion in "'Virtus morum' e 'virtus signorum.'"

temporary churchmen. They demonstrated holiness of life, but for Innocent, this was but a deception that hid their real heresy. They sought to deceive the laity by their show of virtue. On the other hand, there was a danger that some might co-opt demonic power in order to win over the weak-minded (Innocent specifically mentions both the magicians of Pharaoh and the antichrist). Since miracles formed the backbone of lay devotion to the saints, this possibility was alarming. Innocent's response was based on two assumptions. First, those who performed wonders with the devil's aid could in no way be living even apparently holy lives, for they would be plunged in moral turpitude. Second, the heretics who lived simple lives would never be able to accomplish wonders by the help of God and so would be forced back on their example alone. This necessitated the need for a life of both virtue and miracles. The wonders would establish God's confirmation of the holy life lived by the saint, and the virtues of the saint would encourage the gracious distribution of wonders by God; it would be a marvelously symbiotic relationship. Conceived in such a scheme, the saint became the antiheretic par excellence.[9]

This is reinforced by a phrase in the bull of Homobonus's canonization that, though emphasized strongly by Innocent, has attracted little notice among the very real innovations regarding life and miracles. In the initial paragraph the pope outlines his daring rethinking of the quality of candidates for sainthood. He includes a phrase that at first seems somewhat out of place. Innocent avers that the life and wonders of a saint are a gift from God, so that the holy one might be "held up as a Saint among men, and of these principally that the perversity of heretics might be confounded, since they might come to the tombs of such Catholics and see the flowering of miracles."[10] Homobonus had been engaged in his town, during his life, disputing with "Patarene" heretics. This account was inserted among his other pious and virtuous deeds in the bull: "having kept himself apart from the concourse of worldly men, among which he grew, like a lily among thorns, and he showed himself a bitter despiser of the heretics, which perniciously infected those parts."[11] Innocent uses Homobonus's civic-spirited repudiation of

---

9. It is interesting that Innocent puts forward such a program in 1199, perhaps contributing to or at least anticipating the breakthrough made by Diego of Osma and Dominic of Caleruega in the following decade.

10. "Sanctus etiam ab hominibus habeatur, et in hoc praesertim haereticorum confundatur perversitas, cum ad catholicorum tumulos viderint prodigia pullulare." Innocent III, "Quia pietas," Fontanini, 34.

11. "Ipse a saecularium hominum consortio segregatus, inter quos virebat, quasi lilium inter spinas, haereticorum, quorum pernicies partes illas infecit, austerus extitit aspernator." Ibid., 35.

those with heretical tendencies to orient sainthood toward a defense of the
Catholic faith and refutation of heretics. As shown in chapter 2, this was a
critical age for the crystallization of canonization but also for a parallel articulation of a comprehensive critique of rapidly developing papal efforts.
Taken together with these movements, Homobonus's canonization can be
seen as a watershed moment.

It is clear that Innocent was attempting to streamline the canonization process and to reinforce this innovative vision in his subsequent canonizations.
In his glorification of the empress Cunegunda (Cunigunde) in the year 1200,
Innocent reiterates his strong language regarding both signs and life.[12] This
time, though, he explicitly connects both of them to the confutation of heresy. Twice in the bull Innocent places sainthood and heresy in opposition.[13]
While this deployment is understandable in the case of Homobonus (who
had shunned heretics in his own town), the empress Cunegunda had lived
between 975 and 1040, well before the appearance of western heterodoxies.
Innocent was making a clear claim here: it did not matter whether a saint
had direct experience in fighting against heresy but rather that his or her
role in the Church Triumphant in heaven gave the saint the singular role of
defender of the Church Militant on earth. Saints fought heretics because it
was part of the job description.

Cunegunda's exaltation by Innocent demonstrates another remarkable example of that pope's innovation. Innocent used the strongest language to
date regarding the pope's authority to canonize. He speaks with authority as
the "successor of blessed Peter and the Vicar of Jesus Christ." This is one of
the first examples of the stabilization of the term *Vicarius Christi*, which would
become a commonplace title for the popes. What is significant here is that
Innocent describes the desire of the canonization petitioners for recognition
because as "Vicar of Christ" he employs the "plenitude of power." Aside from
the constitutional innovations that Innocent is surely making here, he firmly
situates canonization in terms of the fullness of power that "Christ con-
ceded to blessed Peter."[14] Papal canonization, then, was no simple act of
recognition, no permission to translate, no bare juridical edict or liturgical

---

12. Petersohn, "Die Litterae Papst Innocenz' III," 1–25.

13. "Ad eorum memorias signa faciens et prodigia, per quae pravitas confundatur haeretica, et fides
catholica confirmetur." "Ad confirmationem fidei catholicae et confusionem haereticae pravitatis
evidenter innovat signa, et miracula potenter immutat." Innocent III, "Cum secundum" [April 3,
1200], Fontanini, 37; Potthast, n1000.

14. "Ut ex plenitudine potestatism, quam Jesus Christus beato Petro concessit . . . cum hoc [the
canonization] sublime iudicium ad eum tantum pertineat, qui est beati Petri successor et Vicarius
Jesu Christi." Fontanini, 38.

addendum. No, canonization was a reserved and special case (one of the earliest and most explicit reservations in the history of the papacy). It was to be interpreted through the lens of the pope's supreme authority, granted by Christ Himself. It was to be an extraordinary act, requiring extraordinary process and extraordinary proof. When all of these issues—rigorous public and legal examination, validation by tested miracles, antiheretical orientation, and the fullness of papal power—became joined, Innocent had finally gathered together all the components for the historical unfolding of the process by which infallibility would be claimed regarding canonization, which in the future would stir up strident opposition.

Innocent's later canonizations, of St. Gilbert of Sempringham in 1202 and St. Wulfstan of Worcester in 1203 exhibit no innovations but rather a commitment to retain the theology that he had articulated in his first two. That Innocent did not canonize anyone during the last twelve years of his pontificate is surprising but also demonstrates that canonization was still not commonplace; it did not occur with such regularity as to give rise to sustained meditation about its meaning. Only slowly did the pieces begin to fall into place. A further incident demonstrates how the pope could not canonize according to his own whims. Innocent, in high dudgeon, sent no fewer than four substantial letters regarding what he saw as the martyrdom of his legate Peter of Castelnau by the Albigensians in 1208. While Peter was assuredly killed "in hatred of the faith," Innocent was not able to canonize him.[15] This was not for lack of trying. Innocent tried to follow the models of earlier bulls with an extensive retelling of Peter's story along with denominating him a martyr. In spite of that, Peter did not generate a cult. No miracles were reported at his tomb. Innocent attributed this to the infidelity of the people of Languedoc, but the principle remained: the pope could not canonize in the absence of a legitimate cult.[16] The older model of canonization was still in force; Innocent could not change that, as much as he may have wished to. What he had achieved was to subject genuine cults to analysis and examination at a high level. This is some of the clearest evidence that the pope was innovating in continuity with the past and a robust indicator of the weight of tradition in this matter. Even Innocent, the most

---

15. Being killed "in odium fidei" is the special criterion for assigning the title of "martyr" in the Catholic tradition, distinguishing it from other types of unjust killings.

16. He repeatedly refers to them as a "wicked and perverse generation" and reproves them for their "hardness of heart." Innocent refers to Mt 13:58: "Et non fecit ibi virtutes multas propter incredulitatem eorum." Innocent III, "Rem crudelem" [March 10, 1208], Fontanini, 46; Potthast n3323. For a full exposition of the original texts regarding Peter, see Villemagne, *Bullaire du bienheureux Pierre de Castelnau*.

powerful of popes, could not dispense with the immemorial meaning of sainthood in the church. The pope was not simply making a grab for power, for he was limited and bound by the traditions of Christianity. What he could do, though, was to systematize the process, provide oversight, and—most significant of all—sanction it with apostolic and divine authority.

It is useful to bear in mind that the process of assembling the pieces that would undergird later theories of infallibility is uneven. Up to this point there had been absolutely no effort at articulating a coherent theory of canonization, much less to suggest infallibility in such an endeavor. What I am doing is merely laying out the pieces that will later be collected by theologians and canonists to create and outline such a theory. I also omit many things regarding other aspects of the history of canonization, either because they are tangential or because they have been covered in detail by other authors. For instance, I am not assessing the development of the legal procedures for canonization except insofar as they shed light on a theory of infallibility.[17] This process was so uneven that though most of the tools were in place by the pontificate of Innocent III, he seems to have lost interest in further definition, and even the comprehensive Fourth Council of the Lateran (1215) says nothing about it (unless one includes the brief canon on relics).

✒ After Innocent

Honorius III (r. 1216–27) seemed content to follow the example set by his predecessor (including his predilection for saints from the British Isles).[18] His bulls contain the now-familiar calls for holiness of life and miracles as a matter of course. In his first canonization bull, that of William of Bourges (d. 1209, canonized 1218), he inserts the interesting clause that such investigations have been confirmed by both "divine and human judgment."[19] The testimony of divine grace, confirmed by miracles and assessed by the curia, is now sufficiently certain to proceed to canonization. Honorius also dispatched two bulls, one to the clergy and faithful of Bourges and the other addressed "to all the Christian faithful" announcing the canonization. William had been preparing a mission against the Albigensians when he

---

17. For the legal developments, see Paciocco, *Canonizzazioni e culto dei santi*; and Wetzstein, *Heilige vor Gericht*.

18. Michael Richter argues for the essentially conservative nature of Honorius's canonization policy, while pointing out early *inquisitiones in partibus*, in id., "Canonization of Lorcán Ua Tuathail," 53–65.

19. Honorius III, "Etsi electi" [May 17, 1218], Fontanini, 50; Potthast, n5803.

died, and Honorius does not fail to mention that the miracles at his tomb were there not only for the healing of Christians but for the confounding of heretics. It is interesting that several papal bulls particularly contend that miracles performed locally at the tomb will be of particular use in the conflict with the heretics, who will be refuted by them. Perhaps the sense is that the anti-incarnational attitude of the heretics will be particularly offended by the performance of miracles, at a particular physical place, by a particular material body, at the intercession of a saint. Such a concatenation of materiality and physicality would be a privileged nexus for the refutation of an anti-incarnational heresy.[20] In the letter addressed to the universal church, Honorius does innovate in a small way by introducing the practice of providing indulgences for those who come to honor St. William. Now the popes were actively equating the veneration of their own saints as pious works, worthy of the remission of temporal punishments. With each passing canonization the stakes became a little higher, as papally canonized saints received increasing honors and privileges, setting them further and further apart from merely local and popular saints. Yet Honorius did not slavishly copy the pattern set by his predecessor. At times his canonization bulls were only a paragraph long (such as that for Hugh of Lincoln), and they often lack the exalted language employed by Innocent III, particularly in the definition and injunction of the papacy's "plenitude of power."

In his last canonization bull, that of William of York (d. 1153, canonized 1226), Honorius makes up for his previous lack of prolixity when he engages directly on the question of the validity of particular canonizations. He declares that there can be no doubt that the saint in question has been glorified in heaven, since his life was filled with virtue and his shrine resonates with miracles. Honorius discusses the trustworthiness of the witnesses who have recounted such stories and how such serious matters must proceed only with due discretion. Even considering the possibility that the devil could transform himself into an angel of light, Honorius proceeds to the conclusion that diligent investigations by estimable men of trustworthy witnesses, confirming the divine nature of the miracles and judged by the pope himself, provide the stamp of certainty that allows the canonization to proceed.[21] Perhaps Honorius's previous canonizations did not meet with

---

20. For support the church could turn to Ps 86(85):17 "Do me a sign for good, that they who hate me may be confounded."

21. "Ut sanctae memoriae Willhelmum, quondam Eboracensem Archiepiscopum, qui, sicut ex multurom fide dignorum testimoniis apparebat, tanta fulsit gratia meritorum, quod multa per eum Dominus dignatus est gloriosa miracula operari, et post decessum ipsius, corpus eius multo pluribus dedit mirabilibus coruscare, catalogo Sanctorum, adscriberemus in Ecclesia militanti, cum non esset

universal approbation; we do not know. Here, though, was one of the earliest contentions that papal decisions were absolutely and unconditionally valid. Honorius is asserting here that no good Catholics may impugn the validity of a papally canonized saint, because such a person is already in heaven.

After Honorius III we enter into a new period where three of the mighty streams of thought and activity that we have followed finally come together. In the first place the war on heresy had been fought for nearly a hundred years since vague pockets of heterodoxy had first been identified. The intervening period gave both sides time to refine their arguments and to specify their debating points. This conflict had taken a much more serious turn during the pontificate of Innocent III, who took a personal interest in confronting heresy and launched a multipronged assault on it that would echo through the thirteenth century. This attack roused the heretics to focus their energies most especially on the issue of papal power and papal authority. What had at first begun as an abstract hatred of the material world began to focus on the incarnational spirituality of Catholics and the praxis of the Roman church, in its sacraments and in its earthly authority. This morphed into a critique of saints and saints' cults. In response to this, the Catholic Church began to exercise closer control over its ritual practices and especially began to streamline, systematize, and in a sense professionalize the creation and proclamation of saints. This closer affiliation of saints (already an object of derision among heretics) with the papacy proved to be fundamental for the articulation of infallibility in canonization.

The second stream is that of the practice of papal canonizations as it had been developing since the eleventh century. We have traced the process throughout this period and have arrived at a point where all of the ritual and language of canonization and the plenitude of papal power were ripe for deployment. The terminology used by the papacy had developed significantly during this period, and it had reached a point where the language began to convey the fullness of the papal teaching authority. This was so much the case that canonization bulls became the prototype for papal definitions on faith and morals of any type. Canonization thus became a proving ground for papal authority. As language and ritual became more elevated and formalized, it was only a matter of time before they became focal points of opposition. As the thirteenth century wore on, a new player appeared on stage: the mendicant orders. The approbation of the mendicants by the

---

dubium, ipsum in triumphanti a Domino multipliciter honorari . . . in tam sancto et divino negocio non erat nisi cum maturitate plurima procedendum." Honorius III, "Qui statuit" [March 18, 1226], Fontanini, 58; Potthast, n7551.

church both affirmed the apostolic way of life and was a clever way to defuse the claims of the heretics to religious purity. Because of this the church highly exalted them, and the period from 1228 to 1323 can be called the century of "Mendicant Sanctity." Because these saints were deployed so specifically against the heretics and were so unequivocally bound up with papal claims of supremacy, they became flashpoints of conflict. Sainthood was about to become a privileged battleground in the war between the Catholic Church and the heretics. One of the most stubbornly incarnational beliefs of the Catholic Church would be highlighted against various heresies that critiqued the worldliness of Christianity or that went so far as to deny the goodness of material creation itself.

The final stream was that the age of classical canon law, inaugurated by Gratian nearly a hundred years before, was coming to fruition. The church entered a second spring, as it were, in canonical studies. The period of the Decretists (commentators on Gratian's compilation) gave way to the Decretalists (those who compiled and commented on the living stream of law emanating from the papal curia). These men were worthy heirs of the masterful legal minds who came before them. With that foundation laid, they were able to move beyond the simple application of abstract principles, the reconciliation of divergent authorities, or the effort to make thousand-year-old texts relevant to contemporary situations. What the Decretalists, both the curia and the commentators, did was to use those established principles to formulate new and binding law in response to real-world situations. Canonization is one of the best examples of this. The developed form that canonization now took was foreign to the experience of the first one thousand years of the church's history but, given that very experience, not opposed to it. Gratian himself had almost nothing to say about its practice, ritual, or binding force. Now that the previous two hundred years had seen such an efflorescence of effort in the elaboration of the meaning and purpose of canonization, it became necessary to create a language and a legal superstructure on which to discuss and define exactly what canonization was. In response to rapidly developing situations on the ground, the Decretalists were well equipped to handle this. It is this critical period that I wish to analyze first.

✎ From Reserve to Infallibility

Historians of the papacy and of canon law cite 1234 as the pivotal date for the papal reservation of canonizations. In that year Raymond of Peñafort, the compiler of the Decretals, inserted the decree *Audivimus* into Gregory

IX's *Liber Extra*.[22] *Audivimus* was a letter from Pope Alexander III in 1171–72 stating that no one ought to venerate as a saint someone not proposed by the Roman church. Though it was a personal letter addressed to the king of Sweden, with its inclusion in the *Extra* in 1234 it became official church law.[23] This was the normal way in which the Decretals were assembled, by taking recent particular law and systematizing it in a collection such as the *Extra*. At that point it became normative and binding for the whole church—at least that was the theory. Clearly the law did not have immediate effect, as episcopal translation and local discernment and veneration of sanctity continued as strongly as ever. What the insertion of the letter in 1234 indicates is a new period in the thinking of church leaders and intellectuals on the nature of papal canonization itself. Faced with the de facto continuation of local and popular sanctity, it was up to Catholic thinkers to articulate the particular differences and privileges attendant on papal canonizations that would both set them apart and make them desirable to pursue. In that sense they did not worry overmuch about the continuing popularity of local sanctity; what they did was to ruminate on and develop the positive and qualitative differences involved in papal canonization of saints. In this way canonization finally became a formal constituent of the papal plenitude of power, something so markedly missing from the Gregorian reform. The legal commentators were of one mind on the authority of the pope to elevate saints, but the issue the Decretalists decided to fixate on was the *certitude* provided by such canonizations.

Sinibaldo dei Fieschi, later elected as Pope Innocent IV (r. 1243–54), was the first canonist to take a position on the infallibility question. This indicates that the issue first acquired significance after the time of the incorporation of *Audivimus* in the *Liber Extra*.[24] I do not believe that the canonistic response was at first a reaction against the challenge of heresy. Only later did the interaction between heretical opinion and the developing doctrine

---

22. Alexander III, "Audivimus," in *Corpus Iuris Canonici* II, ed. Friedberg, X 3.45.1. For a recent assessment of this decretal, see Wetzstein, "Audivimus (X 3.45.1)."

23. Kemp, *Canonization and Authority*, 99–103; Kuttner, "La réserve papale," 190–219. Kemp and Kuttner disagree as to the circulation and binding authority of *Audivimus*, but for the present purposes it is clear that the canonists only took up the question of papal infallibility in canonization well after 1234. Kuttner believes that before 1234 the canonists treated *Audivimus* as referring to a single case and not making a broad papal claim, while Kemp thinks that Alexander actually intended to bind the whole church with the decretal. While the evidence favors Kuttner's theory, my contention remains that after 1234 commentators on the decretal treated it as making a broad papal claim. Later in life Kuttner modified his position and emphasized the contributions of Innocent III more than Alexander III; see his *History of Ideas*, Retraction VI in app. 1.

24. Innocent IV probably authored his commentary while pope, sometime after the First Council of Lyons in 1245.

come into play. The issue for these commentators was how to articulate a
difference between papal and local canonizations. The canonists first considered that the papal plenitude of power was the only way to promulgate
and enforce the observance of a universal cult (admittedly a tangential issue
in *Audivimus*, but such a strategy is a demonstration of the brilliant lawyerly
speculations of the first generation of Decretalists). Local cults could have no
purchase outside their specific territories; that is, they made no claims on
the universal church. If the pope, the bishop of bishops, promulgated a cause,
then it was a different story; at that point such a cult could be observed universally. This placed the legal thinkers in a difficult position. What if it was
later found out that the person canonized was in no way saintly?[25] The cases
of dogmas and morals could clearly be established by the immemorial belief
and practice of the church. One could consult scriptural, patristic, conciliar,
and theological sources to confirm papal judgments. No such things existed
for the veneration and exaltation of particular saints. The doctrine of sainthood itself was an established part of the Christian faith, but it was not so
with individuals proposed as saints. So the pope was undertaking an act in
virtue of his universal authority—presenting a member of the church as definitively in heaven, an object of devotion, and a worthy intercessor. This
was a liminal case. It was universal and yet not rooted in the sources of revelation. It was a definitive judgment and yet in its particulars not support-
able from the theological authorities. How was such a delicate point to be
negotiated?

Decretalists began to focus their attention on the issue of certitude by considering whether infallibility was a necessary concomitant of papal canonization. Ironically, while *Audivimus* provided an occasion for discussion of
papal authority in canonization, it did not provide the canonists a frame of
reference for the question at hand: that of certitude in situations not rooted
in the theological tradition of the church. Instead of building castles in the
air with *Audivimus*, rather, when they commented on this topic, they almost
always did so as a gloss on a decretal of Innocent III, *de Sententia Excommunicationis*.[26] This decretal touches on the case of a repentant man who died

---

25. Nor was this fear confined to the lawyers. Angela of Foligno, a late thirteenth-century mystic,
summed up the issue nicely: "Nam multi apud homines videntur dampnati, qui apud Deum sunt
salvati. Et multi apud homines videntur salvati, qui apud Deum sunt dampnati." Angela of Foligno,
Le livre, 516. Cf. Kleinberg, *Prophets in Their Own Country*, 22.

26. "It is often asked of us, whether any excommunicated person, in whom there were manifest
signs of repentance, and with nothing standing between him and being reconciled to the unity of
the Church, and having died without the benefit of receiving absolution, that he ought to have
forgiveness from the Church and whether for such a one alms might be given, and prayers might be
offered by the faithful. . . . We therefore respond that the judgement of God, who neither deceives

excommunicate and without absolution. Innocent III decided that in such a case, since the church might be deceived in its opinion about the man, one might worthily offer prayers and alms for his soul. The early Decretalists used this as a way to protect the faith of the church and, ironically, the power and authority of the pope. What concerned the canonists most was the possibility of fallible human witnesses contaminating the decision of the Roman pontiff.

In commenting on *Audivimus*, Innocent IV alludes to *de. Sent. Excomm.* by making the following contention: "All canonized saints are to be venerated . . . we say, since if the Church might err, which is not to be believed, nevertheless God will accept prayers offered in such good faith."[27] When speaking of canonized saints, Innocent (and subsequent Decretalists) always means papally canonized saints, since he says at the beginning of his commentary, "Only the Pope is able to canonize saints."[28] This is an exceedingly original assertion on Innocent's part. He denies wholesale the title "canonization" to either popular or episcopal elevations. The papacy alone, for Innocent, creates saints for public veneration.[29] In addition, Innocent IV follows the tenor of his predecessor's idea when he declares that the prayers offered for an unworthy saint made in good faith will transfer to a better cause. In spite of his doubt regarding the certitude of infallibility, he is very concerned to protect the church's integrity with the saving clause that the possibility of an errant decision in this matter is "not to be believed." Innocent is primarily concerned with proper order in the church. His commentary strengthens papal prerogatives and reinforces hierarchy. Even if one suspects impropriety in canonization, Innocent maintains that God will sort the prayers made for bad "saints" and that we ought to pray to them in any case. Innocent IV's aggressive papalism (which runs through both his commentary and his career as pope) was still not enough for him to impute ab-

---

nor is deceived, is always supported by truth: but the judgements of the Church sometimes follow opinion, which often happens to deceive, and to be deceived: on account of which it sometimes happens that which is bound before God, is loosed by the Church: and he who is free before God, is bound by the Church: and he who is free before God, might be constrained by a Church sentence." Innocent III, "de. Sent. Excomm.," in *Corpus Iuris Canonici* II, X 5.39.28.

27. "Venerandi sunt omnes sancti canonizati. . . . Item dicimus, quod etiam si Ecclesia erraret quod non est credendum: tamen preces per talem bona fide porrectas Deus acceptaret." Sinibaldo dei Fieschi [Innocent IV], *Commentaria*, 457, on X 3.45.1, *De reliquiis et veneratione sanctorum*, c. 1, 457.

28. "Solus autem Papa potest sanctos canonizare, quod ex eo apparet, quia cum constituatur omnibus fidelibus adorandum, et nullus omnibus praesit, nisi Papa apparet, quod solus Papa hoc potest." Ibid. While he has no alternate category (later to be specified as "beatification"), he certainly paves the way for such an idea.

29. This contempt for local canonizations far outpaces actual lived practices. Long after the definitive reservation of Urban VIII in 1634, the papacy recognized innumerable cults as "immemorial," which was another way of saying it respected the legitimacy of local cults.

solute infallibility to the papacy in canonizing, but neither was that his intention. He was seriously concerned with Innocent III's declaration that "the judgments of the Church sometimes follow opinion, which often happens to deceive, and to be deceived."[30] The problem for Innocent IV was to get people to be docile to those instances where the church *is* deceived, rather than to articulate a more formal statement of papal infallibility at this point. Ironically, the saints created by Innocent IV and his several predecessors were the ones that aroused the opposition that led to a further development in the theory that he himself was reluctant to grant. So here one is presented with the irony of the Decretalists: they are at once conservative and innovative. Innocent IV deftly lays out the sole authority of the papacy to canonize and then, in order to protect the office, hedges with regard to infallibility.[31]

Later Decretalists followed the line set out by Innocent IV. Henry of Segusio (ca. 1200–1271), better known as Hostiensis, gave a very extensive commentary on *Audivimus*. Completing what came to be known as his *Summa Aurea* around 1250, Hostiensis had the benefit of not only Innocent IV's commentary on the Decretals but also the knowledge of how Innocent put those principles into action as pope.[32] In his commentary he gives an extensive description of the twelve things that must be done before a saint is canonized. These include many of the legal apparatuses such as the *inquisitio in partibus*, a written narrative of life and miracles, and an explicit account of the canonization liturgy.[33] In this description Hostiensis includes a new and significant element that was added to the canonization liturgy of the thirteenth century. The pope was to lead all the clergy and people in prayer "that God might not permit him to err in this definition."[34] This is perhaps a liturgical flourish, but it is significant nonetheless. In the first place, the language of infallibility was beginning to appear in public, at the most solemn

---

30. Innocent III's decretal "de Sententia Excomm."

31. This is the inherent tension that Brian Tierney deftly traces in his *Origins of Papal Infallibility*, passim. The Decretalists tended to downplay infallibility in order to defend and exalt sovereignty. Tierney pushes the point too far and, as will be examined in chapters 5 and 6, focuses too much on the poverty controversies of the later thirteenth and early fourteenth centuries and pays too little attention to rapid developments in both theology and canon law in response to developments on the ground.

32. For Hostiensis and his *Summa*, see Pennington, *Popes, Canonists and Texts*, 259ff.

33. The local portion of the investigation, where authorities gathered testimony from witnesses regarding life and miracles. Such was an integral part of investigation from the first third of the 1200s.

34. "Conveniunt Papa et fratres et totus clerus et populus et facit sermonem summus Pontifex processum recitans et probata, inducens populum ad orandum quod Deus non permittat ipsum errare in hoc negotio." Hostiensis, *In Tertium Decretalium Librum Commentaria*, 172, on X 3.45 *De reliquiis* 1, *Audivimus*. For a thorough analysis of this text, see Wetzstein, *Heilige vor Gericht*, 255–58.

moment of the canonization liturgy. In the second place, Hostiensis notes this as one of his twelve essential points for a valid canonization. Finally, he notes this as a prefatory remark to his more developed thought later in the Commentary.

After examining the sole right of the papacy to canonize, Hostiensis declared "If the Church might err in such a canonization, which nevertheless is not to be believed, although it may happen, as is clear in that which is read and noted in *de. Sent. Excomm.* 'A nobis,' likewise God will accept prayers offered in such good faith, for all things are cleansed in the faith of Christ and though it might be that the truth of canonization might be wanting, nevertheless the faith of those [who believe in the canonization] is not wanting."[35]

Hostiensis seems more ambivalent than Innocent IV. Hostiensis, too, cites Innocent III's decretal on excommunication as proof of the fallibility of human judgment, which precludes an absolute assertion of infallibility on the part of the church that canonizes. Neither Hostiensis nor Innocent IV explicitly mentions the pope (though each asserts the sole right of the pope to canonize); they say "the church" might err. Rather than saying the pope is not infallible, they impute the error first to the imperfect witnesses and then to the church as a whole. Papal sovereignty is preserved, fallible witnesses receive the blame, and God sorts it all out in the end—a tidy canonical solution. The Decretalist tradition thus far gives little defense for any real idea of papal infallibility in canonizing. For the Decretalists, it seems that infallibility in this instance is quite nonexistent. Though the canonists were in agreement here, events were already overtaking their carefully worked-out cases.

❧ Papal Actions versus Decretalist Notions

Given the continuing attitude of the canonists on this question, the articulation of the infallibility doctrine seemed to be a dead end. Nevertheless, events continued to transpire that quickly went far beyond the canonists' discussions. In particular, the fertile religious environment of the early thirteenth century created a situation where the discussion of infallibility in canonization became necessary. The apostolic poverty and preaching movement of the twelfth century had reached its maturity and, as Herbert Grund-

---

35. "Quid si Ecclesia in hac canonizatione erret, quod tamen non est credendum, licet accidere possit, ut patet in eo, quod legitur et notatur infra De sententia excommunicationis, A nobis, quod nihilominus preces in honorem talis bona fide porrectas Deus acceptat, omnia enim in fide Christi purgantur, et esto, quod veritas canonizationis deficiat, non tamen deficit fides ipsius." Hostiensis, *In Tertium Decretalium Librum Commentaria*, 172.

mann perceptively recognized, worked itself out into either heresies or new religious orders.[36] I have already considered heresies related to this movement separately, so here I want to focus on religious orders.

With the gradual appearance of the mendicant orders, under the guidance of Francis (1181/82–1226) and Dominic (1170–1221), the church marshaled a powerful new force not only for the refutation of heresy but also for a wholesale renewal of the Christian order. Such renewals had happened often in church history: with the Benedictines in the 600s, the Cluniacs in the 900s, and the canons and Cistercians of the previous century. Each time they injected a powerful spirit of renewal into the life of the church. As such they attracted the best and brightest of their own times: men and women dedicated to a radical living-out of the Christian message. Though sainthood and holiness were by no means limited to these, some of the signal saints of each age came to be associated with these reform movements. The types of spirituality that they practiced exerted a lasting effect on the church and helped to mold ideas of saints and sainthood in sometimes astonishing directions. The prominent religious orders of the thirteenth century—those of the Minorites and Preachers—were no different.

Sainthood and holiness came especially to be associated with the Franciscans and Dominicans in the first hundred years of their existence. Both orders attracted men and women dedicated to a new and, in their eyes, superior way of radically following the Gospel message. The early chronicles of both orders are filled with a plenitude of stories about penance, mortification, strictness, and abstinence as well as more exalted spiritual experiences. The laxity and comfort of the older orders gave way to these new groups that captured the attention of the age by focusing on the needs of the moment. Both appealed to the laity for membership and support and attracted admirers in high places. It was precisely these eminent men who embraced the mendicant movements, particularly the prescient Innocent III, who, learning from his predecessors' errors in handling the Waldensians, embraced the apostolic poverty movement as integral to the church's mission, thereby co-opting their fervor, clericalizing them, and making them weapons in the hands of the church rather than forces ranged against it. Subsequent pontiffs, with few exceptions, continued this policy, and the papacy and mendicant orders entered into a symbiotic and mutually beneficial relationship that was to last hundreds of years.[37] The Minorites and Preachers (including

---

36. Grundmann, *Religious Movements*, 1.

37. The bibliographies of the histories of these orders are immense. For broad overviews, see Moorman, *History of the Franciscan Order*. For the Dominicans, see Hinnebusch, *History of the Do-*

later, lesser-known groups, like the Carmelites) benefited enormously from this papal protection, enabling them to expand their mission all over Christendom, acquiring exemptions that permitted them to circumvent local authorities. The papacy, for its part, benefited in co-opting what became an elite army of preachers, teachers, missionaries, professors, and holy men and women who were immediately subject solely to the Holy See. It was not long before this symbiotic relationship manifested itself in the papal exaltation of many members of both orders to the honors of the altar.

The mendicants were happy to see their brethren raised to sainthood, and each such success further emboldened and reinforced the sense of mission among the mendicants. The papacy, in elevating mendicant saints, rewarded faithful servants, exalted the mendicant model of spirituality for the whole church, and enhanced the already strong connection between the new orders and the pope. It was an advantageous situation for both sides. This rapidly deepening relationship, of course, provoked jealousy and opposition. The mendicants fought to defend and expand papal privilege, for they enjoyed papal favor, and in turn the papacy worked to defend the mendicants from their detractors. Such a mutual defense pact was exceptionally productive in the creation of sustained theological and canonical reflection on the place of both institutions in the church. The rise of opposition spurred both the mendicants and the papacy into detailed articulations of their own self-conceptions, advancing the development of doctrine leading both to the theological monuments of Thomas and Bonaventure as well as the developed papal theology and ecclesiology of the fourteenth century. Nowhere is this development more clear than in the defense of the mendicant saints.

Gregory IX (r. 1227–41) was the catalyst for the exposition of mendicant sainthood to the church. In elevating no fewer than four mendicants to the altar, he completed what his predecessors Innocent III and Honorius III had begun in their initial encouragement and solicitude for the Minorites and Preachers. Only one of Gregory's canonizations was of a nonmendicant, and that was only the confirmation of the historical cult of St. Virgil of Salzburg. The other four were Francis of Assisi, Anthony of Padua, Dominic of Caleruega, and Elizabeth of Thuringia, three Minorites and the founder of the Preachers. Gregory's solicitude for the new orders, particularly the Franciscans, was well known. As Cardinal Ugolino, he had been intimately asso-

---

minican Order. Both of these must be supplemented by many significant newer studies. I have attempted a Dominican bibliography in my "Friars Preachers," 1275–90. As of this writing, I am working on a history of the Dominican order from its foundations to the canonization of Thomas Aquinas, forthcoming from Catholic University Press.

ciated with the development of the Franciscan order as both a friend of St. Francis and a patron of Clare and her sisters. At length he had been named Cardinal Protector of the order in 1220 and was active in promoting the Franciscan mission, advocating for it at the curia and taking a hand in founding Damianite monasteries (after the contemporary name of Clare's order).[38] He was also the prelate who presided over the funeral of St. Dominic in Bologna in 1221, evincing a close relationship with the Preachers as well. Gregory correctly saw that the new orders were a leaven for society, groups that could balance the wealth of the church, counter the heretics by their example, be on the front lines against the emperor Frederick II, and serve as an elite missionary force to the broader world. As such he zealously promoted their interests, a policy that was magnified when Gregory was elected pope in 1227.

As pope he could offer more signal forms of approbation and honor to the new orders. This was particularly effective because both of the founders were now dead, and thus the pope had a freer hand in the arrangement of their internal politics. Gregory's new position enabled him to use the full power of papal authority to continue to patronize the groups that became the preeminent weapons of the papacy in the thirteenth century. One of the supreme honors that could be conferred by the papacy was that of solemn canonization. Gregory lost no time in the elevation of his friends to public recognition as saints of the Catholic Church. Driven from Rome by the supporters of Frederick II, Gregory found refuge in Umbria. Having personally been associated with Francis for over ten years, Gregory moved to canonize him in Perugia in 1228.[39] With this elevation, Gregory ushered in the age of mendicant sainthood.

In spite of the large local following of Francis and the solemnity of the occasion, there were still some disturbing signs. The first was immediate evidence of cultic opposition locally. Confirmation of this opposition can be found in the early lives written around the time of the canonization. One of the keys for tracing this opposition can be found in the miracularies appended to the vitae of the saints. In particular one needs to pay attention to aggression or chastisement miracles that involve punishment for cultic misbehavior, a

---

38. For the office of cardinal protector, see Williell R. Thomson, "Earliest Cardinal-Protectors," 17–80. For the Poor Clares, see the work of Joan Mueller, esp. *Privilege of Poverty* and her *Companion to Clare*.

39. Gregory IX, "Mira circa nos" [July 19, 1228], Fontanini, 60–62; Potthast, n8242. The most significant work on Francis's canonization has been done by Roberto Paciocco; see his *"Sublimia Negotia."* See also id., "Miracles and Canonized Sanctity," 251–74. Bredero also notes that the celerity of this canonization necessitated a startling break in procedure. Francis's vita was composed only after the canonization; see id., *Christendom and Christianity*, 261–63. Bredero speculates that this speed was to prevent an immediate split in the Franciscan order, but I am unconvinced.

popular subset of larger miracle collections and a staple of early and medieval Christian hagiography.[40] The hagiographers' primary purposes in relating these stories are to reinforce the spiritual power of the saint, to defend the reality of their presence in heaven, and to illustrate the intimate relationship between the reputation of the saint and God, meaning that detraction of the saint in question becomes bound up with the sin of blasphemy.[41] If read carefully, such stories also betray a depth of cultic opposition. This opposition did not initially come from heretics. In the first place, there were not enough heterodox men and women to make their presence felt, and in the second place, more than enough opposition already existed *within* the church to create enough material for the writer. As time goes on, heretics do become more and more in evidence, and as a result such opposition to particular saints came to be *conflated with heresy itself by the end of the thirteenth century*. Aggression miracles, then, are the place in which to test the hypothesis of the development of doctrine, whether opposition to a particular canonized saint becomes tantamount to heresy, and what that means for the papal specification of saints.

In Francis's case, some of the opposition was local, with some coming from the nobility and some arising from the lower classes. At first such antagonism was sporadic, and only in the later lives of Francis does one begin to encounter any serious opposition (though less than other contemporary saints). In the two earliest certain sources, Thomas of Celano's first life of Francis (ca. 1228–29) and the Assisi compilation (ca. 1240–41), only straightforward hagiography is found, together with the usual types of miracle stories.[42] It is only as the sources move into the 1240s that one starts to see evidence of cultic opposition. The first example comes from Thomas

---

40. Such miracles have a long pedigree in the Christian tradition (which itself drew from the Jewish scriptural experience of such wonders). One could trace them all the way back to the smiting of Ananias and Sapphira in Acts 5. Early on, the hagiographical tradition began to incorporate similar aggression miracles, e.g., Gregory of Tours, *De gloria confessorum*, PL 71, 889. For the medieval period, the best work on them has been done for French saints before the thirteenth century. See esp. Platelle, "Crime et châtiment à Marchiennes," 156–202; Sigal, "Un aspect du culte des saints," 49–59; and de Gaiffier, "Les Revindications," 123–38. See also a discussion of the aggression miracles of Peter of Verona in my *Martyred Inquisitor*, 163–67. Aggression miracles can also be traced in the cults of the ancient pagan world, e.g., in the cult of Asclepius; see Luck, *Arcana Mundi*. I thank my anonymous reader for the reference.

41. For blasphemy in the medieval period, see Murray, "Piety and Impiety," 83–106; Schwerhoff, *Zungen wie Schwerter*; and Leveleux and Rigaudière, *La parole interdite*.

42. In giving priority to these two sources, I follow Thompson, *Francis of Assisi*, even though the Assisi compilation does bear some marks of proto-spiritualism. See full discussion of Franciscan sources in Thompson, *Francis of Assisi*, 227–45. Later biographies are tainted by various intraorder conflicts. These, too, can be valuable for tracing the outlines of opposition, and I will sketch those as we get to the end of the 1200s and the beginning of the 1300s in chapters 4 and 5. For the

of Celano's *Treatise on the Miracles of Francis*.[43] Increasingly, in addition to hagiographically characteristic wonders such as resurrections, healings, and interventions, new categories were being added to mendicant miracle literature outlining vindication of a saint against his or her detractors. Thomas of Celano included a whole section on punishments meted out to people who failed to keep Francis's feast. A woman called out in birth pangs to Francis, making a vow that she would always observe his feast. She safely delivered but some years after forgot her vow. One day, on Francis's feast, she went out to work and became paralyzed. After she and her husband realized their mistake, her motor functions were restored. Similar things were reported in Campania, and in France, women who went to work on Francis's feast day and were struck with pain or paralysis; they were later healed when they repented.[44] In faraway Spain, a woman in the village of Olite was chastised by her neighbor for working on the saint's day. She opined, "If there were one saint for every trade, the number of saints would be more than the number of days."[45] She became mentally disturbed until her townsmen prayed to Francis for her. Several more similar cases are reported here, underscoring a small undercurrent of cultic resistance. One can sense the irritation in the townswoman of Olite's words. Too many saints, it seems, were being presented to the faithful. Another incident is reported of a cleric in Noto, a Sicilian town: "Henry the priest, though a simple cleric, insulting and vilifying the saint [Francis] with others, lost the power of speech for a long time."[46] Bonaventure, in his *Major Legend*, is content to copy most of Thomas of Celano's aggression miracles, adding one about a scoffing parishioner near Poitiers whose hands seized and became immobile when he tried to work on the saint's day. Was it because Francis was foreign?[47] Or of a different social

---

originality of Thomas of Celano's First Life as a hagiographical work, see Dalarun, *La malavventura di Francesco*, 101.

43. Ed. in *Fontes Francescani*, ed. Menestó et al., and trans. in *Francis of Assisi*, ed. Armstrong et al., 2:2: 399–468.

44. *Francis of Assisi*, 2:442–43.

45. "Si de qualibet arte unus sanctus existeret dierum numerum numerus sanctorum excederet." *Tractatus de Miraculis*, c. 102. *Francis of Assisi*, ed. Armstrong et al., 2:442.

46. "Presbiter autem Henricus, tunc clericus, cum aliis insultans et vilificans Sanctum, amisit loquelam per magnum tempus." "Miracula Sancti Francisci," 386.

47. This is Vauchez's hypothesis; see his *Sainthood*, 134. He has rightly been challenged on sometimes overemphasizing sainthood at the center; see Cormack, *Saints in Iceland*. One could gauge this through an analysis of local calendars. For example, in a Sarum calendar from 1328 that I consulted, Francis was present but Anthony, Dominic, and Peter of Verona were omitted. This was in spite of the fact that the local saint, Thomas of Hereford (sometimes "of Cantelupe"), canonized only eight years before, was present. See Dublin: Trinity College MS 606. For Francis, this was studied in detail in Desbonnets, "Culte de saint François," 155–215.

class?[48] These are some of the suggestions about this opposition, but I do not think there is enough to identify the source with any degree of certainty. It is possible, since so many of the stories deal with banning of manual labor, that there was resistance from the very lowest levels of society. What it may indicate is a nascent irritation about new saints imposed from above challenging traditional and local sanctities. What we do not possess in the early accounts is Francis accomplishing miracles against heretics (as we will see later with Dominic and Peter of Verona). The only mention of heresy in the early hagiography is of Francis's miraculous liberation of a man falsely accused of heresy in Tivoli.[49]

It was not only average Christians who expressed sporadic opposition to Francis. Antagonism also came from higher up in the church. For a variety of reasons some prelates were slow to include mendicant saints in their calendars, and Francis is the first example of this. Gregory felt it necessary to issue a second, briefer bull entitled "Sicut phialae aureae" on several occasions between July 1228 and May 1230, reminding prelates in strong terms that he had solemnly canonized Francis and that the saint's feast ought to be celebrated by the universal church with proper rites on his newly instituted feast of October 4.[50] For various reasons that are rarely clear—with possible responses ranging from ignorance and neglect to outright opposition—prelates and abbots outside Italy were slow to adopt the liturgical commemoration of Francis. This tardiness would be repeated every time a mendicant saint was canonized.[51] A salient example is found in a statute of Bishop Thomas of Cantilupe (himself the uncle of a canonized saint). In legislation for his diocese of Worcester he stipulates, "We desire that the feasts of Sts. Dominic and Francis be celebrated with nine lessons in the Churches. But we do not wish by this to impede the works of the faithful laity."[52] Here one notes a dovetailing of lay and clerical concerns, reflected in a statute about work. Sometimes opposition could be shockingly boisterous. For example, a French priest named William at Dieppe one day completely lost control in front of a stained-glass depiction of St. Francis: "That

---

48. Thompson, *Francis of Assisi*, 213.

49. *Tractatus de Miraculis*, in *Francis of Assisi*, 2:437–38.

50. The full text of "Sicut phialae aureae" is in Fontanini, 63–64; Potthast, n8236. For the connection between the canonization bull and "Sicut," see the discussion in *François d'Assise*, ed. Dalarun, 1:414–15.

51. See Desbonnets, "Culte de saint François," passim.

52. Vauchez, "Stigmata," 71n11. Vauchez correctly intimates that this gave the founders the status of "second-rate saints."

accursed fellow was nothing but a greedy merchant, a coarse and vile figure, and by no means a saint."[53] One can imagine several factors that might play into this phenomenon: a reluctance to venerate foreign saints, the desire of religious orders to focus on their own holy men and women, and perhaps a nascent irritation at what was becoming high-handed papal maneuvering in the arrogation of canonization.

At least one factor about opposition to Francis is clear. It has especially to do with a single aspect of his claim to holiness: the imprint of the wounds of Christ on his body, the stigmata. After the phenomenon became known following Francis's death, scattered but long-lasting opposition to Francis's particular privilege arose throughout the church. Nine bulls were issued between 1237 and 1291 defending the reality of the wounds.[54] Though Vauchez primarily attributes such opposition to conservative spiritualities suspicious of the new movements, something deeper was happening. One factor is Dominican opposition, recorded in two bulls, pointing not only to the growing rivalry between the two orders but also to increasing suspicion about the singularity of Francis's holiness. Around 1340, the aggressive parallelism of Francis to Christ provoked an Italian Dominican to deface an image of Francis's stigmata with a knife.[55] A Sylvestrine monk was hauled before the Assisi inquisition in 1361, complaining that Francis was being divinized.[56] Criticisms of Franciscan excess in their presentation of Francis multiplied in the 1300s with humanists—followed later by Protestant reformers—attacking such over-the-top Franciscan productions as Bartolomeo of Pisa's *Liber de Conformitate*, which maintained aggressive parallelizations between Francis and Christ. Though such opposition was not new with Francis, it was raised to a pique by the adulation of his admirers. The benefit of such conflicts was that they did have the effect of refining resistance and of clarifying the positions of both sides.

Though Francis's canonization occurred just two years after his death, the next glorification of a mendicant saint provided a preview of things to come. Anthony of Padua, a Portuguese Minorite who became a famous preacher in northern Italy, was canonized slightly less than a year after his death in

---

53. This earned him a reproach from the curia, for William foolishly uttered his tirade during the pontificate of the Franciscan Nicholas IV. See Nicholas IV, "Cunctis reverendis" [May 26, 1289], in Bullarium Franciscanum, 4:75; Potthast, n22969.

54. Vauchez, "Stigmata," 66. See also Thompson, *Francis of Assisi*, 388–90. See also Schmucki, *Stigmata of St. Francis of Assisi*.

55. Vauchez, "Stigmata," 83n66.

56. Ibid., 83n67.

1231, the most rapid canonization to that date.[57] Gregory himself notes the impression of haste in the process in his bull "Litteras quas" and, with a rather hand-waving argument, dismisses such charges and reports that the matter had been handled "not suddenly, but with gravity and maturity." In the more extended canonization bull, Gregory rehearses all of the language of canonization up to that point, including the Innocentian addition that such a glorification was directed so "that heretical depravity might be confounded and the Catholic faith confirmed" and that "heretics . . . might be brought back to Christ, who is the light, the way, the truth, and the life." This tone continues throughout the text: a confrontation with heresy becomes the chief hermeneutic of the entire document.[58] Clearly, papal policy had begun explicitly to focus on saints as the heavenly vanguard of the earthly corps of mendicants, who faced off against the heretics then proliferating throughout Christendom. The miracles of the saints, particularly those of Anthony at his tomb in Padua, were an ongoing and powerful sermon contradicting the pretensions of heresy. Just as the mendicants united holiness of life with preaching, so after death did their saints combine preaching with the vindication of a holy life in miracles. This is perhaps the summit of the claims of the new orders and secondarily of the papacy. They who had embraced penance and poverty to the end of preaching and example found confirmation of their holiness in the divine approbation of miracles—in Anthony's case, effusive approbation. The papacy could point to no greater glory or to more certain confirmation of its policies and positions than the tombs of the heroically holy Minorites and Preachers. The symbiosis was in full swing.

The canonization of St. Dominic was another turning point. The two Minorites canonized before him were genuinely and broadly public personages: well-known, accessible saints. Dominic was a holy man, but his genius was behind the scenes, shepherding his small band of Friars-Preachers in such a way as to establish an enduring and balanced religious constitution, navigating his order away from the shoals that would threaten the Franciscan movement over the next hundred years, and aligning them with papal and scholastic orientations. In short, Dominic was an organizational genius, a pa-

---

57. Gregory IX, "Litteras quas" [June 1, 1232], Fontanini, 66–67; Potthast, n8937. This is the letter destined for Padua. The more extended letter was published three days later and addressed to the whole church; id., "Cum dicat Dominus," Fontanini, 64–65; Potthast, n8938. An older but useful study is Huber, *Saint Anthony of Padua*. For Anthony's life, see *Vita prima di S. Antonio*, ed. Gamboso; BHL, 587.

58. It is probable that Anthony, with little recorded confrontation with heretics in his life, obtained the later title Hammer of the Heretics as a result of this theme in his canonization bull.

tient and hardworking friar dedicated to making the lukewarm holy and leading straying sheep back to the fold.[59] His cult was neither immediate nor widely popular. For twelve years Dominic had lain where he wished, in a simple grave under the feet of his own friars in Bologna. It took the charismatic preaching of his follower John of Vicenza to whip up a popular following.[60] Pope Gregory himself had known Dominic personally. He had experienced his quiet and intense holiness firsthand and had at length presided at the founder's funeral. His solicitude for the Dominicans was at least equal to that of the Franciscans, perhaps more, since the Preachers had just the sort of academic training the Minorites lacked and on that account were more suitable for use in diplomatic, inquisitorial, and canonical missions. Wishing to honor the Dominicans, Gregory initiated the process that would lead up to their founder's canonization.

On July 13, 1234, Gregory promulgated the bull "Fons sapientiae," announcing the canonization of St. Dominic. It is one of the most extraordinary canonization bulls in the history of the church. In it Gregory departs significantly from the previous models provided for him. The pope in this letter provides an allegorical roadmap to church history, all leading up to the foundation of the order of Preachers by Dominic. The bull opens with a remark that God produces new signs in every age of the chosen people, particularly for "inconstant minds," and works miracles against the "disobedience of disbelief."[61] Using language from the prophet Zechariah, he describes four chariots, harnessed to horses of different colors, which he interprets to be the four movements that propelled the church through history.[62] The first is the army of the martyrs, symbolized by the red horse, whose sacrifice caused the church to spread through all nations. This army waged war against the powers of the world. The second were the "Knights of the Desert," the monks, typified for Gregory by St. Benedict and allegorically represented by the black horse. These men fought with the weapons of penitence against the lukewarmness of the faithful. A white horse led the third chariot, which Gregory interprets as the Cistercians. Then Gregory resorts to more apocalyptic language, speaking of the "eleventh hour" and the *refrigescens caritas* (the concept of the cooling of charity near the end times). Not only was the love of Christians cooling, allowing thorns to be sown among the fruit, but that favorite symbol of heresy made its appearance, the "little

59. An older but still useful biography of Dominic is Vicaire, *Saint Dominic and His Times*.

60. Thompson, *Revival Preachers*, 59.

61. Gregory IX, "Fons sapientiae" [July 13, 1234], Fontanini, 70–72; Potthast, n9487.

62. Cited from Zec 6:1–8.

foxes" who came to lay waste to the whole of the vineyard. But yet God did not abandon his people, for he called forth a final chariot, led by a gray horse, which meant the Minorites and the Preachers, all of whom in this text are represented by Dominic himself. Dominic was prepared from birth, says Gregory, in prayer, penitence, and liturgical service, all of which Gregory sums up as the purpose of Dominic's life: "That the whole of the assembly of heretics might tremble, and the whole of the faithful Church might rejoice." After noting his personal friendship with the saint, Gregory then proceeds rather formulaically, with the standard and developed language of canonization. No mistake is possible when confronted with this text. Gregory is deploying Dominic as a specifically antiheretical saint, allegorically summing up his mission from God and his whole life as one dedicated principally to the eradication of heresy from Christendom.

Gregory had been pursuing a new course. He had used apocalyptic language in Francis's canonization but had described the Minorite as ministering to the lukewarm rather than the heretical. In Anthony's and particularly in Dominic's bulls, the pope clearly has a new direction in mind. Mendicant saints were to be the hallmarks of the papal antiheretical campaign, the "crown jewels," as it were. In venerating such men, Gregory wanted to make it clear that the Christian faithful were not only to pay homage to holiness and to beg intercession but also to see them as the standard-bearers of orthodoxy, whose lives were confirmed by the very miracles that destroyed and confuted heresy. Pope Gregory IX's final canonization was that of a quasi-mendicant, the Landgravine of Hungary, Elizabeth of Thuringia, who had ended her life as a tertiary of the Franciscans.[63] Her position made her somewhat unsuitable for Gregory's purposes. She had been married, she was a woman and could not preach, and she had been rich before abandoning wealth. She could not, in those senses, then be labeled an antiheretical saint. Nevertheless, Gregory obliquely associated her with his efforts at fighting the enemies of orthodoxy. After enumerating her many virtues in another poetic bull, the pope identified her as the cause of the confutation of heretics on many occasions, without further specifics.[64] No matter what they had done in life, in Gregory's mind all saints naturally fought heresy. The confutation of heretical depravity was something that flowed out

---

63. A complete study of Elizabeth can be found in *Sankt Elisabeth*. See also Klaniczay, *Holy Rulers and Blessed Princesses*, esp. 209–20. For a discussion of her hagiographical sources, see ibid., 419–23. See also Huyskens, *Quellenstudien zur Geschichte der hl. Elizabeth*, 1–109; and Wolf, *Elizabeth of Hungary*. For Dietrich of Apolda's vita, see Rener, *Die Vita der heiligen Elisabeth*.

64. "Et haereticis confusionis multae materia cumulatur." Gregory IX, "Gloriosus in maiestate" [May 28, 1235], Fontanini, 73–75.

of a holy life confirmed by miracles. As saints, holy men and women were, by definition, the sharpest opponents of heretics.

It is clear that Pope Gregory desired to set a pattern for future canonizations. They were of course to be a tool of papal policy, but there was definitely more. Theologically, saints were the vindicators of God's church. They were the exclamation points scattered throughout history, the visible signs of the invisible grace of God and the endurance of his church. Saints were not absent for medievals but were visibly present in their relics and tombs and viscerally present in the impetrations of the faithful and in the accomplishment of wonders. It is not too far a stretch to see the saints as defenders of orthodoxy against heresy. What is surprising is that Gregory constantly deploys the saints against heretics, a vague and undefined lot at this time, rather than at his very specific political opponent Frederick II (though there was surely conflation of the two in the eyes of many churchmen). While papal invective against the German emperor is certainly not lacking, no evidence exists in the canonization bulls that the saints are invoked specifically for political purposes. This makes the link between sainthood and antiheresy easier to understand. It was simply an outgrowth of meditations about sanctity that had grown up over the previous fifty years. Saints had real holiness and performed real miracles. Both of these reinforced each other; both had to be present for sanctity. On the opposite side of the coin, heretics shammed holiness and performed wonders at the behest of the devil, who in the language of scripture "often turns himself into an angel of light."[65] Saints were not only useful against heretics; in their very beings they were the *antiheretic*, the diametric opposite of the heresiarchs. They were the followers of Christ, who had conquered the world, and so stood as beacons to the masses of the lukewarm, beckoning them away from heretical darkness. The air around their bodies, for medievals, fairly crackled with invisible graces, a further refutation to heretical antimaterial pretensions. The church highlighted to the faithful this disjunction in deep relief. This was an understandable theological conclusion. The question was, would it be accepted by the church-at-large or by future popes?

A long interregnum followed Gregory's death between 1241 and 1243. During this period several inquisitors were brutally murdered near the city of Avignonet in the Lauragais. The cardinals, charged with the government of the church during a *sede vacante* (the papal interregnum), sent a short letter of condolence acknowledging the dead churchmen, even calling them martyrs, but with no attempt made to canonize them in any formal way.

---

65. 2 Cor 11:14.

This episode indicates two things. First, papal control of canonization had solidified by this point to such an extent that the cardinals in charge of the church considered it impossible to accord any significant public veneration to the victims. Further, it betokens the increasing animosity between the church and heretical elements. The Avignonet martyrs were not the first. Ever since Peter of Castelnau there had been a rising tide of violence against churchmen dedicated to antiheretical activities. Passion was escalating on both sides. In France the Albigensian Crusade had done its work, with the last Cathar stronghold of Mont-Aimé being burned in 1239. Heretics were attracted to the relative anonymity of the Italian city-states, increasing the temperature of already volatile civic and religious situations. As early as 1199 Peter Parenzo, an inveterate opponent of heresy, had been killed when he was *podestà* in Orvieto.[66] In 1233 the prominent Dominican preacher Roland of Cremona was wounded in an attack in Piacenza. Another Friar Preacher, Ruggiero Calcagni, was wounded in 1239, again in Orvieto. In the spring of 1245 all of Florence was engaged in communal conflict between parties either supporting or combating two Cathar brothers.[67] The stage was set for a serious confrontation. The church had solidified both its teaching on sainthood and its resistance to heresy. This resulted in an increasing cycle of violence on both sides. As saints became weapons in this conflict, the tenor of invective became higher, and both sides began to rush to define their respective positions.

Ironically it was Innocent IV, in his commentary so ambivalent about the question, who was the one who forced the issue. Sinibaldo Fieschi is a difficult character to assess.[68] On one hand, he was very measured and conservative, while on the other hand, he could explode with anger and effort. After all it was Innocent's quiet moderation that enabled him to break the interregnum and become pope in 1243. His steady approach to the emperor Frederick II raised a false hope for reconciliation. Innocent bided his time until unleashing the full might of papal fury at the emperor once the pope was safely at the First Council of Lyons in 1245. One could characterize the pope as erratic. Strongly supportive of the mendicants, particularly the

---

66. The *podestà* was a sort of city manager, usually hired from outside the city, to help manage the day-to-day affairs of the Italian communes and to restrain communal violence. Here it seems not to have helped significantly. For Peter Parenzo, see his vita in AS 18 (May 5): 86–99.

67. For this episode, see Prudlo, *Martyred Inquisitor*, 40–52.

68. No solid biography of this very prominent pope exists, but his registers have been edited in Sinibaldo dei Fieschi, *Les registres d'Innocent IV*. Much on Innocent's policies can be found in works about his bitter rival, Frederick II. See Kantorowicz, *Frederick the Second*. Kantorowicz's almost hagiographical presentation of the emperor is somewhat corrected in Abulafia, *Frederick II*.

Dominicans, throughout his pontificate, the pope did a complete turnabout in the last months of his life, stripping the mendicant orders of nearly all of their privileges (though this imprudent course was almost immediately reversed by his successor). In canonizations one sees a similar bifurcation. In one sense Innocent was a throwback, canonizing much more broadly than Gregory, with only one mendicant saint to his credit. Perhaps this reticence was related to Innocent's own quite temperate approach to the problem as a Decretalist, but when one examines his actions rather than his words, a marked discrepancy arises. The struggle between Emperor Frederick II and the papacy reached its climax while Innocent was in office. As Michael Goodich points out, canonization became another political weapon to train on an enemy.[69] Though I would contend that many other factors were in play in papal canonizations in the period, it is clear that politics was a prime mover.

Innocent IV, over his eleven-year pontificate (r. 1243–54), performed only five canonizations, and all showed a common theme of defending the church against either heresy or the state.[70] Innocent's saints, while all personally pious, were also controversial figures. Certain segments of society intensely loathed them, especially in the case of Peter of Verona, canonized in 1253. The other subjects of Innocent IV's canonizations, while controversial, were often well out of the reach of living memory, leaving little room for substantial opposition to mount against them. In this sense, then, Innocent was a conservative, accepting well-known historical figures and drawing saintly examples from around the Christian world. Unlike Gregory, Innocent did not particularly patronize the mendicants, either. Under his papacy three mendicant causes were introduced only to languish.[71] The fourth, however, would prove to be the catalyst for the definitive elaboration of the qualitative difference of papal canonization: the elevation of the

---

69. See Goodich, "Politics of Canonization," 294–307. However, Goodich sometimes overemphasizes solely political causes.

70. Innocent IV canonized Peter of Verona, Edmund Rich of Canterbury, Stanislaus of Kraków, William of St. Brieuc, and Margaret of Scotland. Of these, four were persecuted for their faith and for their defense of the church. Peter and Stanislaus (d. 1079) were martyrs, both canonized in 1253. Stanislaus died defending the church against the state, while Peter died defending the church against heretics. William and Edmund were persecuted for upholding the rights of the church against the state, and Margaret represented the ideal form of a Christian ruler. Peter is the only mendicant, and from Innocent's perspective was canonized more as a factor of papal policy and popular petition than as a public favoring of the mendicants.

71. These were Giovanni Buono, Simon of Collazzone, and Rose of Viterbo. Vauchez, Sainthood, 52. For Giovanni, see Cipolla, "Appunti eccliniani," 401–8; also, Thompson, Cities of God, esp. 204–6. For Simon, see Pulignani, "Il B. Simone da Collazzone," 97–132; also, Thompson, Cities of God, 203–15. For Rose, see Piacentini, Santa Rosa da Viterbo.

famous Dominican preacher and papal inquisitor to the honors of the altar on March 9, 1253.

Peter's elevation was and remains the fastest canonization in papal history. Eleven months after Peter's murder in the forests north of Milan, Innocent IV enrolled him in the catalog of saints. Besides this swift canonization, Peter was significant for several other pertinent reasons. Peter was born of parents who had Cathar sympathies, and he was raised in an atmosphere characterized by Catharism.[72] His uncle especially was highly committed to the Cathar cause. In spite of this, Peter went to the University of Bologna, where he was one of the first crop of recruits in the fledgling Dominican order. Peter showed a talent for preaching and disputation and committed his life to the conversion of Cathar heretics (whom he, like many other churchmen, often conflated with other enemies of the church). By the end of Peter's life, Innocent IV began to trust him with delicate political and religious missions, culminating in Peter's appointment as inquisitor for Lombardy in 1251. Success brought hatred, and a conspiracy of Cathar nobles and townsmen hired a murderer who accomplished his assignment in 1252. Though Peter was quite popular in Milan and though his cult proved enduring and successful, Innocent IV had further reasons for a quick canonization.

In Peter's death Innocent IV had a golden opportunity. In the past the papacy was unable to canonize churchmen killed by heretics.[73] Innocent III was unable to canonize Peter of Castelnau (d. 1208), whose death partially led to the Albigensian Crusade, for want of miracles.[74] Conrad of Marburg (murdered in 1231) was unacceptable because he was universally vilified.[75] The Dominican and Franciscan martyrs of Avignonet were unfortunate enough to meet their deaths in 1242, the height of the three-year papal interregnum, which stalled recognition of their cults. Neither was any action taken when heretics murdered the Franciscan Peter of Arcagnano, a notary for the inquisition, some years before Peter of Verona.[76] Canonization of these figures could have created a sizable opposition, but political and reli-

---

72. For Peter, see Dondaine, "Saint Pierre Martyr," 67–150, substantially modified and augmented in Prudlo, *Martyred Inquisitor*. Peter's life is printed in a patchwork of texts in *Vita S[ancti] Petri Martyris Ordinis Praedicatorum*, ed. Taegio, AS 12 (April 3). This text is largely drawn from Thomas Agni's ca. 1270 life of Peter. I have translated all of Peter's historical and hagiographical sources in Prudlo, *Martyred Inquisitor*. Hereafter, *VSP*.

73. On the difficulty of canonizing martyrs in this period, see Vauchez, *Sainthood*, 146–58; and Ryan, "Missionary Saints," 1–28.

74. Vauchez, *Sainthood*, 37n16.

75. For Conrad, see Patschovsky, "Konrad von Marburg," 70–77.

76. For Peter of Arcagnano, see d'Alatri, *L'Inquisizione francescana nell'Italia centrale*, 12–15.

gious considerations prevented them from being honored. A further reason also intervened. Conflation of heresy with imperial pretensions sometimes worked against the church. Some could view any antiheretical saint in an anti-imperial light; so as long as the struggle between pope and emperor went on, it was inexpedient to canonize contemporary antiheretical saints. By 1250 Frederick II, the enemy of the papacy, was dead. No longer would it be wildly impolitic to elevate explicitly anti-imperial saints, of which Peter absolutely was. A third reason also existed: according to the standards of the time, Peter was a real saint. In his life Peter had been known for personal mortification, pastoral solicitude, powerful preaching, and the working of wonders. Innocent IV, in his commentary on the decretals, had already stated what had become common belief: both holiness of life and the testimony of miracles were necessary to canonize a saint.[77] Fortunately for Innocent IV, Peter had both. So the canonization of the worthy Peter dovetailed perfectly with Innocent IV's political purposes, positioning the Dominican first as antiheretical and secondly as anti-imperial.[78] Now Christendom was confronted with a genuine saint who was a convert from and battler against heresy and was now reinforced by the full authority of the Roman pontiff. Opposition was sure to arise. As desultory as such opposition had been before, the success of the mendicant saints, culminating with the canonization of Peter, crystallized the resistance. The objects of papal canonization came under direct attack, and the defenders of orthodoxy—the papacy and mendicants together—were forced to refine and define just exactly what papal canonization entailed.

---

77. Sinibaldo dei Fieschi [Innocent IV], *Apparatus in Quinque Libros Decretalium*, on X 3.45.1, *De reliquiis et veneratione sanctorum*, 457, col. ii.

78. For the political purposes of the papacy in canonizing in this period, see Goodich, "Politics of Canonization," 294–307. I disagree with Goodich's position that anti-imperial saints became unimportant after 1266. I argue rather that the anti-imperial became antiheretical (which in papal and church rhetoric often were the same anyway) and that the real battle between saints and heretics was only beginning by that point.

CHAPTER 4

"Hark, Hark, the Dogs Do Bark . . ."
The Assault on Mendicant Holiness (1234–60)

Papal canonization by the middle of the thirteenth century had become one of the most professional endeavors ever devised. It had explicit, streamlined processes, checks and balances, a diversity of legal explanations and defenses, and growing prestige among the membership of the church. It began to be what it had never been before: a tool that the papal curia could use to reward devoted subjects, a method of elevating and underscoring certain types of piety and holiness, and a way to stress certain currents in papal policy. The honing of this process into a precision tool made canonizations a key weapon in the papal arsenal of the 1200s. Canonized saints could also be explicitly deployed against heresy and heretics. This raised the stakes in the medieval battle between heterodoxy and orthodoxy. As a result, heretics began to see that saints were being positioned against them, and in response they began to direct their own opposition against those very saints. In addition, the swift crystallization of papal canonization had left partisans of local sanctity uneasy. While people in the church generally respected papal saints, many were often neglectful of them, and some were outright hostile. This chapter traces the contours of these antagonisms.

Casual blasphemies had existed in human history for as long as people had cultivated religious orientations, and Christianity was no different.[1] It

---

1. See Nash, *Blasphemy in the Christian World.*

was common to curse or swear by this or that saint. Indeed, it was a common part of everyday life in spite of repeated denunciations by Christian moralists.[2] Sometimes this lax speech could cross over into a sustained opposition to various aspects of the Christian cult. Michael Goodich contends that the rise of medieval heresy led to a proliferation of blasphemy about the material aspects of the Christian life, a situation that demanded action from the church.[3] In particular, as papal canonizations came to be more commonplace, it became a matter of course that there would be grumblings from diverse sections of the church's membership: from the hierarchy, from the regulars, and among the laity. The rapidly developing theology surrounding papal canonization, its increasing institutionalization, and its promotion by the mendicant orders were all on a collision course with anticultic sentiment of all kinds and degrees of seriousness.

➤ The Volley of the Heretics

Derision toward saints and saints' cults had been a feature of medieval heresy since its appearance around the turn of the eleventh century. What had started as a general attack on the incarnational materialism of the church had become increasingly specific over time. A critique of relics, shrines, and pilgrimages slowly began to have more focus and had several central aspects. First one sees opposition to Old Testament saints, who came to be viewed as prophets of the Evil Principle (the satanic god of the dualist system). This culminated in a particular assault on John the Baptist, no longer seen as the Precursor but rather as the final and definitive messenger of the Evil God. A Gnostic undertone could also be detected, with a rejection of the physical events surrounding Christ's life, especially his birth and death, along with their soteriological meanings. This led to a neodocetistic understanding of Christ and sometimes of his mother, Mary. Further, one could see rejection of the sacraments, a critique of ecclesiastical ceremony, and an attack on external ritual objects and intermediate material realities (such as relics) that interposed themselves between the believer and God. Finally, there was the general critique of the wealth of the church. At first this was unfocused and rose from the devotional ideal of purity and imitation of the apostles. Later it came to be concentrated on St. Sylvester, the pope of the Donation of

2. For the medieval period in particular, see Murray, "Piety and Impiety," 83–106; for Italy in particular, see Thompson, *Cities of God*, 87, 138, 429, 453.

3. Goodich, *Miracles and Wonders*, 64–65.

Constantine, a development seen by the heretics (particularly the Waldensians) as the moment of corruption. All of these critiques were refined through the twelfth and early thirteenth centuries, and taken together they represented a comprehensive attack on the church's incarnational worldview.

As long as such critiques remained on a general level, the papacy was content to leave prosecution to local authorities. As the influence of heretics increased and as their doctrinal assaults came to be more targeted and specific in the 1200s, the papacy had to take a more direct course of action. It is significant that the increasing papal attention to heresy starting from 1184 dovetailed with the increasing specificity of heretical attacks against the church. This elision accelerated from the time of the Albigensian Crusade through the implementation of the papal inquisitions. Proceeding from a generalized critique of wealth, the heretics began to make particular attacks on St. Sylvester. From opposition to preaching about the Incarnation, the heretics went on specifically to criticize papal preachers and later the mendicant orders. From a blanket condemnation of the cult of saints, they came to castigate recently canonized and papally approved figures. With the rising specificity of these attacks, the church correspondingly rose to meet the challenge.

The thirteenth century saw the refinement of such arguments and their deployment against particular targets. Nowhere did papal policy, heretical sentiment, and popular opinion collide with such effect as in the reservation and creation of saints. Heterodox groups were not slow to notice this rising conflict and so began to prepare a concerted effort against papally canonized figures. Evidence for this shift comes from several sources. One is the writings or testimony of heretics themselves, another is contemporary antiheretical tractates and sermons, and yet another is the hagiographical writings and miracle stories reported surrounding the new saints. Of course this opposition can also be detected in theological writings, but I defer that discussion to chapter 5. Once again it is clear that these texts present interpretive difficulties, particularly interrogations done by the inquisition, written by notaries and translated—sometimes on the fly—into Latin. What we are interested in here, though, is not necessarily the identification of actually held heretical tenets but rather the perception and response of the church to real or presumed threats (though it seems that such beliefs were genuine and sincere among many of the various shades of belief of heterodox men and women). Generalized critiques were not as interesting or pressing to the church authorities. Yet the moment those attacks became aimed at papal saints, the stakes were raised. This heretical enumeration of particularized anticlerical or antipapal grievances was of broader popular appeal than abstract theological musings and drew the attention of increasing numbers of the laity. For this reason, too, such ideas made their appearance precisely when the papacy was securing its rights and pressing its cases.

Cathars professed that salvation could be achieved only through their sect, by the process of becoming "hereticated," to use inquisitorial language, or by being "consoled," the ritual called in their texts *consolamentum*.[4] Being accomplished in law and theology, inquisitors knew that by focusing their attention on this exclusive salvation doctrine they could lay bare the errors of the dualists. They did so from a number of angles. In one approach they targeted heretical doctrines about the Mother of God. Knowing the durability and prevalence of the Marian cult among medieval Christians, it became easy to home in on the disconnect between the *consolamentum* and Marian devotion. Committed heretics would maintain the *consolamentum* alone as salvific, while weaker "hearers" or sympathizers would affirm the salvation of Mary, who had died without being consoled. Several examples exist of inquisitors directly posing such questions to suspected Cathars. Suspects were asked "if the soul of the Blessed Virgin Mary and [the souls] of other saints are in paradise" or, in a similar way—and this time using the popularity of early Roman female martyrs—"if the Blessed Virgin Mary and Blessed Agnes had greater merits than the most recently consoled sinner."[5] D'Alatri, who has written most extensively on this, has speculated that such beliefs may be connected to doubts about purgatory and the particular judgment, or the immediate judgment of individual souls after the moment of death.[6] However, he points to sources about Waldensians and the particular heresy of Hugo Speroni only and not to any Cathar texts. While this hypothesis is possible, I do not think that there was any substantial overlap between these groups. Unlike the others, Cathar beliefs developed in dialogue with their anti-incarnationalism and exclusive salvation doctrine. Their tenets about the particular judgment evolved in response to these issues, and not in dialogue with the doctrine of purgatory. In any case it is difficult to map out a coherent Cathar soteriology, if one even existed. Doubts about the Particular Judgment, when added to an exclusivist salvation doctrine, carved out a gray area for souls after death.[7] In any case, the

4. For the centrality of *Consolamentum* to the Cathars, see *HHMA*, 465–94.

5. From a Dominican inquisition manuscript, Rome: Biblioteca Casanatense, H. 11. 134, "Si anima b. Virginis et aliorum sanctorum in paradiso sunt," ed. Döllinger, 2:320. "Si beata Maria Virgo et b. Agnes sunt majoris meriti quam aliqua peccatrix noviter consolata." Ibid., 325.

6. D'Alatri, *Eretici e inquisitori in Italia: Studi e documenti*, Biblioteca Seraphico-Cappucina 31 (Roma: Collegio San Lorenzo da Brindisi, 1986), 25–26nn8–9.

7. This was the individual judgment accorded to each soul immediately upon death, as opposed to the general judgment over all of creation at the end of time. See chap. 3.

spiritualist Cathars would have seen the liberation from the body as a good thing, with paradise perhaps deferred to the general judgment at the end of time. The inquisitors were on to something: if the Cathars preached exclusive salvation, the salvation of the saints of the Roman church had to be denied.[8]

Though various heretics might have disagreed on the theological implications of their soteriologies, they did agree on one thing: in light of their beliefs it was less than useless to pray to the saints. Inquisitors knew this as well and were quick to attack. A further question to be put to suspects was this: "Do you believe that the saints in heaven are able to be patrons to us on earth and to the souls in purgatory?"[9] The Waldensians were most widely known for their rejection of intercession. An Austrian summary of Waldensian beliefs confirms this denial. "Further they [the Waldensians] say that dead saints or blesseds are not able to assist the living by their intercessions."[10] Similar reports are found about German Waldensians: "they do not seek the suffrages of saints, nor do they venerate any images."[11] The inquisition in Carcassonne, in southern France, reported the same beliefs with an interesting qualification: "They say and hold in secret that the saints in heaven do not hear the prayers of the faithful, nor attend their prayers, by which they are honored on earth, and they say that the saints do not pray for us, and therefore it is not fitting to implore their suffrages, so they spurn the solemnities which we celebrate in honor of the saints . . . but these things they do not publicize among their believers, but rather hold them among the perfects of their sect."[12] Like Marian devotion, the cult of the saints was too

---

8. This line of questioning may have been designed by the inquisitors as a way to differentiate between perfects and ordinary believers. Simple believers may not have been privy to the idea that Mary was an angel and not a woman at all in the docetistic-type abstractions of some Cathar theology, e.g., "Tenets of the Italian Cathars," ca. 1250–60, ed. in *HHMA*, 354. See also, Peter of Verona *Summa contra hereticos*, Perugia: Biblioteca Comunale Augusta MS 1065, fols. 48[vb]–49ra, e.g., "Item cum eam dicit fuisse uxorem ioseph sicut et plurisquam locis sancti evangelii leguntur manifeste declarat eam muliere fuisse. mulierorum enim est muliere et non angelorum."

9. "Credis quod sancti in coelo nobis vivis et animabus in purgatorio constitutus patrocinari possunt?" Döllinger, 2:302.

10. "Item dicunt quod sancti seu beati mortui non possunt juvare vivos suis intercessionibus." Ibid., 305. Confirmed in another Austrian text edited on 345. See similar assertions in Kurze, *Quellen*, 80, 113, 117, 120, 130, 148.

11. "Item sanctorum suffragia non petunt, nec imagines aliquas venerantur." Döllinger, 2: 300.

12. "Item dicunt in secreto, quod sancti in coelo non audiunt orationes fidelium, nec attendunt orationes, quibus eos honoramus in terris, dicuntque, sanctos non orare pro nobis, et ideo non oportet nos eorum suffragia implorare, unde spernunt solemnitates, quas in sanctorum venerationem celebramus . . . haec tamen non manifestant indifferenter credentibus suis, sed inter se perfecti hujus sectae sic tenent." Ibid., 2:9.

dear to the Christian faithful to be attacked all at one go. It was better for the heretics to insinuate their more popular beliefs, drawing people into their circle, before lowering the boom on such matters. Inquisitors knew that if they detected someone who held these beliefs, he or she was already deep in the heretical sect.

When these streams were put together, it became clear that in both Catharism and Waldensianism there was to be a direct frontal assault on the cult of the saints. The doctrine of intercession was the linchpin undergirding all of the other acts of veneration paid to the holy ones.[13] To deny that belief was to undercut all of the exceptionally elaborate rituals and mechanisms for honoring them: the pilgrimages, tombs, masses, relics, images, and everything else that was attendant on saintly devotion.[14] Of course Waldensians were most explicit in enumerating the various ways in which they rejected the cult of the saints, but their attacks were mostly superficial, for they lacked the esoteric theological underpinnings of the Cathars. A typical Waldensian sentiment was "Christians are idolaters on account of the images of the saints and the Crucifix."[15]

While the criticism of outward church ceremony was common in interrogations and descriptions of the followers of Waldo, for the Cathars it went deeper. For them the cult of the saints represented the most sordid wallowing in materiality, the worst sort of religious superstition practiced by the Catholics. In attacking it they went after the most hallowed beliefs of medieval Christians. An interrogation of Italian Cathars in the early 1200s produced this statement: "To visit Saint James [at Compostela], and the tomb of the Lord, and the church of St. Peter they held for nought."[16] They went further than this. For them the veneration of relics was disgusting; it was an "act of rank idolatry towards lifeless bones."[17] Such activity would be horrific to someone who thought the material world crafted by the devil, who believed the body a mere shell whose life prevented the liberation of the

---

13. A prescient Waldensian in Piedmont put it this way: ""We should not pray to saints asking that they intercede with us to God; our prayers should be addressed to God alone." Cf. Audisio, *Waldensian Dissent*, 56.

14. A German antiheretical summa puts this neatly: "Solemnitates et cantus ecclesiae et reliquias sanctorum et peregrinationes damnant." Döllinger, 2:301. In the end they seemed to condemn nearly the whole of the church's communal, ritual, external life.

15. "Item dicunt, Christianos esse idolotaras propter imagines sanctorum et signum crucis." Ibid., 2:338.

16. "Item visitare sanctum Iacobum, et sepulchrum Domini, et ecclesiam sancti Petri pro nichilo habent." Interrogation of Mirisona and Giacomo in Florence, in Antoine Dondaine, "Durand de Huesca et la polémique anti-cathare," *AFP* 29 (1959), 268–71.

17. As d'Alatri puts it; see d'Alatri, "Culto dei santi," 92.

spirit. Images of Mary and the saints and the veneration of their relics are repeatedly termed idolatry by accused heretics in inquisitorial registers.[18] The assault on the cult of the saints was the point of the spear in heretical attacks on the institutional church, though it had to be carefully managed so as to avoid attracting the ire of the faithful. Heretics knew that these core beliefs could not be publicized widely; devotion to Mary and the saints was at the heart of medieval Christian life.

Armed with this theological apparatus and moved by practical consider-ations, the heretics of the 1200s began to focus their attacks on specific saints. They could have more luck with this than a generalized attack, considering the discomfort of some of the faithful with the rapidly developing doctrine of papal canonization. Already contempt showered on the figures of the Old Testament was well established. John the Baptist served as a sort of arch-satanic figure for the Cathars, while St. Sylvester had become an object of particular opprobrium for the Waldensians because of his identification with the acquisition of wealth by the church. As part of generalized anticultic sen-timent, sometimes early Christian saints, including Martin and Nicholas, were condemned, since they were some of the most well-known saints promoted by the Catholic Church.[19] In the 1200s heretical critiques had transitioned to more contemporary saints (while still maintaining their grave disdain for the Old Testament characters). This could only mean one thing: a confrontation with the saint-making authority, for the contemporary church had stakes in this fight. Critics of sainthood in the Roman church were about to begin to attack papally canonized saints.

For at least two reasons, the mendicant saints were the most obvious tar-get for heretical attention. First, they were the most visible opponents of the heretics, the vanguard enforcers of papal policy against heterodoxy. Second, they were wildly successful in nearly all of their endeavors, one of the most flourishing religious movements of the Middle Ages, which turned people away from heresy and toward institutional Christianity. This was a recipe for conflict. Scattered rumblings were heard from the laity about St. Francis (see chapter 3), but the consensus was one of almost undeniable holiness. An-thony, too, was popular, charismatic, and powerful among intercessors and so encountered less resistance. In spite of that, one can discern scattered signs of opposition there as well. In 1325 a renegade Franciscan named Thomas Scotus was fulminating against the church in the Iberian peninsula. His er-rors are all rather abstract, perhaps derived from Averroism, but they became

---

18. See Döllinger, 2:26, 168, 176, 320.

19. Ibid., 340.

all too concrete when he made the assertion "Fra Antonio of the Friars Minor, who was canonized, kept concubines, on account of which the Pope ordered him to be imprisoned."[20] This proved too much for the Franciscan prior, who ordered Thomas incarcerated (and his crime may have been aggravated by impugning Anthony in Portugal, from whence the saint originally came).

It was the Friars Preachers who occasioned the most opposition. Chapter 3 demonstrated how St. Dominic came to be portrayed as a battler against heresy from the moment of his formal canonization. While hagiographers within the order painted a much more complex and homely picture of Dominic, the broader world came to see him primarily as an antiheretical saint (a portrayal that would only accelerate with the canonization of Peter of Verona).[21] Of course there were many stories from Dominic's life, particularly his preaching in southern France, that lent themselves to an antiheretical narrative. Dominic (and his superior, Bishop Diego) were dangerous to the heretics, for they matched Cathar and Waldensian holiness by their manner of life and to that added powerful orthodox preaching.[22] Before this time, the heretics had little to fear from the scattered and halfhearted efforts of the church, but against such successful preachers as these—ones who could beat the heretics at their own game—active antipathy began to build. Symbolic of this was the account of the "trial by fire" held between Dominic's books and those of the heretics. The heretical text was consumed, while Dominic's remained unharmed (and Jordan of Saxony reports it leaping from the fire, not once, but thrice).[23] Because of Dominic's way of life and his success, his order was established, as William of Puylaurens puts it, as "perpetual preachers against the heretics."[24] From the very beginning the Dominicans were to be dedicated to the fight against heresy. The exaltation of the members of such an order would prove a significant flashpoint in the battles with those with heterodox proclivities.

Dominic continued his fight against heresy throughout his life, but increasingly he became occupied with the details of organizing his new order.

---

20. "Fr. Antonius de Ord. FF. Minor. qui fuit canonizatus, quod tenuerat concubinam propter quod mandaverat eum Papa incarcerari." Ibid., 2:616. Also see Lea, *History of the Inquisition*, 2:188.

21. For this cultic focus on antiheresy, see Prudlo, *Martyred Inquisitor*, 101–2. To see an example of this cultic reimagining, one need only read the description of Dominic in Dante's *Paradiso*, canto 12.

22. For this transition, see Lappin, "From Osma to Bologna," 31–58.

23. Jordan of Saxony, *Libellus de Principiis Ordinis Praedicatorum*. Trans. in Jordan of Saxony, *Order of Preachers*, c. 25; BHL 2210; *SOP* 3.2780.

24. William of Puylaurens, *Chronica*, 119–75, c. 10.

While Jordan, his earliest biographer, records no particular aggression miracles, later hagiographers are less reticent in recording opposition to his cult. Gerald de Frachet, whose *Vitas Fratrum* (written ca. 1259) is an early chronicle of the order, records three miracles in which people are punished either for their sins or for blasphemy.[25] One particular nobleman interrupted Dominic in Segovia, because the "long-winded" preacher was keeping him from his dinner. Dominic directly foretold the impatient aristocrat's violent death. The task of preaching was sacred, and was not to be interrupted by those "inflated with a carnal mind," as Gerald says.[26] The order's most famous hagiographer, Jacobus of Voragine—whose work found an overwhelmingly positive reception throughout Christendom—further enhances the aggression miracle tradition and begins to detail its intersection with heresy.[27] While previous biographers had all made the devil a primary antagonist in the life of Dominic, Jacobus makes a concrete connection between the devil and the heretics. One famous episode retells a story of female Cathar hearers who came to Dominic wishing to convert. At this, a "cat as large as a dog . . . with an exposed posterior which issued an intolerable stench appeared." Dominic drove the heretical "deity" away, and the women were converted.[28] Jacobus also dealt with lay impiety. In another postmortem miracle story, a woman was spinning on Dominic's feast, and she mocked other women going to his Mass as "darlings of the friars." She immediately suffered a tumor of the eyes, complete with itching and worms. Recognizing her error, she hastened to the Friars' church and made a vow to be devout on his feast. Having done this, she was cured.[29] Jacobus neatly does two things in these stories. He divides heresy from mere lay impiety, and he aggressively aligns heresy with the devil. Impiety was an enduring problem to be tolerated and corrected, but heresy was another matter entirely. As alarming as it was becoming to church writers, they felt themselves increasingly skilled at discerning between the two.

---

25. De Frachet, *Vitae Fratrum Ordinis Praedicatorum*, 3.45.5; hereafter, *VF.*, translated in de Frachet, *Lives of the Brethren*; BHL 2223. Simon Tugwell has made extensive studies of this work. I defer to his opinion that the correct spelling of the name is "Gerald" and the correct title should be "Vitas Fratrum"; see Simon Tugwell's Introduction to: *Miracula Sancti Dominici*, 29n23.

26. *VF*, 2.7.

27. See Reames, *Legenda Aurea*.

28. Jacobus of Voragine, *The Golden Legend* (1969), 426; hereafter, *LA* (There is a newer translation of *LA* by Christopher Stace [London: Penguin, 1998], but it includes only selections of the whole text); BHL 2227.

29. *LA*, 429–30.

☛ The Controversialists Take the Field

Some of the most valuable material about these issues came from figures who had once been prominent in the sects themselves.[30] One such figure we have met, Bonacorso of Milan, had already written in the 1170s. In the thirteenth century were two writers of particular importance who had formerly been Cathars. The first is Peter of Verona, later canonized as St. Peter Martyr. We have a *Summa contra Hereticos* written sometime between 1235 and 1238 that can, with some certitude, be attributed to him.[31] This *Summa* comes at a transitional point. The papacy had already taken action against the heretics, both in France and in Italy. The papal inquisitions were in their nascent stages of development and had not yet reached the period of their institutionalization achieved with the bull "Ad Extirpanda" (issued after Peter's death in 1252). Minorites and Preachers had been dispatched through Tuscany, Lombardy, and the Veneto on antiheretical (and, frankly, anti-imperial) campaigns. This period also stands between the somewhat more amateur antiheretical tracts of the late 1100s and early 1200s and the more sustained and scholarly efforts of the midcentury, such as the massive *Summa contra Catharos* of Moneta of Cremona. Set in the form of a debate between a Catholic and a Patarene, Peter's *Summa* is a more or less systematic defense of the Catholic faith, from both scriptural and philosophical sources, following the outline of the Christian creed.

In this text, Peter is insistent on both the goodness of the material world and its sanctification brought about by the Incarnation. This is the comprehensive plan of all of the first book of the *Summa*, which proceeds from God as creator all the way to the legitimacy of the consumption of meat products. Having been a former Cathar, Peter is intimately aware of their arguments and knows that the heart of their problem is with the Incarnation.[32]

---

30. An excellent overview of antiheretical literature of the age can be found in Sackville, *Heresy and Heretics*.

31. Some have suggested a date in the early 1240s, but I think comparing the text to the course of Peter's career, as well as the contents of the document itself, makes the 1230s more likely. Kaeppeli, "Une somme contre les heretiques," 295–335. There are two manuscripts of the summa: Perugia: Biblioteca Comunale MS 1065 (N. 16); and Florence: Biblioteca Nazionale MS Conv. Sopp., 1738 A. 9. Kaeppeli edited only snippets; all quotations are from my upcoming edition of the full text. Small parts of it (mostly dealing with Waldensians) are translated in *HHMA*, 274–78. I am completing a full edition and translation, forthcoming from Oxford Medium Aevum Monographs Series.

32. One can also speculate that this realization was a core feature of Peter's entire life, with its foundation of antiheretical confraternities dedicated to Mary as a way to counter Cathar denials of Christ's humanity, not to mention the emphasis on the first article of the creed throughout his

After asserting the goodness of creation and the reality of the Trinity, Peter defends each and every one of the Old Testament patriarchs and prophets from Cathar calumnies. After that, Peter continues on vehemently to safeguard the humanity of Mary, the sanctity of John the Baptist, and the assumption of human nature by Christ. Of particular interest to our present purposes are Peter's defenses of Mary and John. His is one of the earliest testimonies of the absolutist Cathar belief that Mary was an angel (whom Peter names as "Marinum").[33] Peter appears terribly vexed at this point by what he calls the "worst diabolical blasphemy" and calls his interlocutors at this point "wicked dogs." Later, when he speaks of mitigated dualists who accept that Mary was a woman, he does not use the heated language described above; their heresy was not as serious. He sums up his contentions regarding Cathar belief neatly in the section on Christ's humanity. "You Patarenes, who deny the Incarnation of Christ, are Antichrist who has already come, and you are the seducers of souls."[34] Clearly Peter was especially worked up about this, and rightly so, for he had fixed on the key issue of all Cathar theology, their anti-incarnationalism.

Continuing on, Peter fiercely defends the humanity of John the Baptist. In laying out the beliefs of the distinct sects of Cathars, Peter contends that while there exists disagreement regarding whether or not John was good or evil, all concur that John was no man, but a spiritual being, either an angel or a demon. In his effort to promote the goodness and humanity of John, Peter lists no fewer than eighteen privileges that accrued to the Baptist, a significant amount of space in his *Summa*. These proceed through the prophecies of the Old Testament to the miraculous circumstances of his birth, to Christ's own statements, to the details of John's pious life. The eighteenth privilege is very interesting for our purposes. It is an early and very creative use of the idea of canonization. "The eighteenth privilege is his [John's] can-

---

33. "Circa quam periclitantur patareni miserabiliter ipsam negantes feminam fuisse et per consequentiam matrem esse dei minime recognoscunt, delirant namque blasphemantes, ipsam esse angelum nomine Marinum." Perugia: Biblioteca Comunale Augusta, Peter of Verona, *Summa contra Hereticos*, MS 1065, 48vb. The earliest source that describes this belief is the *De heresi catharorum*, in Dondaine, "La Hiérachie Cathare in Italie," 306–12. This text is dated from 1200–1214, and is likely from Milan. It is probable that both the anonymous author of this text and Peter of Verona himself were intimately familiar with the beliefs of the Lombard Cathars, and this belief about Mary in particular is characteristic of the absolute dualists, which finds corroboration in Peter's biography.

34. "Ergo vos patareni qui negatis incarnationem christi estis antichristos qui iam venit et estis seductores animarum." Perugia: Biblioteca Comunale Augusta, Peter of Verona, *Summa contra Hereticos*, MS 1065, 56[ra].

onization which he merited to have accomplished by the heavenly supreme pontiff our lord Jesus Christ praising him as much in life as after his death and by confirming him in the catalog of the saints."[35] This passage opens up an interesting window into the developing theory of papal canonization. In a startling reversal, Christ is referred to as the Supreme Pontiff. As "pope," Christ canonized on earth, providing a pattern and rationale for his vicars to continue the practice. Christ becomes the model for papal canonization, by reading the contemporary practice back into scripture. This illustrates the power of the sovereign pontiff in Peter's mind as well as sanctioning the figure of John the Baptist, whom Peter wishes to exalt. This is novel and unique language and indicates the character of papal canonization as it had developed by the late 1230s. Peter does not directly touch on ritual practices because he was unable to finish his *Summa*. His planned fourth book had to be omitted because he became directly involved in papal missions on the ground in the last years of his life. Neither was Peter able to talk about particular nonbiblical saints, with the exception of Waldensian hatred of Sylvester.[36] In this Peter bears witness to the last period of generalized antisaint sentiment. Ironically, it would be Peter's own saintly cult that would see the final turn of the heretics to particularity.

The most comprehensive summa of the early 1200s was that of Moneta of Cremona, written around the year 1240.[37] In it Moneta highlights the Cathar beliefs that we have come to expect, but he does so in an extended and systematic way. After detailing and refuting the dualism of the various forms of the Cathars, Moneta gives a thorough defense of the material reality of Christ's miracles, a necessary preparation for the defense of the holy men and women of the Old Testament. Moneta presents the Cathar spiritualizing interpretations of nearly every one of Christ's signs and then, using the literal and obvious sense of the text, proceeds to defend the materiality of each one.[38] He then defends the goodness of the primary characters of the Old Testament, drawing a distinction between absolute and mitigated dualists. Interestingly he claims that the absolute dualists, because of their

35. "Octavum decimum privilegium est canonizatio ipsius quam meruit habere a summo pontifico celesti domino ihesu christo quam fecit de ipso tam in vita eius quam post mortem collaudo eum et in cathologo sanctorum approbando." Peter of Verona, *Summa contra hereticos*, Perugia: Biblioteca Comunale Augusta, MS 1065, 51va.

36. Ibid., 127vb and 130va.

37. Moneta of Cremona, O.P., *Venerabilis patris Monetæ Cremonensis ordinis*; *SOP* 3.3025. Small section translated in *HHMA*, 307–28. In addition to this old edition, I have used Munich: Bayerische Staatsbibliothek CLM 14620 and Vatican: Biblioteca Apostolica MS Reginensis Lat. 428.

38. Moneta of Cremona, O.P., *Venerabilis patris Monetæ Cremonensis ordinis*, 98–104.

aggressive allegorization, consider the prophets of the Old Testament to be good, while the mitigated dualists consider them to be messengers of the devil, with the sole exception of Isaiah (who they claim was rapt up to the seventh heaven and heard Gnostic secrets).[39] Having established the goodness of the Old Testament and the materiality of miracles, Moneta then moves on to the continuing possibility of such wonders. If by this time the Cathar interlocutor had been convinced that such wonders were possible in the Old Testament and during Christ's lifetime, Moneta alleges that the next objection would be that the age of miracles was over and that the dead could not perform them.[40] Once again Moneta's Cathar gets to the heart of the matter: if miracles are impossible after Christ, no need exists for a communion of saints or of saints' cults. Uncharacteristically, Moneta does not give him a good answer. He offers two hand-waving arguments and some abuse but no real solution. He first asserts that Christ performed miracles after his expiration on the cross, so the effecting of wonders is not per se impossible after death. He contends next that a belief against postmortem miracles is nowhere to be found in scripture, and in any case the Bible only mentions the death of Stephen and James, hardly enough to build a negative case in support of the nonperformance of miracles by Christian saints. It is an odd passage that surprises the reader, for Moneta is usually not so brief, and he wraps up the section with revilement: "Therefore stop blaspheming and don't attack the Church of God."[41] Moneta then resumes with a less impassioned tone and more scholarly criticism in book three, which he begins by defending the goodness of John the Baptist (a perennial concern) and the humanity of Mary. This he does at length and with far more rigor than with the previous question.[42] In the end, this is the closest that Moneta gets to a comprehensive defense of the communion of saints. He does not delve into questions of particular saints or the papacy's power to canonize.[43] This is for two reasons. One reason is that we are in a transitional period in 1240, and Moneta is

---

39. "Quo ponunt duo principia, dicunt prophetas bonos fuisse; aliquando autem omnes dampnabant praeter Isaiam, cujus dicut esse quemdam libellum in quo habetur, quod spiritus Isaiae raptus a corpore usque ad septimum caelum ductus est, in quo vidit, et audivit quaedam arcana, quibus vehementissime innituntur." Ibid., 218.

40. "Dicunt enim quod licet Dei ecclesia potestatem faciendi materialia miracula habuerit, et fecerit ea, non tamen post mortem; nullus enim sanctus fecit aliquod signum post mortem suam." Ibid., 222.

41. "Cessate ergo a blasphemis, et nolite Dei Ecclesiam impugnare." Ibid.

42. "Videamus de ipso Johanne, contra quem plures dicunt blasphemias. Una est, quia dicunt eum a Diabolo missum." Ibid., 222. Section on John and Mary is 222–34.

43. This is in spite of the fact that Book 5 is an interesting and especially early type of what later came to be called a *Summa de Ecclesia*.

writing around the same time as Peter. The age of mendicant sainthood had just started, and the response of the heretics was being established. The other reason is that Moneta is writing a theological tract concerned with the sources of revelation rather than about a particular historical-ecclesiological situation. As time went on, the theologians would begin to refine their approaches to this problem, as the opposition became more clear.

While much shorter than Moneta's or Peter's efforts at refuting the Cathars, Rainerio Sacconi's *Summa de Catharis et Pauperibus de Lugduno* is irreducibly crucial for understanding the response of the church to the challenge of heresy in the thirteenth century.[44] A convert from heresy, Rainerio had extensive experience on both sides of the struggle. After spending seventeen years among the Cathars, he joined the Dominican order and by 1252 had become an inquisitor himself. He gives exceptionally valuable historical and demographic information, some of which has been challenged by scholars but which remains a unique witness, confirming known divisions and beliefs among Cathar groups.[45] His work is also key for understanding the complex cosmology of the remaining Cathar manual of theology, the *Liber de duobus principiis*.[46] Rainerio's *Summa* is short, to the point, and strikingly personal. The Dominican repeatedly lays bare the antipathy of the Cathars for Catholic practices. "In the seventeen years when I was in intimate converse with them, I did not see any one of them pray secretly, apart from the others. . . . Never do they implore the aid or intervention of the angels, or of the Blessed Virgin Mary, or of the saints, nor fortify themselves by the sign of the Cross."[47] Far from making an abstract theological statement, Rainerio goes right to the lived religious manifestation, the life of the Cathar believers themselves. Their theology has resulted in a practice that is diametrically opposed to Catholicism. In an age where orthopraxis was much more relevant among the laity than doctrinal purity, Rainerio lays bare the outcome of the anti-incarnational assumptions of the Cathars.[48] The physical manifestation of their denial of the communion of saints is made apparent in

---

44. Edited in Dondaine, *Un Traité néo-manichéen*, 64–78; and more recently in Raynerius Sacconi O.P., *Summa de Catharis*, 31–60, trans. in *HHMA*, 329–46.

45. See esp. Zanella, "Malessere ereticale in Valle Padana."

46. *HHMA*, 329. Also edited in Dondaine, *Un Traité néo-manichéen* and *Liber de duobus principiis*, ed. Thouzellier.

47. *HHMA*, 332. "Praeterea dico indubitanter quod in annis xvii quibus conversatus sum cum eis non vidi aliquem ex eis orare secreto seorsum. . . . Numquam etiam implorant auxilium vel patrocinium angelorum sive beatae Virginis, vel Sanctorum, neque muniunt se signo crucis." Raynerius Sacconi O.P., *Summa de Catharis*, 45; Dondaine, *Un Traité néo-manichéen*, 66.

48. See Thompson, *Cities of God*, epilogue, for lay preoccupations with orthopraxis. One can also point to works regarding later periods with the same stress, e.g., Duffy, *Stripping of the Altars*.

their rejection of the practices associated with such a belief. *Legem credendi lex statuat supplicandi*, the law of praying establishes the law of believing, would be the maxim applied by Rainerio (and by the laity themselves, without knowing it). It mattered not what the individual Cather hearers believed, for their belief was made manifest in their practice, an assumption made by the Catholics explicitly and by the heretics at least implicitly, for their rejection of these material signs was itself a material sign, a negative ritual act with profound theological and social implications.

Rainerio then proceeds to give an account of the various beliefs of the Cathars, which accords with previous accounts yet is precise in assigning beliefs to the various subgroups. He addresses the absolute dualists, particularly those Albanenses who follow the beliefs of the older Cathars. These are outright docetists, denying the assumption of human nature by Christ, the humanity of Mary, and the reality of the physical actions of Christ on earth. They also consign the characters of the Old Testament, chiefly John the Baptist, as "enemies of God and ministers of the devil," who for them is the real author of the Old Testament.[49] Concerning the mitigated dualists, or those of the church of Concorezzo, Rainerio is somewhat kinder, having given them credit for belief in only one eternal principle, for admitting the real humanity of Christ, and even for coming "recently to believe correctly about John the Baptist."[50] This last is especially interesting and represents a real turn for the Cathars; the Baptist had long been their standard bearer for the Evil Principle. I propose that this softening toward John and characters of the Old Testament is less a genuine theological development than a natural declension of Cathar beliefs. First, it represents a gradual wearing down of the edges of strict dualism, making it easier for Cathar hearers outwardly to conform in a Catholic world. Second, it represents a change of tack. By admitting the sainthood of biblical figures, the Cathars did not give up much and allowed them to conventionalize their heterodoxies more easily—especially in the case of Mary. This left the Cathars open to finding new targets that focused on the institutional church, in particular, the new saints of the papacy. In proposing biblical figures for veneration, the church had behind it the testimony of scripture, the witness of tradition, and well-established lay piety. These did not generally apply when one considered the new saints. They were not immemorial figures embedded in sacred texts and loved for

49. *HHMA*, 338. "[All the Old Testament characters] atque Johannes Baptista fuerunt inimici Dei et ministri diaboli." Raynerius Sacconi O.P., *Summa de Catharis*, 51; Dondaine, *Un Traité néo-manichéen*, 71.

50. *HHMA*, 344. "Multi ex eis [Concorezzans] modo bene credunt de B. Johanne Baptista, quem olim omnes damnabant." Raynerius Sacconi O.P., *Summa de Catharis*, 58; Dondaine, *Un Traité néo-manichéen*, 76.

generations. They were externally imposed by a novel method and inserted without significant organic development into the stable calendars of the church. In pivoting to attack the new saints, Cathars more fully aligned themselves with movements significantly more popular and mainstream than their own. In doing so, they also allied themselves with the Waldensians, whom Rainerio describes as saying "the Church of Christ subsisted in the bishops and other prelates down to the time of blessed Sylvester, and in him it fell away until they themselves restored it."[51] So the attention shifts from biblical saints and high theology to the very practical details of the Christian life, rituals and saints. For the heretics, Sylvester is a placeholder for the institutional Roman church. All precepts of that church might be willingly jettisoned in favor of the restoration of the primitive truth. This was particularly true of those new saints, proposed by the false Catholic Church, who themselves were glorified precisely for opposing heresy and who in their cultic form were sent into battle against the heretics themselves. At stake was no less than the pure form of the Christian religion, and the new saints were seen as the vanguard of either orthodoxy or false Christianity.

✒ From Peter of Verona to St. Peter Martyr: The Tide Turns

On the Saturday after Easter, April 6, 1252, Peter of Verona was returning by foot to Milan.[52] As prior of the Dominican convent in Como, Peter had been spending the holy season with his brothers, but Easter week having concluded, he had to return to his other occupation. In 1251 Pope Innocent IV had named Peter, already an exceptionally famous and charismatic preacher, as inquisitor-general for Lombardy.[53] Peter was especially suited for this task, having spent over twenty years debating and preaching against the heretics of northern Italy. The offspring of a Cathar family of absolute dualist sympathies in Verona, Peter had received an excellent education and had been converted to the Dominican life in Bologna. He dedicated his career to preaching and peacemaking, which in the thirteenth century involved the reconciliation of communal forces in order to attack heretical elements

---

51. *HHMA*, 346. "Ecclesia Christi permansit in episcopis et aliis prelatis usque ad B. Slivestrum, et in eo defecit quousque ipsi eam restaurarunt." Raynerius Sacconi O.P., *Summa de Catharis*, 60; Dondaine, *Un Traité néo-manichéen*, 78.

52. The death of Peter of Verona is treated in detail in Prudlo, *Martyred Inquisitor*, 56–65.

53. Peter was the first to hold this title; see Innocent IV, "Misericors et Miserator" [June 13, 1251], trans. ibid., 185–86; Potthast, n14333.

in the cities. For years Peter battled heresy, often quite successfully, and it was for this reason that Innocent named him to lead the inquisitorial efforts in Lombardy, in cooperation with the local towns and bishops. Peter's success bred fear and resentment, and a plot to assassinate him was in the works even before the papal bull announcing his appointment. After nine months of reconnaissance, fund-raising, and planning, the Cathars were ready.

So it was on that fateful sixth of April that an assassin hired by the Cathars ambushed Peter and his companion, one Brother Dominic, in the forest of Barlassina north of Milan. Peter was dispatched fairly quickly, and with his dying breath he uttered the first sentence of the creed, "I believe in God," an anti-Cathar, pro-incarnational affirmation springing to his lips as he expired. The reaction was stunning. Martyrs were exceptionally rare in the Middle Ages, and in an age when martyrdom was still treasured, Peter's cult gained immediate popularity, much like that of Thomas Becket.[54] Peter had been popular and exceptionally well-known in life, as the itinerant, orthodox preachers of the thirteenth century were the closest medieval analogues to modern celebrities.[55] Known and respected by all within the church, he had cultivated good relations with laypeople and with towns, with prelates and the papacy, and with those in his own order and had earned a reputation for holiness. When such a life was combined with the uncommon and venerated condition of martyrdom, the effect was electric. The Cathar conspirators were stunned by the reaction of both the laity and the church.[56] Some turned themselves in, while others ran, pursued for decades until finally caught. Heretical strongholds were reduced to dust by the city of Milan, and within a generation Catharism was a spent force in northern Italy. On the positive side, popular veneration was ecstatic and, as had been the case with Anthony of Padua, Peter's cause was introduced not by his own shocked Dominican brethren but by the laity, commune, and clergy of Milan, not the least of whom was the Franciscan archbishop. Miracles began to be reported from the very day of the martyrdom, and Peter's tomb became a popular shrine. The lay piety, popular pressure, miracles, and the testimony of a holy life all combined and coincided perfectly with papal policy. Sometimes opportune moments truly do arise in church history.

---

54. For descriptions of medieval conceptions of martyrdom, see Vauchez, *Sainthood*, 149–51; and Ryan, "Missionary Saints," 1–28.

55. For the public perceptions of medieval preachers, see Thompson, *Revival Preachers and Politics*; see also Muessig, "Sermon, Preacher and Society," 74–91; and the essays in Muessig, *Preacher, Sermon, and Audience*.

56. See Prudlo, *Martyred Inquisitor*, 74–76.

Innocent IV could not tolerate the murder of one of his highest officials, recently appointed by name and while on official papal business. Having recently emerged victorious over the German empire with the death of Frederick II, Innocent was not about to let northern Italy spin out of control again. At the request of the people and clergy of Milan, Innocent opened an *inquisitio in partibus* into Peter's life and miracles. This having been satisfactorily concluded, he proceeded on March 9, 1253, to inscribe Peter's name on the roll of the saints, thus effecting the swiftest canonization in all of papal history. Such was Innocent's resolve that he canonized Peter on the First Sunday of Lent, an intensely penitential time for holding a solemn canonization. In many ways Peter's canonization represents the coming together of the old and the new, for there were certainly an efflorescence of popular enthusiasm and an outpouring of devotion in terms of the construction of the shrine and the reporting of miracles. The local bishop, the Franciscan Leo da Perego, was involved from the outset and coordinated the appeal to Rome, ran the *in partibus* inquiry into life and miracles, and orchestrated the elevation and translation of Peter in the summer of 1253, finding the saint wholly incorrupt.[57] Peter's cause gained international attention, finding mention in most contemporary chronicles throughout Christendom. Miracle stories began to proliferate from all over Europe. The papacy capitalized on this rapidly growing cult. Innocent seized on both the testimony of miracles (absent in the murdered Peter of Castelnau's case, much to Innocent III's chagrin) and the witness to Peter of Verona's holiness of life (absent in the murder of Conrad of Germany) to glorify the new Dominican martyr.

The Dominicans themselves, thrown into confusion by the murder of Peter, seemed to have responded somewhat more slowly than the papacy and laity. As time went on, though, the Friars began to see the possibilities inherent in the martyr's cult. Peter came to be seen as "Dominic's Perfect Follower." Indeed, Peter became the symbol of the ideal Dominican life: the elite antiheretical preacher, founder of confraternities, consoler of the laity, peacemaker between communes, and servant of the papacy.[58] Sometimes this aggressive parallelization of Peter with the ideal Friar Preacher caused the founder to fade into the background or even to come to look like Peter himself. For example, the Dominic portrayed in the *Divine Comedy* seems modeled on Peter Martyr. The later incorrect attribution of the office of

---

57. Though translation had, in former times, preceded canonization, in this period the elevation of saints began commonly to occur after formal papal recognition, another development that qualitatively differentiated papal canonization.

58. Ibid., 98–100. See also Ames, *Righteous Persecution*, esp. 57–93.

papal inquisitor to St. Dominic is also a legacy of the concentration of the Friars Preachers on Peter's cult. The church had a new saint, the laity had a new and successful intercessor, the Dominicans had a model, and the papacy had successfully aligned itself with the burgeoning cult. Given the aggressive promotion of Peter as the summation of the apostolic lifestyle, of orthodoxy, and of holiness, the response of those who were in opposition would not be long in coming.

☛ Orthodox Opposition

At the outset one must remember that opposition to Peter was sporadic and local, whereas his cult was popular on a broader level. It is those very pockets of opposition that are of particular interest to this study. As in previous cults, the resistance to the saint comes from two directions, from the orthodox and from heretics. This bifurcation is thrown into relief in Peter's hagiography. Formerly the line between orthodoxy and heresy was not drawn clearly and is sometimes indiscernible, but in Peter's case, the division becomes more vivid. The orthodox among the clergy and laity are clearly distinguished in the stories. Of course, one can certainly allege that the biographers themselves are not clear on who is or is not a heretic or about what exactly constitutes heresy, but here we are examining the attitudes of medieval churchmen. They clearly discerned a difference among the various actors, and it was precisely that difference that drove them to act in order to defend the validity of Peter as a saint as well as to safeguard the cults of the other mendicants.

As with other saints, one can trace the opposition of some conservative orthodox clergy and laity. These were slow to appropriate Peter's feast. There is nothing new here. Given that bishops and religious orders were dubious of the new saints and attracted to their revered local holy men and women, it is not surprising that the papacy had to issue several pointed reminders to them to include the newly canonized among their calendars. Opposition such as this to Peter's cult was contemporary with his canonization. In the earliest biographical sources (all within fifteen years of Peter's death), many so-called aggression or chastisement miracles appeared. The most common tale involved people from all walks of life (such as nobles, professors, and wool spinners) who impugned the cult of the saint. Following their detraction, Peter visited them with immediate punishment. The hagiographers and cultic promoters wanted to make clear that Peter would in no way tolerate denigration of his cult. One notes an interesting turn in the stories about

Peter. In them an attack on a saint's cult is not simply cast into the old topos of ignorant, lazy, or venal laypeople. Rather, such opposition, in the minds of the cultic biographers, became fused with heresy. To impugn Peter's cult was to make one not just a bad Catholic but a heretic. In this way developments in hagiography began to mirror developments in theology. Whether this conception of heresy had yet trickled down to the laity is questionable. The casual blasphemers among them were perhaps still simply ignorant, lazy, or venal, without knowing that as a result of the swiftly developing doctrines of papal canonization, their sentiments were being swept down the road into heresy.

The crystallization of the distinction between impiety and outright heresy did not prevent hagiographers from continuing their attacks on the former. Long a classic topos in hagiographical literature, part of a saint's heavenly mission was to confirm the saint's holiness on earth by correcting the erring and encouraging the pusillanimous. As time went on, though, church interpretations of criticisms leveled by mordant mockers began to take on a more serious edge. In light of the practical and theoretical critiques of the cult of saints and of sainthood generally made by the heretics, simple impiety began to be reexamined. As the doctrine of papal canonization advanced, opposition by the orthodox laity, no less than from heretics, was a challenge that spurred development. Such critiques had been common throughout the history of Christianity, with the people who made such criticisms being considered at the very most weak Christians. A saint would come along and punish their impiety, and that would be the end of it. In the thirteenth century there is a shift. To attack the cult of a papally sanctioned saint was not only to challenge the validity of the new mendicant orders; it was a direct threat to papal claims. This new viewpoint was bound to cause friction, for the seriousness of papal claims about canonization took a long time to reach the laity.

Previous chapters dealt with the evidence that the claims of papal superiority in the saint-making process were making themselves felt. Resentment about this fact could exist even in the midst of popular devotion and pilgrimage. It was present in the cultic biographies of all the mendicant saints: Anthony, Dominic, and even Francis. This increased tension is especially evident in the cult of Peter of Verona. In his hagiography are several examples involving lay indifference or opposition. One of the earliest miracle stories about Peter involved wool-spinners in Utrecht. They were engaged in their trade across from the Dominican convent on Peter's feast when they saw people congregating there. They began to remonstrate with the devotees, revealing many things about contemporary criticisms of Peter's cult and the Dominican order. "Behold these Preachers have found every way to make money, for instance they hoard up cash and build wide palaces, and now they do honor to a new martyr."[59] Perhaps economic motives were again coming into play, indicating that the women are not interested in yet another saint's day. In any case they clearly are irritated at the "new," whether it be the new feast, the new order, or the new martyr.[60] The ingrained traditionalism of the laywomen here is offended. The Dominicans are upsetting the established order, and because of this they come under a popular type of lay criticism: the appropriation of too much wealth. As befits a hagiographical story, the women are suitably punished. Their looms become covered in blood and they rush to confess their indiscretion to the Dominican prior.[61] The story did not end there. The bloody cloths became a preaching aid for the friars. A German grammar master was passing through and mocked the miracle: "See how these Preachers deceive the hearts of the simple, for example, when some silly women declared to their friends that their threads were stained with blood and it happened 'miraculously,' the Friars retell it."[62] He was made mute and later brought to repentance. It is no mistake that these miracles appeared in most of the early sources of Peter's vita, for they diffuse two type of orthodox criticism at once, one popular and one learned. They gave the preachers tools to cut off cultic opposition before it went too far. While such opposition does not appear to have been widespread, it was still a worry to the church, in particular to the mendicants and to the papacy. They would have to respond to such contention, since they were no longer generally directed at saints indiscriminately but rather to individuals, mostly of the new orders, elevated by the papacy.

✎ The Challenge of Popular Sanctity

Latent and passive opposition to the new saints was evident in the endurance of older models of saintly veneration. Sainthood was one of the most perennially popular of all the forms of Christian life and devotion. The or-

---

59. "Ecce isti Praedicatores omnes lucrandi modum invenerunt; nam ut magnam possent pecuniam cumulare, et lata aedificare palatia, novum nunc invenerunt Martyrem." *VSP*, 8.60[1], 705 [Agni, ca. 1270; also in *LA*, 431].

60. For the implications of the term "new martyr" in Peter's cult, see Prudlo, *Martyred Inquisitor*, 119–21.

61. For a literary analysis of this miracle, see Jongen, "Legenda de Sancto Petro Martyre," 41–55.

62. "Videte, quomodo et qualiter isti Fratres simplicium corda decipiunt: nam cum aliquibus mulierculis de suis familiaribus condixerunt, ut filum ipsum in aliquo tingerent sanguine, et sic quod miraculose accidisset, narrarent." *VSP*, 8.60[2], 705 [Agni, ca. 1270; also in *LA*, 431–32].

thodox lay critics did not attack sainthood per se in their assaults on the new saints but rather trained their attention on the types of persons and the methods of elevation employed. While saintly veneration, if anything, became more popular than it had been (and that is a debatable claim, so deeply embedded is sainthood in the fabric of historical Christianity), the traditional forms of veneration and canonization endured. While the church, together with the mendicant orders, was advancing on a path of systematization and reservation of canonization, the customary forms of saintly veneration continued. In particular this meant that the vox populi was long considered the indispensable first step in canonization. If the *sensus fidelium* discerned holiness, then it was unlikely to be wrong, and so sainthood was a grassroots phenomenon. It caused irritation when the papacy chose to impose a new saint, just as friction ensued when the local churches had to make provision for the new orders in terms of pastoral service. Further, the papal reserve caused consternation among the bishops, who had been the supervisors of cultic activity for nearly one thousand years. Until the 1100s it was the bishops who canonized after a solemn translation of a holy person's body. Now the groundwork was being laid for depriving them of that ancient right, though such a transition took centuries. The process would conclude only with the outright abolition of episcopal canonizations as a result of Urban VIII's reforms in 1634.

Most Christians were content spontaneously to recognize holiness, which for them came in two varieties: immemorial and local. Anything outside those two categories was suspect. People were content with the saints of the Bible and of the early church, for these had the hallowing of tradition. This was one reason why the heretical attack on ancient saints such as John the Baptist eventually lost steam. While there was not much lively devotion to the figures of the Old Testament, for someone to come along and cast aspersions on the patriarchs was *male sonantes*: it left a bad taste in people's mouths. This effect was multiplied in heretical attacks on New Testament saints, including John the Baptist, but especially Mary. In attacking these figures the heretics had come up against the bulwark of popular devotion. They had to find more productive areas for critique and conversion if they wanted to promote their beliefs more widely.

Equally precious to medieval people was locally discerned and recognized sanctity. The familiarity and neighborliness of a local saint were extremely powerful, and local sainthood ensured that a holy man or woman was focused on the needs of the community.[63] Here was a person who had lived,

---

63. For a general summary of this phenomenon, see the essays in Petersohn, *Politik und Heiligenverehrung im Hochmittelalter*. For Italy, see Peyer, *Stadt und Stadtpatron*; Webb, *Patrons and Defenders*;

worked, and died in charity and holiness of life and was raised up by the people themselves, who had spontaneously recognized his or her holiness. A symbiotic relation was created. The local saint was the epitome of a *patronus/a*, not like the fickle, overbearing, and sometimes intolerable character of a local magnate, but rather one who was raised from the locality, a friend of God, and an advocate on behalf of his or her neighbors. The people received a near a dear intercessor, while the saint received glorification on earth that he or she may have been denied during life. Such local saints could be found in every corner of Christendom: advocates who stood between believers and the awful judgment of God while at the same time bowed close to bring the mercy of the Lord home to their people. As Augustine Thompson put it, "The city made the saints."[64] The relationship between city and local saint was intense.[65] Townspeople celebrated the feast with special pomp, legislated cultic donations and protections, and practiced civic devotions. It was not that this local saint displaced other saints on the Christian calendar. No, the local saint merely enriched the tapestry of the sanctoral cycle, embedding it in particularity and connecting the locality to the larger whole. Incarnational Christianity in particular has always had the tendency of the concretization of the abstract, taking eternal verities and embedding them in particular times, places, and situations. In a certain sense Christianity can be seen as a "missionary to particularity," whether it is in the mediation of God's grace to individuals through the sacraments, the catechizing of the masses, the sanctifying of places and times, or the manifestation of local holiness. Such recognition of holiness was still necessary in the thirteenth century; devotion was still needed before official veneration. Yet new questions were being asked as a direct result of developing doctrine and challenges toward the cult of the saints.

Bad Saints?

As with all other questions of church life, the doctrine of canonization and sainthood was confronted with the explosion of learning in law and theol-

---

Golinelli, *Città e culto dei santi*; Golinelli, "Antichi e nuovi culti cittadini," 159–80; and Frugoni, "Cities and the 'New' Saints."

64. Thompson, *Cities of God*, 179.

65. For local and civic saintly patrons in the Middle Ages, see for Britain and France Thacker and Sharpe, *Local Saints and Local Churches in the Middle Ages*; for Germany, Beissel, *Die Verehrung der Heiligen*, particularly the first vol., which covers up to the thirteenth century; for Scandinavia, DuBois, *Sanctity in the North*.

ogy in the twelfth and thirteenth centuries. Confronted with papal central-ization and using the methods of scholasticism, church intellectuals began to ask questions about the way in which saints were recognized in the past. These thinkers had no interest in checking lay devotion but had become wor-ried that it was possible that the faithful could be deceived about the sanctity of a particular individual particularly in a single locality, for they did not rep-resent the universality of the church. As Innocent III himself had said, it was possible for someone to simulate holiness, while at the same time de-mons themselves could perform material miracles. This is why Innocent had required both holiness of life and the testimony of miracles for the identifi-cation of a saint. The canonists then pushed the matter further. In order for there to be recognition of holiness of life and the veracity of miracles, there had to be an investigation, and witnesses had to be called. For the canon lawyers, this entailed a process: the *inquisitio*. This was apart from the canoni-cal problem of the fallibility of witnesses or the possibility that a formal in-quiry might be corrupted or fail in its task. What was happening is that the church began to overlay a methodology onto the existing mechanisms for the discernment of saints. In reality this was not a change as much as an added layer of discretion. The spontaneous devotion of the Christian faith-ful was still the prime mover for the calling of such an investigation, and in many cases these local *inquisitiones* confirmed popular devotion (and most were a result of local petition). Such a tack, while understandable from an institutional perspective and while generally leaving popular devotion intact, was bound to conflict with lay sensibilities, for what was to happen if the church authorities suspected deception or corruption or, even worse, scented heresy in the life of a popular saint?

The problem had been around for a while and could be seen in the ten-sion between the virtues of the local saint appreciated by the community and the clerical perceptions usually emphasized by the authors of the saints' vitae. The virtues valued by the Christian people were service, charity, hon-esty, and neighborliness as well as civic duty. In particular the laity valued lived piety, especially as manifested in partaking of the sacramental and li-turgical drama of the church.[66] Often local saints were converts to a more radical form of Christian observance or asceticism. Though their clerical bi-ographers wanted to categorize this as a transition from lay to clerical (or at least monastic) life, the local saints in reality continued to be part of their

---

66. This is how heretics were often unmasked by the laity. They would not participate in communal ritual. For the medieval laity, orthopraxis was the *sine qua non* of holiness. If it looked like a Catho-lic and acted like a Catholic . . .

communities. While medieval people looked to liminal moments such as conversion, it was the moment of death that became the most favored. If a person made a "good death," then he or she could be acclaimed as a saint, even if that person had lived a horrible life before that point. Michaele Delicti, executed for various crimes in 1225, made a very holy death with communion and confession, a pious passing that resulted in a small cult surrounding him.[67] The clergy had repeatedly reinforced the idea that a holy death merited forgiveness of sins and entrance into heaven. Of course, one who publicly died making a good death as a repentant criminal was admitted to heaven and was therefore a saint.[68] A further example communicates such attitudes well, even though it is in the context of a preaching exemplum. A lustful man who nonetheless was devoted to Mary found himself in bed with a beautiful woman. When he learned her name was Maria, he died from compunction on the spot. At that moment the bells of the town began to ring, and a cult immediately sprang up.[69] While such stories attest to the historical attitude of forgiveness in the Christian church, they also illustrate the spontaneity of the creation of medieval cults. One begins to get a glimmer of how churchmen might begin to be uncomfortable with some of these new "saints."

In some of their first efforts to come to grips with the local saints, rather than simply acquiesce to them as had been the practice in previous ages (under the supervision of the bishop), clerical biographers began to underscore certain virtues and reinterpret others.[70] Thompson notes that in clerical biographies asceticism, charity, and pilgrimage came to dominate, for they were categories of holiness with which the clergy could relate.[71] As time went on, the clerical writers became more and more concerned about the veracity of the holiness of local saints, as the challenges posed by heretics became more pronounced. A favorite tactic circa 1200 was the emphasis of antiheretical activity in the lives of the local saints. In his canonization bull,

---

67. Thompson, *Cities of God*, 189.

68. The ethos of Christianity was suffused with such stories of repentance and of the love of God for conversion and penance. The Gospels are replete with stories such as the prodigal son. The laity was also surrounded by examples of saints who were venerated for their public and extraordinary conversions, e.g., St. Mary Magdalene or St. Mary of Egypt. The one most probably recalled in this case was St. Dismas, the good thief on the cross who accompanied Christ to heaven.

69. Pisa, Biblioteca Cateriniana del Seminaro Arcivescovile, MS 139, "Miracula de Beata Virgine," fol. 149r, cited in Thompson, *Cities of God*, 189. Similar stories of salvation by simple Marian devotion are a staple of Marian literature.

70. For an excellent introduction to hagiography, its audiences, and its purposes, see Heffernan, *Sacred Biography*, esp. chaps. 1 and 2.

71. Thompson, *Cities of God*, 190.

Pope Innocent III had proposed Homobonus of Cremona as a lay saint spe-cifically preoccupied with antiheretical activity. This interpretation har-monized with papal presentation of saints in canonizations performed by Innocent and his successors. There should be no mystery concerning why this was. Heretics were attacking the cult of the saints; as a result, the antiheretical activity of saints had to be emphasized. It is not clear if this type of hagio-graphical presentation was a product of papal policy or something realized by the literate clergy as a whole. The phenomenon is real and directly parallels increasing heretical attacks on incarnational sanctity. To be a saint in the thir-teenth century meant that a primary characteristic of one's holiness was fight-ing heresy. While saints became venerated for a multitude of reasons, when their cult became presented in literary form, antiheretical themes came to predominate. In spite of saints' being multifaceted people, their cultic identi-ties could become victims of tunnel vision. For example, there were many reasons that Giovanni Buono of Mantua and Pietro Parenzo of Orvieto came to have cults, mostly having to do with their charity, asceticism, and peace-making.[72] As time went on, the clergy came to see them as antiheretical saints, particularly Pietro Parenzo.

The laity indeed was antiheretical after its own fashion. From laypeople's perspective, heretics rebuffed the fellowship of the community by refusing to take part in devotional and liturgical orthopraxis. Laypeople's perception of heresy differed from that of the clergy but had the same result. For the laity, it was not the niceties of doctrine that made saints. It was the miracles. If miracles began to proliferate around a tomb, the Christian people were of-ten ready instantly to proclaim a saint. Notice that it is clearly not an ex-ample of a bifurcation of society; the local clergy was generally just as ready to proclaim local saints and proclaim miracles. People immediately began to announce their cures, and a sort of paraliturgical preaching ensued, some-times circumventing clerical control. The recipient of a miracle in the Mid-dle Ages received not only healing in mind and body but, as it were, a quasi-official preaching license from heaven itself that permitted him or her to announce the virtues of the new saint wherever he or she went. Hagiog-raphy from the middle of the century attempted to establish some form of oversight, such as the youth who experienced a miracle from Peter of Ve-rona and was given permission from his confessor to retell the miracle.[73] It is difficult to believe he would not have done so in any case. This pattern is

---

72. For Giovanni Buono, see *Processus Apostolici*, 778–885. For Pietro Parenzo, see Lansing, *Power and Purity*, 23–42.

73. Prudlo, *Martyred Inquisitor*, 234.

continually repeated, as saints' reputations for healing and intercession grew like wildfire among the laity. Even St. Dominic himself was the subject of a nascent cult among non-Preachers, yet it was quickly smothered by the Bolognese friars for a variety of reasons (though one thinks they would have been happy with that sort of spontaneous cult when, twelve years later, they began to agitate for his canonization).[74]

The clergy and laity together had a serious stake in promoting miracles and the shrines that went along with them. Both were critical intersections where clerical and lay orthodoxy united to oppose dualist trends. Saints healed broken bodies, which the Cathars claimed were mere "tunics" or "shells" fashioned by dark powers. From heaven the holy ones of the church prayed for spiritual and divine power to heal material vessels. Miracles were at the heart of incarnational Christianity. No less were the shrines of the saints, where many of the miracles occurred and where most were reported to a notary who was usually (but not always) a cleric. Here was the nexus between heaven and earth, centered on the very thing most hateful to the dualists: the body of the saint whose soul now beheld the beatific vision. By controlling access to the shrine, maintaining notaries to record miracles (necessitating traveling to the shrine if one wanted to report it), and coordinating liturgical functions there, the clergy began to exercise some measure of control over the access to sanctity. The shrine also incorporated another aspect of holiness critical to lay piety: the pilgrimage. In the end, though, when a saint was spontaneously recognized, all the clergy could really do was respond, for the church was only just starting to cross the line into active promotion or condemnation of living cults.

✤ Developments in Heterodox Theology

Among the heretics themselves, one can trace a development of doctrine as well as an increased focus on sainthood in particular. As the transition to the latter half of the thirteenth century occurred, heretical attention moved away from generalized attacks on the cult of saints and more toward a concentration on opposition to recently canonized saints and saints whose cults were being extended by mendicant preaching and papal authority. This transition

---

74. *Processus canonizationis sancti Dominici*, ed. Walz. Trans. in *Saint Dominic*, ed. Lehner. Bologna Process, c. 9, 105. Many came with votive offerings and candles and wanted to venerate the tomb but "the fearful brothers forbade this so that the Order might not be troubled by the multitude and lest some might say that the friars did this or permitted it to be done because of cupidity or ostentation."

had several effects. For instance, there was a softening toward biblical saints, particularly to the old bugbear John the Baptist. This is probably a result of the increasing transition away from absolute dualism to a more mitigated (and therefore more easily integrated and hidden) dualism. The saints of the Old Testament no longer represented the avatars of Satan the Evil Principle but were increasingly viewed as tangential to the current situation. One can see the cracks in the common front in the description of the mitigated dualists of Concorezzo given in the 1250s by a Franciscan inquisitor. They manifest some disagreement about whether John was evil, but the Concorezzenses all agreed concerning the reality of the Incarnation.[75] Abstract dualism was becoming more and more conventionalized while at the same time directing itself against new targets. Rainerio Sacconi, writing circa 1250, agrees with this assessment and makes special mention of this doctrinal development.[76] He mentions that while their understanding of the Incarnation was theologically unsophisticated, the mitigated dualists did have the common belief that Christ received a real body. That said, there was nothing special about the body that Christ assumed and that the souls of Mary and the saints were in a sort of celestial waiting-room until the Second Coming.[77]

All of this evinces a growing disconnect between Cathar belief and practice. As Cathar belief developed, it became quite sophisticated in its soteriology, while at the same time the practices of the Cathar hearers were becoming more conventionalized. The equality of future rewards and punishments challenged the theology of supererogation of the Roman church. This led to the downplaying of the evil of biblical saints while at the same time permitting sympathizers to go about the daily religious life of their towns. The Lombard inquisitor Anselm of Alexandria, who was Rainerio Sacconi's successor, confirms this. Writing around 1270, he stated, "[They] believe that all future punishments are equal, so too are the rewards of the good. . . . Also, no Cathar fasts on the vigils of any saint, or of the apostles, or of the Blessed Virgin."[78] Such thoughts allowed Cathar theology and Cathar practice to converge. It was counterproductive to spend much energy attacking the established cult of the saints and Mary, for that was assaulting the faith of the laity at the place where it was strongest.[79] What was of more

---

75. *HHMA*, 354, 358.

76. Rainerio Sacconi, ibid., 344.

77. Ibid., 344.

78. Anselm of Alexandria, ibid., 365.

79. Smart mendicants, like Peter of Verona, recognized this and organized countless lay confraternities dedicated to the saints and Mary, making them vanguards for the defense of orthodoxy among the laity.

immediate moment than the saints of dim past ages were those recently canonized, whose cults were sent into battle specifically targeting the heretics.
They turned their attention to the new saints such as Dominic, Peter, and
the others. In doing so, heretics not only deflected attention away from their
unorthodox theology but in a certain sense made common cause with the
orthodox laity, already suspect of saints recently created.

Conversely, the Waldensians remained fairly fixed in their attacks on the
cult of the saints. Their dislike did not proceed from deep-seated theological
disagreements; it had always been rooted in a critique of the practices of the
Catholic Church with its panoply of apparently nonbiblical cultic ceremony.
They continued in their attacks, particularly on Sylvester and Laurence, the
standard-bearers both for temporal entanglements and for the Roman church.
According to Rainerio, the Waldensians claimed that the church of Christ
subsisted in the Roman church until Sylvester, and then it went underground
until restored by the Waldensians.[80] Stephen of Bourbon, a colorful inquisitor
from France, writes about the practical outcomes of this belief. It concurs
with what had characterized the Waldensians from the period of their falling
out with the church: a rejection of immediate possession of the beatific vision, derision toward those who participate in the cult of saints through
piety and ritual, and that the only sanctity is that of a good man or woman.[81] Berthold of Regensburg, a famous preacher of the mid-1200s, echoes
this in his sermons describing the "new" heretics, who say "that the saints
in heaven are not to be invoked, neither the Blessed Virgin nor any other
saint, and so neither fasting, nor feasts, nor any other thing should be done
to honor men."[82] Anselm is more specific around the year 1270. While he
concurs that Waldensians reject the feasts and fasts of the Roman church, he
makes specific reference to the corruption of the church under Sylvester.
He claims that all Waldensians agree—for there had been a schism between
the trans- and cis- alpine branches of the sect—that Sylvester and Laurence
were specifically not saints.[83] Their belief that the Roman church had lost
the faith, coupled with their contention that the cult of the saints was not to

---

80. Ibid., 346. Very similar to the Restoration Movement among the Churches of Christ in America
after the Second Great Awakening.

81. Stephen of Bourbon, ibid., 349.

82. "Tertia hereticorum modernorum via est quod sancti in celis non sint invocandi, nec beata virgo
neque aliquis aliorum sanctorum, et ideo nec ieiuniis, nec festis nec aliquibus hominis fuit hon-
orandi. Ecce quanta stulticia, si enim hic martyris et multas aliis impetravit ut patet indiversis multo
melius et efficacius nunc possunt impetire in celo. vultus dei purissimi assistentes." Berthold of
Regensburg, "Sermons on Eight New Heresies," Munich: Bayerische Staatsbibliothek CLM 2951a.

83. HHMA, 372.

be found in primitive Christianity, set the stage for the aggressive Walden-sian rejection of the new saints. Forces were being lined up in opposition that would in turn drive the Roman church to a clearer articulation of its own beliefs.

As time went on, heretical opposition to Peter and his cult grew, while at the same time his fourteenth-century biographers blurred the line between scoffers and heretics. Now any and all opposition to Peter's cult came to be lumped in as heresy, a significant transition over the course of fifty years, for the early biographers heretics mocked Peter simply because they were he-retical in other areas. For Peter's later chroniclers, people who mocked Peter *were heretics for that very reason.* Heretics made efforts to thwart the growth of Peter's cult, going so far as to chop down the woods of Barlassina, the site of his martyrdom. At the first cut of the axe, blood flowed copiously from the tree, preventing the achievement of their ends.[84] Others who uttered blasphe-mies about Peter were later found violently killed, having called down a curse from heaven by their impiety.[85] Something had transpired that completely altered the perception of opposition. This was precisely the articulation of the definitive nature of papal canonization. To attack the cult of the saints was an error, born of misunderstandings about the revelation of Christ, which had been evident since the beginnings of medieval heresy. To attack and disparage a papally canonized saint was something of a different order. Not only was one impugning the Petrine office and assaulting the papally sanc-tioned mendicant orders, but one was undermining the very fabric of faith. Something significant had come to pass.

---

84. Prudlo, *Martyred Inquisitor,* 233 [Miraculary of Berengar, ca. 1316].

85. Ibid., 234–35 [Miraculary of Berengar, ca. 1316].

CHAPTER 5

"That God Might Not Permit Us to Err"

The Articulation of Infallibility in Canonization

By the 1250s several long-simmering issues and resentments came to a head in lived religion and in the intellectual circles of Christianity. These had been developing in parallel, sometimes unrelated ways for years. The papacy had successfully (indeed, spectacularly) co-opted the tendencies toward apostolic poverty and preaching and mainstreamed them into the mendicant orders. Yet rival claimants to apostolic religion still abounded, in particular the Cathars and the Waldensians. These groups had been weakened by this time but not yet eliminated, as attested by the dramatic murder of Peter of Verona. In creating the mendicant orders the popes had brilliantly created a shield of holiness, as it were. The friars had become a buffer between the papacy and heretical groups. In reality it was the mendicants and the heretics who faced off, nor were the new orders arrayed against the heretics alone. Resentment against mendicant privileges was also building within the church among the laity, the secular clergy, and the prelates, not to mention the intellectual class. In the last case, the bitterness broke into open warfare in the middle of the 1250s at the University of Paris and would arise again in the early 1270s.[1] The secular masters, irritated at the erosion of their privileges and at the lack of professional solidarity from the

---

1. For the backgrounds to these episodes, see Douie, *Conflict between the Seculars and Mendicants*; for the mendicant response, see Traver, "Forging of an Intellectual Defense," 157–96.

friars during university labor disputes, broke into open revolt against the mendicants, led by William of Saint-Amour.[2] On the part of the prelates there
was irritation at the exemptions that the papacy granted to the mendicants
and annoyance at their ability freely to preach and hear confessions without
episcopal authorization. Connected to this was the new orders' assumption
of the promotion and supervision of the cult of the saints, formerly under
the purview of the bishops. As papal agents, the mendicants took their new
saints with them throughout Christendom, creating competition where
earlier there had been none. For its part, the laity was mixed in its assessments. On the one hand, many friars were wildly popular preachers and confessors, and the laity did tend to flock to their convents on feast days, but on
the other, there was a lingering undercurrent of resentment, as some of the
miracle stories related in previous chapters testify. The continual imposition
of new saints from the top contributed to this antagonism and grumbling.
All these matters boiled over in the 1250s. While it is not the purpose of
this book to trace all of those movements in detail, I want to discuss how
each of them played a role in driving the development of contemporary
thoughts about papal canonization and in particular to challenge Brian
Tierney's interpretation of the evolution of papal infallibility.

✒ "Innovators" on the Defensive

In the 1250s resentment toward the mendicant masters broke into outright
war at the University of Paris, but as so often happened in church history,
this virulent assault produced rich theological development. Led by William
of Saint-Amour, the mendicants came under attack for various innovations
in church discipline, not the least of which was their novel approach to religious life. Thinly veiled behind this onslaught, one could discern inchoate
accusations of heresy, for some mendicants had become involved in the matter of the *Eternal Gospel*, a Joachite work that seemed to imply the imminent coming of the end times and the transition into a purified church of
the Holy Spirit (of course to be dominated by the mendicants).[3] By no
means were all mendicants implicated in such esoteric speculations, but they

---

2. For William, see Dufeil, *Guillaume de Saint-Amour*. For his main antimendicant work, see *William of Saint-Amour*, ed. Geltner; for his shorter works, see Traver, *Opuscula of William of Saint-
Amour*.

3. One can trace the spread of the thought of Joachim of Fiore and the Joachite work the *Eternal
Gospel* in Reeves, *Influence of Prophecy*; see also Burr, *Olivi's Peaceable Kingdom*, 14–21; and Whalen,
Dominion of God, esp. chap. 4.

did have to respond as a corporate body to such attacks. What William and his allies attacked specifically were their "novelties," and in particular their shifting the language of holiness away from the cloister and cathedral and toward apostolic poverty and preaching.[4] For William in particular, the mendicants were barely distinguishable from the heretics of apostolic poverty themselves, and their embrace of the *Eternal Gospel* simply proved it.

Confronting this attack on the academic front, the mendicants—active at the universities for over a generation—went on the offensive. The two best known exponents of mendicant privileges at the University of Paris were Thomas Aquinas and Bonaventure. They both came of age in a period where there was a grave university reaction against the friars, and in many ways both of them cut their teeth, so to speak, on this controversy. Each wrote tracts defending the Franciscan and Dominican presence at the university against their detractors. In so doing they addressed a multitude of issues, many of which were actually tangential to the central axis of the debate but nonetheless laid the groundwork for fruitful theological development. By firmly planting themselves in the midst of scripture and church tradition and emphasizing the authority of the papacy that had created them, the two friar-professors emerged victorious and in so doing created a new ecclesiological language.

Bonaventure had been one of the rising stars of the Franciscan order in the 1240s, studying under its first famous masters.[5] In 1253 he was appointed to the Franciscan chair at the University of Paris, almost at the precise moment that the controversy with the seculars broke out into the open. One of Bonaventure's main thrusts in the defense of the orders comes in the context of saints and canonization. Bonaventure situates the question in terms of his defense of mendicancy and apostolic poverty, while throughout offering a spirited affirmation of papal privileges. This was because the popes had approved the Franciscan order, established its rule, granted it exemptions, and confirmed all of the foregoing by the canonization of its saints. For Bonaventure, the canonization was the most solemn form of papal (and ecclesial) approbation of the mendicant way of life. In *On the Poverty of Christ*, written directly against William, Bonaventure railed against anyone who impugned the mendicant orders and their saints, since they were the objects of papal commendation and constant curial attention throughout the previous

---

4. Though this does not mean that the mendicants wholly cast aside older, monastic visions of holiness. See Prudlo, "Living Rule."

5. Bonaventure's complete works are found in two collections: Bonaventure da Bagnoregio, *Opera Omnia*; and Bonaventure da Bagnoregio, *Doctoris seraphici*. For biographies, see Corvino, *Bonaventura da Bagnoregio*; Robson, "Saint Bonaventure"; for an overview of his thought, see Cullen, *Bonaventure*.

forty years. For Bonaventure, if the popes erred in this, then "the whole of the universal Church has erred and has been deceived, and of those who are found in such error and have approved it, all are damned, which is most horrible and most incredible, that God might permit the whole of His holy people to err universally."[6] Further, if one dared to judge the Holy See, "which is judged by God alone," then the result would be "to thrust all holy men into the inferno."[7] For the Franciscan theologian, the heart of the matter was the judgments of the popes, which he concluded were above reproach (after all, they confirmed the Franciscans and Dominicans and canonized Francis and Dominic). Such decisions were not merely disciplinary; for Bonaventure they touched the fabric of the faith. The church cannot have been deceived in the recognition of the mendicants or in the discernment of sanctity. Bonaventure equates the authority of the pope to make such decisions with the integrity of the faith of the whole of the church of God. Pull those strings, and the fabric of the faith would unravel. Since the church is protected by Spirit who leads her into all truth, such a defection is, for Bonaventure, utterly impossible.

Further on, Bonaventure asserts that he can demonstrate the infallibility of papal canonizations. The miracles of the saints that "today amaze the Church" are the striking and irrefutable proofs of divine favor, enabling the pope clearly to confirm his proclamation of the sanctity of a certain individual.[8] For Bonaventure, true miracles are the definitive proofs of the divine sanction on any holy man or woman. What he lacks here is any sense of reserve present in the Decretalists such as Hostiensis and Innocent IV. Bonaventure makes no mention of and has no concern about the trustworthiness of the witnesses who report the wonders. If a true miracle has occurred, the person through whom it has been effected has given categorical proof of his or her holiness. What is striking from this passage is that Bonaventure assumes it as normative that the definitive sentence of the pope in

---

6. "Quod universalis Ecclesia tota erravit et decepta fuit, et qui huiusmodi statum erroneum invenerunt et approbaverunt, omnes sunt damnati, quod est horbilissimum et incredibilissimum, quod Deus permitteret errare universaliter populum sanctum suum." Bonaventure, *Opuscula de Paupertate Christi*, in *Opera Omnia*, Vol. 5, cited from Schenk, *Die Unfehlbarkeit*, 13. Tierney briefly gives half of this quotation without referencing its relation to the apostolic see: Tierney, *Origins of Papal Infallibility*, 87n3.

7. "Quod si hoc non est sapientia, sed potius temeritas, sedem apostolicam velle iudicare, quae a solo Deo iudacatur, et eius iudicium et sententiam reprobare, et tot viros sanctos in infernum retrudere." Schenk, *Die Unfehlbarkeit*, 13.

8. "Rursus si miracula, quae fecerunt non sunt testimonia efficacia ad sanctitatem eorum astruendam, stultizat hodie Ecclesia, quae propter testimonia miraculorum sanctos canonizat, et catalogo sanctorum adscribit." Bonaventure, "De paupertate Christi contra magistrum Guilelmum," *Opera Omnia*, 14:395. For the context of this quotation, see Schenk, *Die Unfehlbarkeit*, 14.

the creation of saints is absolute. While Bonaventure goes on at length to defend the utility and holiness of the mendicant orders, he does not seem to feel that he has to do so in regard to canonization. In his mind, an appeal to the papal canonization of saints bolsters his contentions about papal supremacy in the church and about the legitimacy of the mendicants. Bonaventure presumes that canonization is so thoroughly grounded and recognized as an aspect of the faith that it gives him a foundation to build his argument for the continuity of the mendicants in church history.

Though he overstated his case (in the nature of a logical *reductio ad absurdum*) and is surely acting in the interests of his order, he is still making a theoretical claim: if it is absurd to say a pope can err once, then it is absurd to say the pope can err at all times. For Bonaventure the issue is clear, and he was the first church thinker to make an implicit argument in favor of infallibility in canonization. Yet two problems plague Bonaventure's analysis. First, the validity of his *reductio* is questionable because of his lack of precision about the different types of papal decisions, whether they be doctrinal or disciplinary. Second, his reliance on miracles as reliable proof discounts the possibility of human fallibility in *describing* those miracles to responsible authorities. Nevertheless, Bonaventure represents a significant step in the development of this doctrine.[9]

Bonaventure is far from the field of Decretalist law here, but neither is he simply talking about canonical praxis. Rather, the Franciscan thinker is making a bold theological claim, a claim about the faith of the church. Here he has the bare rudiments of what will become the theological argument for the infallibility of canonization. Because Bonaventure only briefly refers to the decision of the popes to elevate the mendicant saints, some have doubted that he was writing directly about canonization here, but since the seventeenth century the consensus is that he was.[10] Brian Tierney argues

9. I must emphasize that I am not making a claim as broad as Tierney's about infallibility in general, merely about the ascription of infallibility to the popes in canonizing saints. Tierney, *Origins of Papal Infallibility*, passim.

10. Shenk asserts that since the time of the Jesuits Turrianus and Tanner in the 1700s there has been unanimity that Bonaventure was here referencing canonization. Ibid., 14. Schenk himself concurs. He, too, sees the passage clearly as directed toward the glorification of the saints. The miracles passage makes it crystal clear that Bonaventure asserts papal infallibility in canonization. Ratzinger and Congar concur that Bonaventure lies at the root of the doctrine of personal papal infallibility; *pace* Tierney, *Origins of Papal Infallibility*, 82–88. See Ratzinger, "Der Einfluss des Bettelordensstreites," 720–21, who says that Bonaventure laid all the groundwork for papal infallibility during the Mendicant crisis; and Congar, *L'église de Saint Augustin*, 223. In a study of St. Bonaventure, Heinrich Berresheim confirms the Bonaventurian root of the infallibility doctrine, particularly citing the infallibility of the canonization of Francis; see id., *Christus als Haupt der Kirche nach dem heiligen Bonaventura*, 221–23.

that Bonaventure and the Franciscans were the first to give a substantive impetus to the doctrine of papal infallibility. However, Tierney neglects to discuss infallibility in canonization at all in his book. Though very thorough on Decretist commentary, he completely neglects the Decretalist discussions detailed in the present work. While he cites Bonaventure as one of the pioneers of this doctrine, he gives very short shrift to *On the Poverty of Christ* and instead focuses on Bonaventure's other polemical writings. Because of this omission, Tierney's analysis of the development of infallibility becomes overly fixated on the poverty controversies and thus ignores the long maturation of the infallibility question precisely where it had its origins: in the debate about papal canonization.

Soon after confronting the seculars, Bonaventure left Paris on other missions, but his Dominican associate, Thomas Aquinas, continued to teach there. Remaining after the controversy, Thomas was free to frame his investigations in a more systematic manner than if he wrote them at the time of the debate.[11] In his quodlibetal questions, Thomas addressed precisely the problem outlined in this book. For the first time in the history of theology, Thomas directly framed the question of the infallibility of canonization. Quodlibet IX, question 8, asks "whether all saints who are canonized by the church, are in glory, or if any of them might be in hell."[12] In this question Thomas patiently explores what Bonaventure had only alluded to. Modern critical consensus dates this quodlibet to Thomas's first mastership in Paris, between 1256 and 1259.[13] This was precisely when opposition to mendicant saints was building; many signs had appeared of outright denial. Quodlibets answered the occasional and contextual questions that came up in the course of history, and few issues were so topical at that precise time as the status of canonized saints.

Thomas, in good scholastic form, gives two strong arguments against infallibility in canonization. First, since one cannot be sure of one's own salvation, how can the pope be sure of another's? In his response to this argument, Thomas takes it as a given that it is the pope's exclusive right to canonize saints (of course the standard canonical position since 1234 publication of the *Liber*

---

11. Thomas did write several polemical tracts at the time of the controversy itself. For these, see Torrell, *Saint Thomas Aquinas*, 1:75–95.

12. The quodlibetal questions are edited in the Leonine edition: Thomas Aquinas, *Sancti Thomae de Aquino*, vol. 25. For Quodlibet IX in particular, see Glorieux, "Le plus beau Quodlibet de Saint Thomas est-il de lui?," 235–68. Doubts about Thomas's authorship of this question have disappeared. I include my own complete translation of IX.8 in the appendix. I do not believe it has been translated before.

13. For the dating of the quodlibets, see Torrell, *Saint Thomas Aquinas*, 210–11. Most Thomistic scholars agree on a late 1250s dating. The editor of the Leonine Commission edition, Fr. R.-A. Gauthier, is the most recent authority, and he dates IX to Christmastide 1257.

Extra, though de facto the position had been working itself out since the late 1100s). He replies that the pope is able to rely on witnesses in assessing the condition of the blessed, but this leads him directly to the next objection. In the second argument against infallibility, Thomas cites the concern of the canonists: "whoever relies upon a fallible medium in judging, is able to err." Here he gets to the heart of the matter: canonization does not appear to be directly derivable from divine revelation. Bonaventure completely omitted this objection, but Thomas does not make the same mistake. He is very aware that it is the decisive problem in ascribing infallibility to the act of canonizing. In answering this, Thomas takes an innovative position by outlining a third way of judging beyond the two cited by the Decretalists. For them, either a thing was judged on the basis of human testimony and so was fallible, or a thing was judged by faith and so was infallible. For the Decretalists, canonization was obviously of the first type: it relied on human witnesses for testimony on both life and miracles. Though it was temerious to say the pope could err, nonetheless it was altogether possible. Thomas denies this interpretation and claims that canonization is a particular type of judgment that lies between fallible human testimony and infallible faith, and this is the really creative part of his solution. Thomas does not deny the fallibility of human witnesses (as it seemed that Bonaventure was close to doing, at least regarding miracles). Rather, he turns his attention to the pope who canonizes. For Thomas, the pope is unable to err in canonization for three reasons: (1) he makes a thorough investigation into holiness of life, (2) this is confirmed by the testimony of miracles, and (3) the Holy Spirit leads him (for Thomas, the clincher). When a pope elevates a saint, he proclaims that the saint is in heaven. The pope asks the faithful to give honor to the saint, which means that the faithful are making a quasi-profession of faith in the glory of the saint.[14] Since, as Thomas says, no damnable error can exist in the church and since it would be a damnable error for the faithful to honor a saint in hell, therefore no canonized saint can be in hell. For Thomas the church, then, is not "liable to error" in this case. Thomas would say that the canonization of a saint involves a declaration that relates materially to a dogma of the church. Thomas articulated, for the first time, the infallibility of the papacy in the glorification of saints. For him, though, the definition of a dogma is a very strict business. Since nothing without at least its seed in the scriptures can be an article of faith, Thomas would not call infallibility in canonization in itself a dogma. He makes a rather fine

---

14. Theologians in later centuries would specify such decisions as "secondary objects of infallibility," which were necessary to safeguard the primary objects of infallibility directly derivable from revelation.

distinction. Each canonization was infallible considered in itself, because no damnable error can exist in the church, but since it cannot be absolutely derived from the scriptures, the doctrine of the infallibility of the pope in canonization is a matter of pious belief only. Later thinkers would follow Thomas's reasoning but would not be as reticent in their thoughts on the binding authority of the doctrine.

Tierney, in places, uses selective quotations and strategic omissions to deny that Bonaventure and Aquinas had a doctrine of papal infallibility, in order to give the primacy to Peter Olivi in the 1270s. First, he claims Bonaventure's and Thomas's positions are identical (they are not) and that they are merely parroting the Decretists (they are absolutely not). In citing what he calls the *loci classici* of the infallibility question, Tierney *entirely omits* a discussion of both Bonaventure's *De paupertate* and Thomas's Quodlibet IX, question 8 (as regards canonization). When read in conjunction with the whole of their work, Bonaventure and Thomas differ markedly from the canonists and make a very explicit argument that the infallibility of the Roman church is lodged in the persons of the individual Roman pontiffs. In order to advance Olivi as the foundation of the doctrine, Tierney asserts "virtually all the scholars who have written on Olivi's attitude towards the papacy have been misled by the widespread but quite unfounded assumption that papal infallibility was a generally received doctrine in the church in the second half of the thirteenth century."[15] The reason that "virtually all the scholars" claimed this was for the simple reason that it was true.[16] Tierney is flatly incorrect here. The early mendicant theologians had already made the connection, and the place where that connection was first established was in the papal canonization of saints. The language of infallibility of such canonizations had been in the air for decades, with both Decretalists and theologians weighing in. What Tierney was doing was merely repeating the arguments of some of the anti-infallibilists of Vatican I. He did so by ignoring canonization utterly throughout his book, by overemphasizing the Decretists to the detriment of the Decretalists, and by reawakening debates that had long since ended.[17] Indeed, Thomas is downplayed throughout Tierney's text.

---

15. Tierney, *Origins of Papal Infallibility*, 95.

16. Tierney himself lists scholars like Ehrle, Maccarone, Leff, and Ratzinger as accepting that papal infallibility was well under discussion before Olivi, not to mention the whole of the Thomistic commentating tradition. Given such authorities and the foregoing information presented, one should hardly consider this "unfounded." Ibid., 94, 245.

17. Other authors have gone past Tierney's argument in this case. E.g., Wetzstein recognizes this as the origin of the discussion and is good on his focus on the quodlibet but does not pay much attention to Bonaventure as a source; see id., *Heilige vor Gericht*, 250–70.

Tierney vigorously asserts that nothing of importance exists in Thomas's writings about infallibility and that he lacked any of his customary clarity whenever he mentioned the pope. Thomas is often confined to footnotes in Tierney's text. Tierney's interpretation of IX.8 is especially tendentious.[18] The quodlibet makes no mention of a "preference" for the pope's teaching over that of "private doctors." Thomas clearly states,

1a. There is no damnable error in the church.
1b. The universal judgment of the church is not able to err.
2. It belongs to the pope to make determinations on faith.
3. Divine Providence and the Holy Spirit will protect the church in such determinations; therefore, plainly.
4. Divine Providence and the Holy Spirit will protect the pope, to whom it belongs to make such determinations.

It is not clear how Thomas's "usual clarity of expression deserted him."[19] How could Thomas be clearer? With good reason this became the *locus classicus* for papal infallibility.

➴ The Papacy Opens Its Defense

At the same time that mendicant theorists were defending the infallibility of the papacy in canonization, the popes were busy enforcing that authority on the practical level. It is worth noting that the formula for canonization was increasingly becoming formalized, elevated, and standardized during this period. With the canonization of Francis in 1228, Gregory IX wrote, somewhat informally, "Having the consultation and assent of our brethren, we decree that he be enrolled in the catalog of the saints to be venerated."[20] A second bull was sent several months later and circulated throughout Christendom in 1229. This bull was more formal in its declaration.[21] Perhaps Gregory had encountered opposition to his first declaration. In canon-

---

18. Tierney, *Origins of Papal Infallibility*, 95n3.

19. Ibid., 246n4.

20. "Habito fratrum nostrorum consilio et assensu, ipsum adscribi decrevimus Sanctorum catalogo venerandum." Gregory IX, "Mira Circa Nos" [July 19, 1228], Fontanini, 62; Potthast, n8242.

21. "De fratrum nostrorum consilio et Praelatorum omnium, qui tunc temporis apud Sedem Apostolicam consistebant, Sanctorum catalogo duximus adscribendam." Gregory IX, "Sicut phialae aureae" [September 12, 1228], Fontanini, 63; Potthast, n8236.

izing Anthony of Padua, Gregory used much more formal language. He spoke of the canonization as "holy undertaking, made not suddenly, but with great gravity and maturity."[22] With a long preface, Gregory built up to the canonization proper. While the same language of elevation was used as was present in Francis's second bull, the pope added a long paragraph that would become common in later bulls. It enjoined an indulgence for pilgrims to honor Anthony, which Gregory granted "by the mercy of almighty God and of the blessed Apostles Peter and Paul." Such indulgences would become a prime tool for the papacy in promoting its cults.[23] Gregory's canonizations of Sts. Virgil, Dominic, and Elizabeth of Hungary followed very similar models in terms of the sections on formal canonization. Innocent IV also hewed to that standard formula, but in his canonizations he became more verbose, making sure to include affirmations that these canonizations were the result of systematic inquisitions and including short biographies with the requisite virtues and miracles briefly enumerated. It is with Peter of Verona, though, that Innocent modified the formula and established the pattern that continues to exist today, still the standard phrasing for the papal canonization of saints. It was Innocent who elided the language about indulgences into the formula. "After expert investigation, studious examination, and also many solemn consultations, we know more concerning him whose cause was introduced; then by the counsel and assent of our Brothers and all Prelates now living with the Apostolic See, having confidence in the power of Almighty God, and likewise by the authority of His Apostles Peter and Paul, and also Ours, we order him to be inserted in the Roll of the Holy Martyrs."[24] Innocent IV clearly intended with this canonization to invoke the maximum level of papal authority, invoking God, the

---

22. Gregory IX, "Cum dicat Dominus" [June 12, 1232], Fontanini, 64–66; Potthast, n8938. Of course this was also to offset claims of an overhasty process, concluded in only eleven months.

23. It is precisely the language used for the indulgence—appended at the end of such bulls—that will begin to elide into the formal declaration of canonization through the 1200s.

24. "Et quia post inquisitionem solerem, studiosam examinationem, et discussionem solemnam, plura et majora de ipso comperimus, quam insinuta fuissent, eum de communi Fratrum nostrorum et Praelatorum omnium, tunc apud Sedem Apostolicam existentium consilio et assensu, confisi de omnipotentis Dei virtute, auctoritate quoque beatorum Petri et Pauli Apostolorum ejus, ac nostra, Sanctorum Martyrum catalogo duximus ascribendum." Innocent IV "Magnis et crebris" [March 25, 1253], Fontanini, 85–86; Potthast, n14926. One need only compare this to the modern canonization formulae to see their similarity. See Frutaz's excellent linguistic comparisons in id., "Auctoritate beatorum apostolorum Petri et Pauli," 435–501. For the period after Innocent, see Otfried Krafft, "Kanonisationen von Urban IV bis zu Bonifaz VIII," in Krafft, *Papsturkunde und Heiligsprechung*, 667–74.

apostles, and his own personal authority.[25] Innocent wanted no mistake here; Peter is a saint absolutely and simply. As if to underscore this, for his next canonization, that of St. Stanislaus of Kraków that same year, Innocent moved the ceremony from the forecourt of the church to the interior nave, further tying the canonization to the liturgy and elevating its formality.[26] Alexander IV used nearly identical language when he canonized Clare of Assisi in 1255, and thereby a precedent was set.[27] By the time of the compilation of Ordo Romanus XIV (the ceremonial for papal liturgy) by the beginning of the 1300s, the ritual was set, and the formula was fixed.[28] As the popes raised the stakes in terms of their actions and declarations, they and the mendicants were forced to defend their actions accordingly.

Between 1254 and 1266 many records come down to us of the popes enjoining cultic observance of the mendicants. On February 8, 1255, Alexander IV had to remonstrate with the people of Barcelona to get the city to celebrate the feast of St. Anthony of Padua.[29] During that time the popes issued no fewer than nine bulls commanding that various groups observe Peter of Verona's feast with all due solemnity throughout the Christian world—an early and exceptional demonstration of papal will to enforce devotion to saints it itself had created. The first bull, "Magna magnalia," issued in 1254 by an irritated Innocent IV, commanded that bishops insert Peter's name in all of their calendars. The pope commanded the whole church, lest forget-

---

25. It is this increasing formality and seriousness of papal declarations that engenders further development of the idea of infallibility in canonization. Indeed, it is the gravity of papal language that drives that development. In time not only will such language become standard for canonization; it will also serve as the template for the most formal of papal pronouncements, being incorporated into the language of infallible definition in the nineteenth and twentieth centuries. One can see this in the pronouncements of Boniface VIII ("Unam Sanctam," 1302), John XXII ("Cum inter nonnullos," 1323), and Benedict XII ("Benedictus Deus," 1336).

26. See notes on Stanislaus's canonization, Fontanini, 91. For the development of the Canonization liturgy, see Klauser, "Die Liturgie der Heiligsprechung," 230–33. By 1131 the Te Deum was included in the ceremony, and as early as 1174 Alexander III sang Solemn Mass after the canonization of St. Bernard. Interestingly some bishops tried to mimic this increasing solemnity in their local canonizations, for instance, the episcopal elevation of St. Boniface of Lausanne by the archbishop of Malines in 1603. See Beaudoin, "History of Canonizations," 28.

27. Alexander IV, "Clara claris praeclara" [September 26, 1255], Fontanini, 95–96; Potthast, n16025.

28. See "Ordo Romanus XIV," PL 78, cols. 1249–50. Compare to Peter's canonization "Ad honorem Dei omnipotentis Patris et Filii et Spiritus Sancti, et exaltationem fidei et christianae religionis augmentum, auctoritate ipsius omnipotentis Patris et Filii et Spiritus Sancti, beatorum Petri et Pauli et nostra, de fratrum nostrorum consilio decernimus et definimus bonae memoriae N . . . sanctorum catalogo ascribendum." By the mid-1250s the canonization was increasingly tied to liturgy, with the most solemn liturgical paraments and insertion of the new saint's name in the prayers.

29. Gilliat-Smith, *Saint Anthony of Padua*, 17.

fulness intervene, to "mark with care the name of the same saint [Peter], with the designation of the Order of Preachers."[30] The failure of his canonization to find universal approbation clearly exasperated him. Perhaps it was the realization that the papal reserve of canonizations was tenuous at best, but in reality the cause was deeper. In Peter's case the pope did not want merely to canonize but rather to enforce devotion to Peter in the Christian world. These bulls clearly demonstrate that the proper veneration of papal saints was quickly becoming bound up with the assertion of papal authority itself.[31] The church began to equate failure to venerate as an actionable offense; popes were not content to be the sole proposers of new cults but sought to impose uniformity on the whole church in their celebration. Here was something new. The papacy had proposed such saints to the broader church, for political reasons certainly but primarily as models of holiness and devotion that the popes wanted to advance before the whole of Christendom. That people dared to ignore, or worse impugn, papal saints was now rapidly becoming a singular problem. It is no mistake that the secular-mendicant controversy occurred at precisely this time. The papacy was "innovating," according to William of Saint-Amour, and he attacked it through the medium of the mendicants. An assault on the papacy was evident behind William's contentions. If the papacy could not defend these actions, it would be difficult to enforce the claims it had been making in principle since the Gregorian reform.

The status of the mendicant orders was inextricably bound up with the assertion of papal authority in this period, and the friars were also quickly becoming identified with the cause of Roman centralization and of orthodoxy itself. This excess of papal favor caused friction within the church. The controversy over Francis's stigmata in the late 1230s was an emerging example of this tension.[32] "Magna magnalia" commanded that people commemorate Peter specifically as a member of the Friars Preachers, indicating some previous reticence to do so. In the next year, Alexander IV, himself a staunch supporter of the mendicants, issued a command to the general chapter

---

30. Innocent IV, "Magna magnalia" [August 8, 1254], *BOP* 1, 252; Potthast, n15482.

31. The popes were eager to aid mendicant cults. Dominic was also the subject of some of these and other bulls, while even Francis of Assisi's cult was promoted a year after his canonization: in Gregory IX, "Sicut phialae aureae" [February 21, 1229] *Bullarium Franiscanum*, 1:49; Potthast, n8236. If one adds the papal admonitions over Francis's stigmata, then one can see the intense curial solicitude for mendicant cults.

32. For a history of this controversy, see Vauchez, "Stigmata of St. Francis," 61–89. For a broader overview, see Schmucki, *Stigmata of St. Francis of Assisi*; for another view of the sources, see Frugoni, *Francesco e l'invenzione delle stimmate*. See Thompson's recent comments in his *Francis of Assisi*, 391–93.

of the Cistercian order to get the white monks to celebrate Peter's and Dominic's feasts.[33] In the year 1255 St. Clare of Assisi was solemnly canonized. She was the latest in a series of saintly elevations that heavily favored the mendicants; six of eleven saints papally created in this period were of mendicant orders.[34] When opposition boiled over at the University of Paris in the 1250s, the papacy and the mendicants began to act as if an attack on one was an attack on the both.[35] Caught up in this development were not only the traditional model of saint-creation and various forms of lay and clerical traditionalism but also the contentions of various heterodox groups within the church. The conflict was coming to a head.

An interesting component of the foregoing arguments and events is the question of their context. Why had the two renowned mendicant professors chosen to address the issue of infallibility at this place and time? Why had they situated the question in terms of the creation of saints? William had not directly impugned the legitimacy of Francis and Dominic. Given the doctrinal development that had occurred by the 1250s, he would not have dared. While the Decretalists had said that a pope might err, nonetheless they declared it temerious in the extreme to attack a papal canonization. This is telling in itself. For his part, Thomas had made canonization a centerpiece of his thoughts on papal supremacy. Of all the citations about papal authority from his works, this quodlibet was most often referenced by those on both sides of the infallibility debates of the nineteenth century. Thomas and Bonaventure were certainly engaged in refuting a specific challenge both to the papacy and to the authenticity of their mendicant saints. Both saw infallibility as the logical and necessary working out of the papal reservation, but their teaching failed quickly to trickle down into their orders.

---

33. Alexander IV, "Licet Apostolica Sedes" [July 21, 1255], *BOP*, 1:285; Potthast, n15490.

34. Numbers taken from Vauchez, *Sainthood*, 253–54, table 9. Out of twenty-three processes from this period, eleven were mendicants. Forty-two percent of the nonmendicants were canonized at this time, while 55 percent of mendicant cases concluded successfully.

35. Their victories were also one. In 1256 a triumphant Dominican order met in Paris for its Chapter General under the able Master Humbert of Romans. Using Peter's relics as the centerpiece, he organized an exultant meeting that celebrated the order's victory by focusing devotion on its new martyr. The pope had confirmed mendicant rights, and Peter was the chief symbol of the victory; both mendicancy and papacy emerged victorious. This was amply demonstrated by the concourse of nobility and prelates who came to the chapter to venerate Peter, including King Louis IX. Humbert had skillfully choreographed the Dominican and papal triumph. See Prudlo, *Martyred Inquisitor*, 158. "Quia tantus fuit concursus secularium ad sermones et generale capitulum nuper ibidem celebratum cum tanta solempnitate vidimus celebrari. Sed et reliquie beati Petri Martyris, presente rege cum archiepiscopis et episcopis multis, principibus et populi multitudine copiosa, preter morum Parisiensem cum tanta tunc temporis recepte sunt devotione et reverentia; quod vix antea credi potuisset." Letter of Humbert of Romans to the Order in *Chartularium Universitatis Parisiensis*, ed. Denifle, 1:317–19.

Ironically, the mendicant defense of papal infallibility came at a time when the Franciscans and the Dominicans were deriding each other's saints. When the pope canonized Peter in 1253, the Franciscans failed to add him to their calendar, ostensibly because the Dominicans failed to celebrate the feast of St. Anthony. This tension lasted until 1260 when, under presumed papal pressure, the orders came to a bilateral agreement to celebrate the two feasts.[36] Apparently Thomas's teaching had not penetrated very deep into the order, because in that same year, 1260, a Dominican in Vienna derided the sanctity of St. Clare of Assisi. Further, this wayward Dominican claimed that "she was not joined to the company of the Saints, and that the judgment of the Holy See in ascribing heaven to her was in error."[37] Alexander IV was unimpressed. In his bull responding to the Austrian Dominican, it was clear that the pope fully considered Clare to be in heaven; this fact was proved by the canonization itself. Opposition to it was both "insane" and actionable. The unnamed friar in question was to be made publicly to recant his intemperate language. This particular friar must have been a serious outlier, but the episode shows that cracks could still appear in an otherwise unified papal-mendicant front. For a long time Dominicans had lacked saints with the sort of open and accessible charisma that Francis and Anthony had. In Peter, for the first time, Dominicans had a popular preacher and wonder worker. Franciscans for their part made a studious effort to avoid Peter and his cult. In the period from Peter's death to 1350, only four Franciscan sermons for his feast are extant, as opposed to over a hundred by Dominicans and others.[38] I believe that there was a rising Franciscan jealousy of Peter. Not only was Peter similar to the Franciscan saints in terms of charismatic personality and miracle-working ability; he was that rarest of canonized commodities in the Middle Ages: a martyr. Not even Francis, whose imitation

---

36. This was not necessarily a denial of their respective sainthood, simply a reluctance to give the saints a public cult. It would not have been much of a problem, since laypeople would go to whichever convent had a feast that day in order to hear a sermon. Humbert of Romans, intent on presenting a united front in the antimendicant furor of the 1250s, attempted to cajole his friars into "making nice" with the Franciscans. He so often refers to the ideal of concord in his works that the underlying rivalry comes across just as strongly. This is especially true as one reads the somewhat strained attempts to read back harmony between the two orders into early Dominican history during his tenure as master general in the *Vitas Fratrum*. See Brett, *Humbert of Romans*, 26–29.

37. "Quod eadem S. Clara, cujus felix anima in conspectu fulget Altissimi, Sanctorum non erat aggregata Collegio: et quod praefatae Sedis judicium in ascriptione praedicta erroneum extitisset." Alexander IV, "Profundi doloris aculeo" [June 3, 1260], *Bullarium Franciscanum*, ed. Sbaralea, 2:398; Potthast, n17882.

38. This is perhaps attributable to fewer occasions for Franciscans to preach on a Dominican feast. Most of the laity would have gone to a Dominican church on his feast, and the Franciscans had little reason to promote the cult themselves. Prudlo, *Martyred Inquisitor*, 122n129.

of Christ the hagiography often recounts, could, like Peter, claim to be really *another* Christ, who had gone even to death with his Lord.[39] In conjunction with rising tensions in all areas of mendicant life in the late 1200s, it is understandable that competing visions of sanctity came into conflict. In spite of all these things, though, the friars were able to maintain a unified front.

❧ War between the Saints

By the latter half of the thirteenth century, the Roman curia and the mendicant orders were clearly moving to protect their saints. These actions shored up the international cults of canonized Franciscans and Dominicans and catalyzed the first discussions of personal papal infallibility. These activities had a flip side, however. As the doctrine and practice of papal canonization began to be systematized and the implications sounded out by the theologians, there was a reaction against more traditional manifestations of popular piety and canonization by the vox populi. Because the church had now plumbed the meanings of canonization, such *sublimia negotia*, that is, such lofty matters, could not be left to the faithful alone. While popular devotion could certainly discern holiness, a cult had to pass through the sifting process of legal measures: witnesses, testimony, and the sanction of the divinely conferred authority of the Roman church. So while the lawyers, the theologians, and the papacy went about the positive process of creating saints, developed over the previous hundred years, the church began to shine a light on the saints of popular devotion.

Possibly by the 1260s and certainly by the 1280s, both Franciscan and Dominican inquisitors were investigating local saints and attempting to quash popular canonizations that they considered beyond the bounds of orthodoxy.[40] One of the most famous of these was the investigations of the Dominican inquisitor Stephen of Bourbon. When preaching in southeastern France, he heard people talking about a "St. Guinefort." He went to the place and found that the saint in question was no less than a loyal greyhound that had mistakenly been killed after protecting a baby from a snake. The dog was buried and, because of its undeserved death, somehow came to be considered to be a martyr. People began to frequent the grave, and a minor

---

39. Ibid., 122–24.

40. Augustine Thompson proposes that a systematic review may have been undertaken by inquisitors of popular cults in Italy; Thompson, *Cities of God*, epilogue.

cult grew up. Of course this is an outrageous and sensational example, and no others like it are to be found, but this was precisely the thing the church had been fearful of in terms of popular canonization. Churchmen began to fear that the laity lacked theological sophistication and could be credulous of miracles and so could not be trusted in such a grave matter as the discernment of sanctity.[41] Stephen preached against the practice and "had the dead dog dug up and the grove of trees cut down and burned along with the dog's bones. Then we had an edict enacted by the lords of the land threatening the spoliation and fining of any people who gathered there for such a purpose in the future."[42] This would be a common reaction of mendicant inquisitors to questionable cults.

The cult of Guinefort illustrated for churchmen like Stephen a particular problem in terms of the discernment of holiness. For example, it was common for medieval people to associate any unjust death with martyrdom, which would then be followed by the creation of an attending cult. Again one detects an enduring traditionalism among the Christian people. Medievals remained attached to the ideal of martyrdom as the absolute guarantee of sanctity. Though martyrdom was exceedingly rare in the Middle Ages, the figure of the martyr remained popular.[43] Laypeople filled the vacuum created by a dearth of genuine martyrs from actual persecutions with guiltless wives murdered by jealous husbands, men killed in pursuit of justice, or wild popular takes of children killed by Jews.[44] Only tenuously could any of these be accorded a theologically sound title to martyrdom. The church was rightly concerned about this and refused to recognize any martyrs after Thomas Becket for the rest of the Middle Ages, with the sole exceptions of St. Stanislaus (killed in the eleventh century) and St. Peter of Verona. No

---

41. I am in no way making an argument for a Humean two-tiered model here. Medieval Christians valued the same things: they desired holiness and valued its recognition. It is simply that the mendicant theologians and inquisitors began to home in on what those things actually meant and to articulate concepts for its proper recognition and praxis.

42. "Canem mortuum fecimus exhumari et lucum succidi, et cum eo ossa dicti canis pariter concremari, et edictum poni a dominis terre de spoliacione et redempcione eorum qui ad dictum locum pro tali causa de cetero convenirent." Stephen of Bourbon, *Traité sur les sept dons du Saint Esprit*, 327–28, section *De Supersticione*, 370; *SOP* 3.3633. A full analysis of the story can be found in Schmitt, *Holy Greyhound*.

43. One can see this in the stunning popularity of Thomas Becket, recognized by the laity and promoted by the church. This is also true to a lesser extent of Peter of Verona's cult, which became quite generally and immediately popular. For an analysis of his popularity, see Prudlo, *Martyred Inquisitor*, chap. 5.

44. Vauchez gives a list of these "martyrs" in *Sainthood*, 148–51.

popularly reputed martyrs were ever accorded formal canonization in this period. Just as Innocent III could not canonize without a popular cult, so neither could these local saints achieve formal canonization because of a lack of systematic virtue, reliable miracle stories, or various theological considerations about martyrdom itself. From the church's perspective, it was correct in not honoring such people as formal saints, but on the other hand, such refusal to recognize these cults evinced a widening gulf between popular and institutional ideals of the recognition of sanctity. Vauchez is correct that for the most part the church was content to let these cults die by a "silent rejection." The curia refused to give any sort of formal sanction at all to any of these, and in refusing to take notice of them, most of them passed into memory rather quickly. Sometimes the papacy was content to let local prelates forbid cults, for this reinforced the papal reserve. Deprived of their ancient right of canonization, all the bishops had left was the negative enforcement of cultic discipline in forbidding veneration of uncanonized saints.[45]

This is not to say that the papacy was passive. Especially in Mediterranean countries, the mendicants, empowered by their offices as inquisitors, sometimes engaged in a cultic purification of their own. Here university-trained preachers, proficient in the logical discourse of the schools and steeped in the scholastic method, went out into the world of lived Catholicism. What they encountered were lay realities that failed readily to align with the categories that they themselves had learned. Seen from the perspective of academic Catholicism, some of these beliefs and practices could seem to fall outside the mainstream of orthodoxy. Here was the crux of the problem. Medieval Christians tended to see faithful Catholicism through the lens of orthopraxis—that is, the correct performance of and communitarian attendance and participation in the rites, rituals, and devotions of the church—in addition to the pious and good works of charity and asceticism. They were people steeped in the liturgy, for, according to this model, if one performed the deeds demanded by Christianity, how then could one fail to be a good Christian? By and large the clergy agreed with this assessment, yet from the mendicant and inquisitional perspective orthopraxis could be feigned, so the only real test of authentic Catholicism was orthodoxy, or right belief. From this angle, if one did not believe correctly, if one did not accept the Trinity and the Incarnation, how then could one be a faithful Christian? What emerges here is a clash of perspectives, in tension certainly but not mutually exclusive. The mendicants themselves came from the heart of the laity; they

---

45. A very few, such as the cult of St. Werner, endured through episcopal disapproval to make it through to modern times. See ibid., 149n4.

had grown up with the same mindsets. No vast chasm existed between learned and lay Christianity; that is to create a false dichotomy.[46] The well-educated mendicants had taken lay Catholicism and had mapped it onto the world of orthodoxy. Onto the top of lay piety, the church had overlaid a superstructure of well-defined belief. It was analogous to a layperson who sees and smells a beautiful flower and a biologist who sees and smells the same beautiful flower and yet can explain in detail its classification and all its biological processes. The tension was not then so irreconcilable. Rather, it arose around the question of identity: what was the source of the features that distinguished one as a Christian? When orthodoxy and orthopraxis coincided, as they did in the vast majority of cases, there was no problem. If lay devotion began to transgress the bounds of proper Catholic orthodoxy, though (for example, according saintly veneration [dulia] to a dead dog), then the conflict of the two visions would become apparent, as happened in some cases.

As the institutional church had raised the stakes over the meaning of papal inquisition, the mendicants began to challenge the veracity of local saints. Such a tack had several purposes. It would enhance the purview of the saints proclaimed universally by Rome by proclaiming the holiness of such individuals to be beyond reproach. It would underscore the significant and growing chasm between the theory of papal canonization and local canonizations. Finally, it would assert the growing significance of religious orthodoxy as the normative means of discerning holiness without thereby discounting the importance of orthopraxis. One of the first instances in which one can detect this push was in the case of Giovanni Buono.[47] Throughout his vita and miracles, one sees the theme of orthodoxy related repeatedly. He was described as having an inveterate dislike of heretics. This hatred was mentioned in the same breath as his love for the Eucharist. He was versed in all manners of pious lay devotion, though he was not educated. He was even the object of persecution by heretics (which ended in the conversion of the same). His last instructions to his disciples commanded them to help him make a last trip to Mantua, "that my death might forward the destruction of the many heretics living there . . . and for the confirmation of the Christian faith."[48]

---

46. I fully concur with Peter Brown's dismantling of David Hume's unfortunate two-tiered model of religious life that can be found throughout Brown's works but especially in the first chapters of his *Cult of the Saints*. See also Duffy, *Stripping of the Altars*, 1–8; and Thompson, *Cities of God*, 1–4.

47. See *Processus Apostolici Auctoritate Innocentii Papae IV Annis 1251, 1253, et 1254 Constructi de Vita, Virtutibus et Miraculis B. Johannis Boni Mantuani*, AS 51 (October, IX): 778–885.

48. "Et mors mea erit ad destructionem hereticorum multorum ibidem existentum . . . ed ad corroborationem fidei christianae." Ibid., 783. Cf. Vauchez, *Sainthood in the West*, 432n23.

His canonization proceeded apace with major impetus from his home city of Mantua. The entire inquest was complete by 1254. Yet something was not quite right. In 1253 Innocent IV remanded the process back to Mantua in order more fully to investigate Giovanni's faith.[49] In the 1260s a slight doubt about Giovanni's orthodoxy was voiced by a mendicant inquisitor. It was enough to bring the process to an end, permanently.[50] It is possible that rivalry among the mendicants had gotten in the way of the process, for Giovanni had been one of the founders of what later became the Order of the Hermits of Saint Augustine. It is also possible that Giovanni's earthy lay Catholicism and his status as *illiteratus* did not jibe well with the forms of sanctity then desired by the papacy. By this time explicit orthodoxy seemed to be not merely a baseline but rather a fully manifested requirement for papal consideration.

In addition to increased oversight of canonization processes, it seems that the mendicants undertook an analysis of extant popular cults, though the comprehensiveness of such efforts is unclear. In any case, there were several high-profile attacks on saints' cults, similar to Stephen of Bourbon's assault on the cult of St. Guinefort. The objects in these instances were perhaps not so undeserving of Christian veneration as the Holy Greyhound. One of these local saints was Guido da Loca of Brescia. During the 1250s Brescia had a famous Dominican preacher as bishop, Bartolomeo of Braganza, a veteran of the Alleluia revival of the early 1230s. Here was a sort of test case for the power and influence of the mendicants that had been increasing over the previous generation. Bartolomeo united the authority of his office as bishop with inquisitorial duties and made an inquest into the life of Guido da Loca. Judged to have been a heretic, Bartolomeo ordered Guido's tomb destroyed. After an apparent miracle in Guido's favor, the people of Brescia were ready to do injury to the bishop and his men, and it was only after exposing the supposed relics to the power of the Eucharist that the near-riot was quelled. The cult of Guido da Loca was suppressed. Only the authority of the bishop united to his supervision of the Eucharist—the very heart of the Christian life—was enough to mollify the townspeople agitated

49. Vauchez, *Sainthood in the West*, 54n78, also 333–35.

50. Paolo Golinelli, "Dal santo del potere al santo del popolo: Culti mantovani dall'alto al basso Medioevo," in id., *Città e culto dei santi*, 58–66.

at the overthrow of the cult of their neighbor. The universalizing tendencies of the mendicants had begun to hit home.[51]

Perhaps the most blatant and unjustifiable attack on a local saint happened to Alberto Brentatore of Cremona.[52] Alberto had been a wine porter renowned for his piety and holiness. After his death there was an efflorescence of miracles around his tomb, and he became an archetypal patron saint of his home city. He became renowned throughout Lombardy, and pilgrimages began to his resting place. Devotees collected an amount of money sufficient to erect a hospice in his honor. Acquiescing to the developing veneration, the clergy and bishop of Cremona began to sponsor and promote his cult. Alberto appears as a typical lay, popular saint, the type of which could be found throughout Christendom. One might say that he was the right man at the wrong time, for he died in 1279. The age of unchallenged popular canonizations was drawing to a close, while the age of inquisitorial and papal oversight had come. The irascible Franciscan chronicler Salimbene is one of the main witnesses for Alberto's cult. Salimbene describes the rise of the cult, but when he gets to the creation of images of Alberto for use in churches and the veneration of his relics, he begins to object. Such an action is "contrary to Church law, that relics ought not be held in honor unless first one is approved by the Roman Church and added to the catalog of saints, nor can one paint any image of a saint, if first his canonization has not been proclaimed by the Church."[53] Salimbene is up on the latest law from Lateran IV and the *Liber Extra*, but in the traditional order of things, Alberto had already been recognized by the "church," that is, the local bishop. Therein lay the tension.

The clergy and people of Cremona probably sensed nothing amiss. When they thought of the church that is authorized to do such things, they thought locally. When Salimbene thinks of the church, he clearly means the Roman

---

51. Unfortunately we possess no life or miracles of Guido da Loca, only a late entry in some town chronicles. Thompson, *Cities of God*, 403. Creytens, "Le Manuel de conversation," 120–21.

52. Thompson, *Cities of God*, 430. The case of Alberto, who according to Salimbene was a drunkard, was strangely similar to the classic Decretal *Audivimus*, which condemned the Swedes for venerating a man killed in a drunken stupor. While Salimbene may have read the *Liber Extra*, it is clear that the people of Cremona had not. For the episode, see Salimbene da Adam, *Cronica*, 2:761–64; and Salimbene da Adam, *Chronicle of Salimbene de Adam*, 512–14.

53. "Quod contra statuta Ecclesie expresse cognoscitur esse, quia reliquie alicuius in reverentia haberi non debent, nisi prius a Romana Ecclesia aprobentur et sanctorum cathalogo ascribantur, nec etiam alicuius ymago ad modum sancti alicubi debet depingi, nisi prius ab ecclesia eius canonizatio divulgetur." Salimbene, *Cronica*, 2:761–62. Of course images of the dead, including those not yet canonized, continued to proliferate in the Middle Ages, but Salimbene's particular concern (aside from more general narrowmindedness) is liturgical use in a church setting.

church. Mendicant attitudes have shifted away from the lay piety of earlier ages. Salimbene calls the attitude of the local clergy and bishop an abuse, going so far as to suggest that such actions merited the deposition of the local bishop from office. The Franciscan chronicler even reported a scene that painted the whole of the lay and secular clerical world as foolish, when he described a translation of a bit of Alberto's relics to Parma. During the ceremony the bishop's vicar discovered that the relic was a garlic clove. Only the mendicants came out smelling good in this story, which is Salimbene's whole point. Alberto, associated with such a menial job as wine porter, must also have been, in Salimbene's scornful turn of phrase, a "carrier as well as a quaffer."[54] Thompson suggests that Salimbene means this as a blanket statement to cover laypeople as a whole, which is very possible. In any case, for Salimbene, the recognition of the saints is no matter for local churches, which are made up of wine-bibbers, silly women, and outmoded secular clergy. Only the Roman church and its elite vanguard—the mendicants—were suited to such a task. The popes agreed. When Padua tried to have the cult of St. Anthony the Pilgrim confirmed, the Franciscans would have none of it. The pope (unnamed in the story) replied, "One Anthony is enough for you."[55]

A difficult case involved the cult of Armanno Pungilupo, a widely admired layman of Ferrara who attracted a large following after his death. Apparently converted from heresy, he became a model Catholic and made very public his regular practice of confession, going so far as to confess to the bishop's chaplain. He was known for his charity and for his regular observance of the sacrament of penance. Though Armanno participated in other rituals, it was confession that he made the centerpiece of his devotion. The idea of conversion still exercised a certain fascination among medieval people. Not only was Armanno a convert from heresy, but he frequented the very sacrament of conversion. By the marks of orthopraxis, Armanno was a model medieval Catholic: penitential, devout, charitable, and neighborly. The townsmen of Ferrara had no doubt that he was a saint in their very midst, and after his death, miracles began to multiply around his tomb. The mendicants were not fooled. Armanno had been haled before the inquisition in 1254 and had admitted and abjured his Catharism. In the minds of the mendicants this made him suspect. As regarded his devotion to confession, was it not the one sacrament that was considered permissible by the Cathars, for it passed through no material medium; rather, it was by word, one soul com-

54. "Cuiusdam Alberti qui stabat Cremone et fuerat unus vini portator simul et potator nec non et peccator," Ibid., 761.

55. Rigon, "Dévotion et patriotisme," 259–78; Thompson, *Cities of God*, 206.

municating to another?[56] Inquisitors began to build a case against him after his death in 1269. The clergy of Ferrara, for its part, had fully embraced the cult and had begun the initial steps in the canonization process: the gathering of miracles. Meanwhile, the inquisitor sent in his report in 1288. It is significant that by this time both the mendicants and the secular clergy were appealing to the papacy for vindication. At the same time the cult was flourishing, a new inquisitor was appointed in 1299 named Fra Guido da Vicenza. He reopened the investigation.

What the inquisitor found was a mixed bag. Many of Armanno's neighbors were convinced he was a good Catholic. The inquisitor turned up a streak of anticlericalism, or more specifically, an animosity toward the friars (perhaps a result of Armanno's citation before the inquisition in 1254). Such anticlericalism was part and parcel of lay life at the time.[57] It did, however, clue the mendicants in to one solid fact: this person was not a saint. Saints respected the clergy, even when they disagreed or thought them corrupt (St. Francis was a sterling example of such cases). The difficulty for the inquisitors was fixing Armanno's religious identity in a world where such things were fluid, passing from Catholic to Cathar and back. In the absence of the subject himself, the inquisition latched onto moments of "heteropraxis."[58] This left them analyzing orthodoxy through the lens of practice, much as the laity did. Armanno did some very suspicious things that were set apart from common anticlericalism. At the very least, Armanno was virulently antimendicant, flippant, and duplicitous. He was no saint. The evidence against him also seems to indicate that he was a hidden heretic, feigning holiness, especially his exaggerated and defensive devotion to confession. He mocked and denied transubstantiation. He had been consoled in 1266 and even presided over Cathar rituals. He was a very clever dissembler who clearly violated the spirit of confession and communion. Some of the miracles at his shrine had been faked. In spite of his cult, the inquisition had demonstrated that popular piety could be tricked. Armanno really was a secret heretic.[59] Fra Guido reached this conclusion as well and in 1301 ordered Armanno's tomb destroyed and his bones burnt. When some of the laity found out,

56. This Cathar confession was called "The Service" by Cathars and *apparellamentum* in church sources and involved aural confession and penance. It can be found in their own Provençal Cathar service book, ca. 1250–80, edited in Wakefield and Evans, *HHMA*, 484–85. Rainerio describes it similarly; ibid., 332–34.

57. Murray, "Piety and Impiety," 83–106.

58. I borrow the term from Hull, *Banished Heart*.

59. I agree with Lambert, *Cathars*, 281–82. In this I disagree with Zanella, *Itinerari ereticali*, 52–62. Most recently Thompson has concurred with Zanella: Thompson, *Cities of God*, 430–33.

they formed a lynch mob to kill Fra Guido, who was saved only by the opportune intervention of the local authorities. These things are indicative of an increasing insistence on the papal reserve and, more to the point, of the mounting mendicant desire to mold and control lay piety and to clericalize and standardize devotion to the saints. It was the capstone to one hundred years of the articulation of the difference between papal and popular canonizations. Papal canonizations were certain because of the matter and authority involved. Popular canonizations were invalid at best and wildly wrong at worst. The seed of the doctrine had successfully been sowed, but the harvest would prove difficult.

The growing mendicant and papal insistence on the authenticity of their saints and the growing discomfort of heretics and some laypeople against them were at cross purposes around 1300. During the Bologna anti-inquisition riots of 1299, many people intemperately bandied about hasty declarations in the streets. These were later compiled in the testimonies given to the inflexible inquisitor Fra Guido of Parma, whom we met above.[60] One of the depositions that concerned one Andrea di Miglo of Florence was colorful to say the least. He hoped for no less than a "war between the saints in heaven, so that one would kill another, and so that pieces of their bodies would fall to earth."[61] This statement sounds like general uninformed bluster, but it is interesting nonetheless. Perhaps he means a war between the good men and the Catholic saints; it is not clear. In any case the saints were at war, bringing with them rival visions of both holiness and ecclesiology.

❧ The Heretics Respond

Chapter 4 traced the beginnings of a leitmotif in the hagiography of the new saints: the attribution to them of aggression miracles against heretics. These stories were a way for the cultic biographers to defuse tension created by the expanding cults of their saints and to respond to heretical dissension that sought to minimize or detract from them. The reimagining of this hallowed piece of hagiographic convention did several things. It demonstrated the proper attitude toward the saints while discouraging scurrilous attacks.

---

60. The depositions are contained in *Acta S. Officii Bononie, ab anno 1291 usque ad 1310*, ed. Paolini and Orioli. The episode of the anti-inquisition riots is described in Thompson, *Cities of God*, epilogue.

61. "Item dixit quod audivit dictum Andream Migli de Florencia . . . dicentem quod libenter vellet quod prelium esset in celo inter sanctos, et quod unus occideret alium, et quod interiora, sive membra sanctorum, caderent in terram." Deposition of Geppo da Firenze, *Acta S. Officii Bononie*, 1:97–98.

The power and holiness of the saint received a startling public demonstration, leading not only to a quelling of resistance but perhaps also to
positive growth for the cult. In Peter's case slightly more aggression miracles
are reported than average for contemporary saints, but it is how the cultic
promoters present them that is key.[62] Of course one reads standard tales of
cultic "backsliders": those who made vows to the saint and failed to keep
them, most notably in the fertility miracles of Peter.[63] These are part and
parcel of medieval hagiography of all sorts. It is the other aggression miracles
that begin to shed light on the change in sentiment and doctrine. In the early
sources, such stories are continuations of Peter's earthly struggles against the
heretics. One of these stories records Peter in his last public sermon of Palm
Sunday—after having been warned of the heretical plot—as saying, "Let
them do as they will, I shall be worse to them in death than in life!"[64] It was
up to Peter's early biographers to make sure they recorded the ways in which
Peter kept his promises.

In one of the earliest examples, a youth of Florence saw a representation
of Peter's martyrdom in the Dominican convent of Santa Maria Novella
sometime before 1259, making it perhaps the first instance of an aggression
miracle in his hagiography. "If I had been there, I would have dealt a worse
blow!" the youth intemperately bragged to his friends. The story states that
he was made mute and fled from the Dominican church, careening through
the back streets of western Florence until he came upon Orsanmichele. There
he made a mental vow to confess and to abjure his heresy. He returned to
the church, confessed and converted, and received permission to tell his tale
publicly. This youth "infected by heretical depravity" moved freely throughout Florence, even into the center of the Florentine inquisition, an indicator of the fluidity of confessional identities and the absence of any pervasive
social control exercised by the inquisition. That said, though, his opposition
to Peter was visceral. The young man knew why he would have struck Peter
harder than the murderer: life had been made immeasurably more difficult

---

62. See Prudlo, *Martyred Inquisitor*, 146, table 3. In the thirteenth-century sources, Peter is nearly
identical in the percentage of published aggression miracles, while in the fourteenth-century
sources he has slightly more than average. For an explanation of this, see ibid., 147–48.

63. For an analysis of Peter's relation to female supplicants, see Prudlo, "Women, Wives, and Mystics," 313–24.

64. "Sed faciant quod volunt, quia deterius faciam eis mortuus quam vivus." Both in Agni (*VSP*,
5.35, 698) and in the *VF*, 239, it is interesting to note that this is the converse of some of St. Dominic's last words. The *Acta Canonizationis* from Bologna relates that Dominic said, "I will be more
useful to you and more profitable after death than I have been during my life." Cf. Hinnebusch,
History of the Dominican Order, 1:106.

for heretics after the death of the Dominican. The equation of antiheretical activity with sanctity had begun to sink in. A similar episode, indicating the initial fluidity of interactions between heretic and Catholic, happened in Milan. A heretic by the name of Obizo was loitering around Peter's tomb and stole some offering money to get a drink. He was frozen in place, and not until recanting and returning the money was he able to move.[65] Peter's early hagiographers were not heedless in their attributions of heresy. Four other early aggression miracles occur against orthodox laypeople. Once again we see the bifurcation in the sacred biographers. Not only do orthodox laypeople get punished for irreverence, a well-established trope, but also heretics are specifically chastised—but their punishment involves conversion. Peter's earthly mission to convert the heretics continued from heaven. While initial cultic presentation of Peter was much broader, as time went on he came more and more to be pictured as an antiheretical saint. By the end of the Middle Ages, he had become the Inquisitor Saint, a severe narrowing of his cultic persona. This image was also appropriated by heretics, who focused their ire on Peter in order to contest the very specific assimilation of holiness to inquisition.[66] It was this narrowing and the resulting opposition that led to the crystallization of the papal canonization doctrine.

Heretical theology was not far behind the sentiments of the characters depicted in the aggression miracles. Already there had been a generalized movement away from a theoretical assault on the cult of saints in general and criticism of the biblical saints in particular. To take one example, the typical Cathar irritation with St. John the Baptist is found less and less in the sources as the thirteenth century wore on. Indeed, some Cathars had come to embrace the sanctity of the Precursor. Heretical groups began to turn in two new directions. First, they began to train their sights on the new saints, in particular the mendicant saints. In doing this they were reacting against a deployment of these holy men and women that was consciously directed against them personally. By attacking them they were also able to assail the foundations of papal authority and to contest the mendicant claims to holiness. Second, and more surprising, heretics began to fashion a cult of saints of their own. They began the construction of a pantheon of holy heroes, persecuted perfects, and individuals handed over to the secular arm by the inquisition. In so doing they began to create another, parallel group of holy men and women, to contest the meaning of sainthood with the

65. Prudlo, *Martyred Inquisitor*, 234, *VSP* 8.59[4].

66. See Ames, *Righteous Persecution*, esp. 57–93.

Catholic Church. I am convinced that these two trends represent the conventionalization of heresy in the late thirteenth century. Whereas before much effort had been expended in order to create a coherent and logical presentation of anti-incarnational dualism, now with the rise of persecution, inquisition, and ecclesiastical attention, heretics were forced to conventionalize their beliefs. The fluidity of identities in Christendom enabled them to continue to mount a critique of the institutional church and the mendicants while appearing outwardly orthodox. This sometimes made them look like standard anticlerical laypeople. Ironically it was this collapse of theoretical beliefs that made it so hard for inquisitors to tease out orthodoxy. It was as if the heretics (particularly the Cathars) had forgotten their theology and had conventionalized their practice to such an extent that it became difficult to discern real heresy.[67]

The first reaction of the heretics was one of outright rejection of the new saints proposed by the papacy and the mendicants. This was not always systematic or thought out. The accusation of sexual impropriety was not uncommon. If it hurt mendicants to have their saints attacked, it cut them to the quick to hear that their saints were not holy at all but had died as the result of some love affair. For the laity such a claim was sensational, gossipy, mildly seditious, and offensive to the friars. It proved to be a popular line of attack. When the heresy of the Fraticelli flourished, St. Anthony (along with those salacious monks Bernard and Benedict) was repeatedly charged with having concubines.[68] The alleged sexual indiscretions of saints were not the central problem for the inquisition. The real issue was the result of these sinful activities, since now, according to one heretic, "Blessed Francis and Blessed Anthony and Blessed Benedict are in hell."[69] Peter of Verona was also a subject for such accusations. One heretic in Gubbio said, "I have it for certain that it [his murder] was not on account of the faith, but that he was

---

67. By the end of the thirteenth century, Catharism was nearly defeated. When added to the increasing precision of scholastic theology, this forced the inquisitors to peer into corners (like lay anticlericalism) where heresy could be discerned only with difficulty. In this sense we do have the "creation" of heresy by the inquisitors, as James Given has argued, but it is not "creation" in a vacuum; rather, it is a determination based on the development of doctrine, theological precision, and the lived practice of the Catholic faith. See Given's argument in *Inquisition and Medieval Society*.

68. "Fr. Antonius de Ord. FF. Minor. Qui fuit canonizatus, quod tenuerat concbinum, propter quod mandaverat eum Papa incarcerari," Errors of Thomas Scotus, apostate Franciscan, in Döllinger, 2:616.

69. D'Alatri, "Culto dei santi," 36n62.

killed on account of a wicked woman."[70] Of course all of this might reflect simple lay anticlericalism and was probably treated as such during the 1200s. Yet by the year 1300 such loose language applied to canonized saints became officially unacceptable to the inquisition. While ignoring most cases of generalized anticlerical sentiment, as we will see, the inquisition began to focus on any derision directed toward officially authorized cults of the new saints.

The Waldensians maintained a strong disposition and clear theology throughout this period. Wherever they were found, they were fairly unanimous in their rejection of the cult of the saints. A German antiheretical manuscript of the fourteenth century lists the following error of the Waldensians: "Further they do not preach about the martyrs, confessors, or hermits, Nicholas, Martin, Ambrose, Catherine, Margaret, nor of any saints at all; they believe nothing about them, but they say that they may possibly be damned."[71] Their critique of the new saints followed their old animosity toward the institutional church of St. Sylvester. Dominic, Francis, and Peter of Verona were not really saints, since they served the authority that had received the secular power. For the Waldensians, the mendicants were likened to the biblical locusts; they mimicked poverty yet enjoyed copious worldly honors, "especially the Dominicans."[72] Such a reaction was common among the Waldensians and was an enduring preoccupation. In the famous Fournier register, an exceptionally lengthy deposition exists for Raymond de la Costa, a self-identified Waldensian deacon.[73] Testifying in late 1319 and 1320, Raymond laid out an exceptionally detailed account of transalpine Waldensian belief. In an extended passage surrounding the power of the Roman pontiff, Raymond said "that he did not believe that a person was a saint, even if the Roman church canonized him as such,

---

70. From the miracles of St. Peter of Verona, collected at the order of Master General Berengar (ca. 1316), *VSP* 8.61; cf. Prudlo, *Martyred Inquisitor*, 235.

71. "Item de martyribus, confessoribus, eremitis, Nicolao, Martino, Ambrosio, Catharina, Margaritha et omnibus aliis sanctis quodcumque predicatur, nihil credunt, sed dicunt, quod fortasse in inferno sepulti sunt." Döllinger, 2:340. Attacks on these prepapal saints was not of main concern to the church; they merely represent a particularization of Waldensian claims about the corruption of the post-Constantinian church, or other doubts about postbiblical observances, or generalized antimaterial sentiment.

72. "Iste locuste (Apoc 9:3) sunt religiosi qui habent caudas caputiorum et habent coronas aureas quia propter coronas capillorum suorum inter homines multum honorantur et iste percutiunt homines in ore scorpionum maxime qui dicuntur fratres predicatores." Perugia: Biblioteca Comunale Augusta MS 1065, Peter of Verona, *Summa contra hereticos*, fol. 130rb. Peter later replies that the heretics are the real locusts whence they "wear their hair long" and are many and divided among themselves.

73. *Le Registre D'Inquisition de Jaques Fournier*, ed. Duvernoy, 1:40–122.

and that he would not believe such a person to be a saint, since the church that believed such a thing was that which persecuted them."[74] The terminology (if not the theology) of the Roman church is clearly attributed to the heretics here. Raymond point-blank refused belief in a Christianity that persecuted what he considered to be the true church.[75] Nonetheless, Waldensians often outwardly conformed to the cult of the saints, understandable in confrontation with this massively popular aspect of lived religion.[76]

Waldensian theology seemed to remain very stable. In an inquisition conducted near Pinerolo in northwest Italy in 1387 and 1388, the Waldensians had held the line. They condemned the feasts of the saints, continued to advocate the doctrine of soul sleep (whereby no one was admitted to the beatific vision before the Final Judgment), and continued to mock the outward expressions of Christian veneration.[77] In an Austrian antiheretical text of the 1390s, a rather original reason was adduced by the Waldensians as to why the cult of the saints was of no avail. The text asserts that they believed "the blessed Virgin and the other saints in heaven to be so full of joy that they are utterly unable to think of us."[78] As a result of this, they are not able to help us and are not to be invoked, honored, or served. As late as 1395 Waldensians in Piedmont continued to declare that Peter of Verona was not a saint and was damned, since he persecuted the servants of Christ.[79] This idea that persecutors could not possibly be saints was something very com-

---

74. "Item dixit, quod non credit aliquem fuisse sanctum, licet ecclesia Romana eum canonizasset pro sancto, qui non crederet illud, quod eorum ecclesia credit, et qui eos persequutus fuisset." Deposition of Raymundus Costa before the inquisition of Pamiers, ibid., 108. Also in Döllinger, 2:114.

75. Euan Cameron claims that Raymond did accept the cult of the saints, which in a certain sense is true. Raymond only accepted the saints that his own church embraced, however, making the key difference the application of the Power of the Keys of the papacy. See Cameron, *Waldenses*, 91. Waldensians did accept some saints. We still have a Waldensian liturgical calendar preserved at Trinity College Dublin, MS 267. This calendar includes the feast of Francis but omitted all Dominican saints.

76. Gabriel Audisio considers that it would have been impossible for them to omit the cult of the saints, no matter how much they would have liked to. "The Waldensians hold in contempt the solemnities which we celebrate in honor of the saints, as well as other signs of veneration and homage, and on saints' days, if they can do so without too great a risk, they work." See id., *Waldensian Dissent*, 56, 96.

77. See the depositions in Döllinger, 2:254 and 256.

78. "Item credunt beatam virginem et alios in patria sanctos tantum impletos esse gaudiis quod nichil possint cogitare de nobis." Ibid., 2:306. This passage may be an expansion of Bernard Gui's discussion of Waldensians and the saints from 1325 in his *Practica Inquisitionis*: see *HHMA*, 391.

79. Merlo, "Pietro di Verona," 473–74.

mon (understandably so) among the heretics of the late Middle Ages. It crossed sectarian boundaries, since similar sentiments are to be found among nearly all the heretical groups of the time. Though we see stability in the small surviving Waldensian communities,[80] the Cathars, always a more urban and therefore visible phenomenon, were quickly morphing into different forms. Beyond the Cathars, who were quickly becoming marginalized, there was a host of new heresies to fill the pages of fourteenth-century inquisition registers.

---

80. The Waldensian doctrine on the saints and the developing idea on the sole sufficiency of God in the Christian life formed the backdrop for later Protestant approaches to the cult of the saints. In 1451, one Philip Regis from San Martino in Piedmont said, "No saint has the power to realize actions or miracles or to bestow grace, which God alone can do"—a perfect proto-Protestant sentiment. Cf. Audisio, *Waldensian Dissent*, 96.

❧ CHAPTER 6

Sancti per fidem vicerunt regna
"The Saints, by Faith, Conquered Kingdoms"

The concerted efforts made by the papacy and their mendicant allies achieved significant progress in consolidating the cult of the saints by the year 1300. In several ways, the fourteenth century was a "mopping up" operation in terms of the integration and elaboration of the doctrine of papal canonization. In the first place, the papacy was largely successful in facing the heretical challenges of the previous centuries. Catharism was nearly spent as a force, and the Waldensians had been reduced in numbers and driven into remote Alpine valleys. Further, the mendicants—especially the Dominicans—had acquired a formidable reputation for orthodoxy, carrying with them the developing theories of their most significant commentators, not the least of whom was Thomas Aquinas. The process, formula, and liturgy of canonization had been, for all intents and purposes, thoroughly established in the previous one hundred years, necessitating little more than elaboration and commentary. Episcopal canonizations were, by and large, marginalized, though they occasionally would take place until their legal demise in 1634. The papacy and the mendicants had also gone a long way toward establishing a supervisory role over the cults of local saints. In addition, the cults of papally canonized saints were thriving and growing in popularity, eliding the devotion of the laity with the policies of the Roman church. In many cases these cults were beginning to displace more local and traditional holy men and women. Finally the mendicants had successfully assimilated doubts about the sanctity of various papally canonized saints into the machinery of the inquisition, effectively elevating the denial of these into a heresy. All of the pieces were on the board for a harmonization of these disparate trends into a common approach to the cult of the saints that would endure for centuries, even surviving the Protestant assault of the 1500s.

While the church had been dealing—mostly successfully—with the Cathars and Waldensians for over one hundred years, there arose new forms of heterodox religious life around the year 1300. These lacked the substantial theological background and experience of the older groups, and given the Roman church's development of both doctrine and inquisitional practices over the previous century, the Catholics were well equipped to deal with them. In this vein were the followers of the Milanese Guglielma, who, filled with Joachimite apocalypticism, expected the imminent purification of the church and the rise of a Christianity dominated by women, including the coming of a female pope. Dominican inquisitors pursued the case from 1284 until 1322, when the sect was finally eliminated. Guglielma might have become a standard local saint were it not for some of her followers who began to spin wild stories and prophecies about her. It was mostly because of these followers (several of whom were executed at the behest of the inquisition in 1300) that Guglielma's bones were disinterred and destroyed.[1] The heresy surrounding Guglielma was thoroughly eradicated, yet later a "Saint" Guglielma, radically softened and reimagined, did reappear in rural Lombardy.[2] This episode indicates the enduring lay appropriation of local holiness well into the period of the papal reserve while also demonstrating the necessity of "domesticating" such a person as Guglielma in order to match conventional expectations of sanctity and so as not to draw the attention of the church, so recently interested in the supervision of such cults. A similar fate awaited the cult of the "Pseudo-Apostles" or Apostolici, founded by Gerard Segarelli and then continued by Fra Dolcino, who claimed to be the prophet of the final age of the church. He went so far as to declare that his movement was superior to the mendicants because it practiced a more rigorous poverty. Ironically the very arguments used by the mendicant professors at Paris were now turned against the Minorites and Preachers. Dolcino, too,

---

1. For the Guglielmites, see Benedetti, *Io non sono Dio*, based on the trial transcripts edited by id., *Milano 1300*.

2. Newman, "Heretic Saint," 1–38. Newman makes the interesting observation that Guglielma's initial cult was two-tiered. One was the standard portrait of lay devotion to a holy woman, while there was also an esoteric inner circle around a female "pope" that betrayed the truly heretical locus.

was apprehended and burned at the stake in 1307.[3] Once again the inquisition had intercepted the possible creation of a popular saint.

Other heretical groups were more successful than the Guglielmites or the Apostolici in promoting cults of alternative saints. Indeed, the creation of a parallel pantheon of holy men and women was one of the most original achievements of late medieval heresy. Since this development was born out of the exclusivist salvation doctrine of various sects such as the Cathars, it stood to reason that only the dead of a particular sect would merit the title "Saint." Whereas the attribution of sainthood to the dead of a particular group was a logical outworking of its soteriology, its creation of external cults for such people was quite unexpected and creative. For instance, with the Cathars, it was astonishing that a group so rooted in antimaterialism could have come up with a version of saint veneration. It is perhaps related to the various practices of adoration of the perfects on earth. Even this most anti-incarnational and antisacramental group still found the need to have organized, structured ritual. If one venerated these men and women here on earth, oughtn't they be venerated even more after death? In creating this parallel group of saints, the Cathars not only were faithful to their economy of salvation but also comprehended the massive lay popularity of sanctity and patronage. In that sense the creation of a heretical communion of saints was yet another conventionalization of their rather esoteric theology. It indicates the exceptional popularity of the cult of the saints in medieval Europe while at the same time evincing the genius of various heretical groups in co-opting the orthopraxis of lived medieval religion.

↜ The Response of the Classical Heretics

There were two ways of creating saints among the heretics. One was merely to co-opt the existing catalogue of holy men and women, claiming that they were really of the sect in question (similar to a restorationist idea of a "hidden church of the just"). In the early and mid-1200s, heretics were explicit in damning particular saints (or most saints) to hell, but by the latter part of the century one begins to hear claims that all of the holy men and women of past ages had been members of their own sect, which was the true church. "All saints and especially all martyrs were of our sect" was a common expression.[4]

---

3. See Lambert, *Medieval Heresy*, 202–3. See also Orioli, *Venit perfidus heresiarca.*

4. "Omnes sanctos et precipue martires fuisse nostre secte." And see d'Alatri, "Culto dei santi," 98, esp. n63. I am indebted to d'Alatri's work in this section.

Heretics could also draw inferences from the lives of the saints themselves. "It is read that many saints would not eat meat, just like us."[5] At the heart of such claims was an ecclesiological and soteriological issue. The Cathars may have been influenced by a sort of Waldensian "remnant theology" whereby the true church, small and persecuted, endured in hidden pockets through the centuries. One can see this in the *Liber de duobus principibus*, John of Lugio's extant Cathar treatise, which says that the true Christians are those called heretics, from whom all the legitimate prophets, apostles, and saints came.[6] This is because the only holiness possible came from the Cathar faith, from the secrets of the *consolamentum* passed from perfect to perfect. The "good men," particularly in Languedoc, seem to have generated something of a living cult, perhaps like the *starets* of Russian Orthodoxy. In late Catharism we see a conflation of roles. Guillaume Belibaste, caught by Jacques Fournier's famous Pamiers inquisition, commented that the believers of the Cathars "adored (the perfect) as a saint," but we must be wary of pushing the text too far.[7] In the scholastic world "adoration" had already come to mean the worship of *Latria*, which was due to God alone. It is possible that the ceremony of "adoration" was merely a local custom of politeness.[8] Yet the reality seems to lie somewhere in the middle. The actions of Cathars toward their perfects throughout its history most resemble the cultic acts directed toward the saints, not like the *adoratio* due to God alone but also not simply politeness. Rather, it was most similar to what was called by the theologians *Dulia*, or the veneration proper to the saints. Perhaps Guillaume was really getting at something here. Using the orthopractic rituals of saint veneration, Cathars considered their perfects to be living saints. Most likely this avenue of saint creation was the logical outworking of their exclusive salvation doctrines, which leads to the second possibility for heretical saints. In their soteriology, only consoled Cathars could be saved. Some of those consoled on their deathbeds partook of the ritual called *Endura* or ritual starvation.[9] If one was consoled, then one was saved and, by extension, a saint. This was a corollary to the Catholic doctrine that a purified and justified soul immediately apprehended the beatific vision and so could

---

5. "Item multi sancti leguntur non comedisse carnes, ergo et nos." *Summa contra hereticos*, ca. 15 Döllinger, 2:282.

6. D'Alatri, "Culto dei santi," 98nn66,67.

7. "Se dicebat sanctum et se faciebat vocari Petrum, cuius ipsi credentes et quem adorabant ut sanctum." Döllinger, 2:236.

8. As argued in Pegg, *Corruption of Angels*.

9. The frequency (and sometimes even the existence) of the *Endura* ritual is a subject of academic debate. See Rottenwöhrer, *Der Katharismus*, vol. 2, pt. 2, 586–604.

rightly be called a saint.[10] If one was saved, then one was a saint. The Cathars began to apply this doctrine to their own practices, in effect creating a parallel corps of saintly men and women. In 1320 Bernardo Franca made this point during his interrogation: "These heretics were good men and saints and suffered much persecution on account of the good God."[11] In the end they formed a new pantheon; those "alone were the Church, where the Cathars were, and that those who were burned for the defense of the faith or died in the *endura*, are the Martyrs of God."[12]

Some evidence also exists that the Waldensians were not as thoroughgoing in their rejection of saints as the inquisition made out. As we saw in chapter 5, individual Waldensians were ambivalent about the cult of the saints.[13] In the summa attributed to the Franciscan inquisitor David of Augsburg from the second half of the 1200s, the author twice asserts that Waldensians paid veneration to relics of their own saints.[14] Around the same time Stephen of Bourbon reports something similar. Jealous of the miracles of a Christian bishop, heretics—who were probably but not necessarily Waldensians—gathered the ashes of a burned heretic and kept them as relics, attempting to use them ineffectually to cure blindness.[15] This was similar to aggression miracles in other sources in which heretics claimed power for relics or for the performance of miracles. Even latter-day Cathars began to evince respect and veneration for the bodies of their dead. In the late 1200s a weaver named Simon took the body of the perfect Giuseppe da Viterbo off the gallows and buried it with devotion.[16] This may have been an act of simple

---

10. A later outworking of this idea was that all those in heaven were "small *s* saints," while those who had been canonized by the church were "capital *S* Saints."

11. "Dicti haeretici erant boni homines et sancti et sustinebant multas persecutiones propter Deum bonum." 2:234. Also in d'Alatri, "Culto dei santi," 99n68.

12. "Quod solum erat ecclesia, ubi ipsi erant, et quod illi qui moriuntur en la endura, sunt martyres Dei." Döllinger, 2:235. Also in d'Alatri, "Culto dei santi," 99n69. At the same time, this veneration did not seem to include appeals to intercession, which would still set them far apart from traditional Christian beliefs regarding the saints. I thank Augustine Thompson for this observation.

13. Euan Cameron was of the opinion that the inquisitors extrapolated views from Waldensian confessions that seemed to make them more antisaint than they were in practice. See Cameron, *Waldensees*, 93. While this is probably true, I would contend that their particular animosity toward saints like Sylvester, Laurence, and later Peter Martyr came to be construed by the inquisition as heretical in itself. To deny one saint was to deny all saints, not to mention the power of canonization. Such a view had not trickled down, as it were, quite yet.

14. Praeger, "Der Traktat des David von Augsburg," 222, 228.

15. Stephen of Bourbon, *Traité sur les sept dons du Saint Esprit*, 283, sec. 333. Stephen is probably abbreviating a miracle from another source.

16. "Prophanum corpus Joseph dampnati heretici deposuit de furcis et devotissime sepelivit." Cf. d'Alatri, "Culto dei santi," 99n71.

charity, but it sometimes went further.[17] Some heretics expected their holy men and women to perform miracles. Giuliano Borsaio, questioned by the Bolognese inquisition in 1299, was certain of it. Speaking of the execution of some heretics in Mantua, he said, "They burned certain heretics, and a great light appeared over them, and they performed miracles and wonders."[18] All of this is a conventionalization of heretical theologies to make them conform more closely to contemporary lay piety. Relics and veneration were central to the medieval experience of saints and sainthood. Premodern Christianity of any kind could not exist without the tangibility of holiness. Immemorial practice acted as a lodestone, drawing heterodox theologies toward it.

❧ Latent Resentment among the Orthodox Laity

The tension between orthodoxy and orthopraxis really came to a head in Bologna in 1299. As Augustine Thompson rightly says, "by the 1290s heresy hunting was on a collision course with lay piety."[19] During that summer one Bompietro di Giovanni was handed over to the secular arm to be executed as a *relapsus*—a relapsed heretic. Bompietro had unquestionably consorted with heretics, lied to the inquisition, refused to fulfill his enjoined penances, and ran a virtual hostel for traveling perfects. When he was haled before the inquisition in 1283 he seemed repentant and was let off with a light sentence. After this he lived as an exemplary Catholic, though he continued to offer hospitality to Cathars. In 1299, when he was arrested again, the inquisition took astonishing care over his case, asked for opinions from leading canonists and theologians, and at length declared him relapsed. Bompietro's neighbors were unimpressed and began to make public (and sometimes impassioned) defenses of the reality of his conversion and of the authenticity of his Catholicism. After his condemnation by the city officials, Bompietro begged for confession and communion, declaring he had abjured heresy twenty years ago. For some inexplicable reason (one imagines that the inquisitor doubted his sincerity) his request was refused. This caused immediate uproar. The laity, which earlier had opposed the inquisitors and thought Bompietro a good man, now broke into open rebellion. How dare

---

17. For short but insightful comments on such phenomena, see Wakefield, "Burial of Heretics," 29–32.

18. "Fuerunt combusti quidam heretici et apparuerunt magna luminaria super wis et fecerant miracula et virtutes. Interrogatus si credebat ita esse, respondit quod sic, quia bene credebat quod haeretici facerent virtutes et miracula." "Acta Sancti Officii Bononiae," 253.

19. For the full story, see Thompson, *Cities of God*, 430ff.

the inquisitor refuse such a good and Catholic final request (one whose validity had been guaranteed by several popes)![20] The scene began to resemble
a riot, and there was open talk of murdering the inquisitor and burning down
the friars' home church of San Domenico.

The situation the next day was more restrained, but serious resentment
was fermenting against the inquisition. Bompietro was burned, and the inquisition turned its attention to those who had murmured against its sentence. These impending investigations did nothing to quell the issue. Leading
men of Bologna began to rise in open revolt against the inquisition and to
speak loosely of Bompietro's goodness and the corruption of the Dominican tribunal. The inquisitor quickly and deftly assessed the situation, arrested
the leading nobles, and made them submit publicly. This swift action un-
leashed a flood of self-denunciations. Dozens of people were impenanced
and fined, seeking to avoid further proceedings. This episode has much to
teach about conditions at the turn of the 1300s. First, the anger of the Bolognese populace was directed against the execution of Bompietro because
of his expressed sentiments of repentance. Hundreds of people reported having voiced sentiments of support for him, while almost none mentioned the
burning of the self-confessed Cathar who was executed alongside him. The
laity opposed heresy; that was not the issue. As Thompson correctly asserts,
the laity's definition of orthopraxis had been satisfied in Bompietro's case:
an apparently good man had asked for the sacraments, and he could not
be refused. The inquisitor, on the other hand, working more on experience and a clearly defined vision of orthodoxy, thought differently.

More to the point, the issue began to spread beyond the fact of Bompietro's unfortunate demise. Broader antimendicant issues began to make themselves apparent as people began to report on their neighbors. During the
tense period after the unpopular burning of Bompietro, neighbors denounced
one Oddo del fu Albertino Lasagnoli, a carpenter of Bologna, who apparently went about town denouncing the friars and generally making a nui-
sance of himself. He was well known as an inveterate opponent of the
mendicants and a casual blasphemer. Many probably reported him so that
further inquisitorial attention would not be focused on their own parishes.
In addition to his normal blasphemies, he heaped particular opprobrium on
St. Peter of Verona. Oddo, it seemed, was all swagger. Appearing before the
inquisition, Oddo confessed almost everything and received a stiff fine. One
of his neighbors claimed Oddo opined that the Dominicans "had made

---

20. E.g., Alexander IV had demanded that the sacraments be presented to heretics who asked for
them. After that point, God alone would judge their veracity.

one Peter Martyr a saint, while he was not and is not, and derided the said saint Peter Martyr, and made many slanderous statements about him."[21] Oddo was very open about all this. He admitted to everything he was accused of except, interestingly, defending the good name of Bompietro. Oddo flatly claimed (repeatedly and ad nauseam, considering the number of his neighbors who accused him) that he thought that Peter "was no saint . . . and that the friars made him a saint through bribery."[22] Oddo was a compulsive anticlericalist, and he equally derided all orders of the clergy.[23] In his own eyes and in those of his neighbors, Oddo was not a heretic; in fact, he expressed a lay position that was not uncommon. Unfortunately for him the development of Catholic doctrine that had taken place up to that point meant that from the perspective of the papacy and the inquisition, such sentiments had begun to smack of heresy. The decline of the mendicant orders by 1300 and the high-handed activities of the Dominican inquisitor provided fertile ground for a reaction against them. Oddo knew that by attacking the well-known Dominican saint, he was hitting the Dominicans where they were most sensitive. People derided saints because they knew it offended the friars: sometimes it was their only means of rebellion. Such casual blasphemies, not uncommon in any age of Christian history, had now taken on a new meaning. Such claims now began to be equated with heresy. The inquisition let Oddo off with a fine because his words, while offensive and intemperate, did not yet indicate pervasive heresy. Even the inflexible Guido could see that, but as time went on sentiments similar to Oddo's would elide more and more with a heretical attitude when viewed from an official perspective. Other inquisitors began to discern a much more common pattern. In 1301 the citizens of Albi decided to make a public demonstration of their dissatisfaction with the inquisition and the Dominicans. To this end they proceeded to deface the images of Peter and Dominic, which were graven on the city gates. This was an act of civic and lay defiance to be sure, but the fact that many took part and that it occurred in an area rife with Catharism was a matter of some concern for the church authorities.[24]

---

21. "Quod fecerunt unum Petrum martirem sanctum, cum non sit sanctus nec est, et derridet dictum sanctum Petrum matrirem et multam detrahit sibi." *Acta Sancti Officii Bononie ab anno 1291 usque ad annum 1310*, ed. Paolini and Orioli, 1:234.

22. "De beato petro martire, dicendo quod non erat sanctus . . . et quod fratres fecerant eum santum per baratariam." Ibid., 256–57.

23. "Locutus fuit male de domino papa et cardinalibus, clericis et fratribus et specialiter de beato Petro martire." Ibid., 256.

24. Bernard Gui, *De Fundatione*, 201–2.

✦ The Challenge of Spiritual Franciscanism

By the 1310s and 1320s the church was quite experienced in dealing with those who tried to create parallel communions of saints or who denied the sanctity of the papally canonized. One primary example was the Spiritual Franciscans, whose remote founder was Peter John Olivi (1248–98).[25] After his death, a small but rapidly growing cult began to develop in the Franciscan order and around Provence. The Spiritual party in the Franciscan order attempted to focus devotion on him as a visible symbol of their theological struggle and began to orchestrate a cult around his tomb. Some saw him as more than just a saint, filled as they were with Joachimite apocalypticism. When one Pierre Tort was investigated, he stated that "more had been revealed to Friar Petrus Iohannis than to any other doctor. . . . They considered him to be on a par with Augustine, Jerome, Gregory and Ambrose."[26] Many reported attending sermons on his feast day: his spiritual descendants were fostering a cult around him. Some reported mystical experiences at his tomb.[27] One, named Na Prous Boneta, went so far as to claim that Olivi was the incarnation of the Holy Spirit, but this was an uncommon assertion.[28] Surely the promotion of devotion to Olivi was common piety, the recognition and cultivation of the cult of a reputedly holy man, but in the case of the Spirituals more was at stake: the acceleration of the end times and the correct interpretation of the evangelical poverty of Christ and Francis. As the Spiritual Franciscans came under pressure in the early part of the fourteenth century, the inquisition in particular focused on their fomenting of Peter's cult.[29] One of the first to bring charges against the Olivi sect was Raymond of Fronsac, an inveterate opponent of the Spirituals. He listed among their three main errors that they venerated someone publicly who was not canonized as a saint. That this was recognized as one of their chief errors is very significant and dovetails with other inquisitorial

---

25. The best treatment of this movement is Burr, *Spiritual Franciscans*. See also Duvernoy and Manselli, *Spirituels et béguins du Midi*. A good treatment of the cult in comparison to Louis of Toulouse is Grieco, "Boy Bishop and 'Uncanonized Saint,'" 247–82.

26. Burr, *Spiritual Franciscans*, 225.

27. Ibid., 231.

28. For Prous Boneta, see ibid., 230–37; and May, "Confession of Na Prous Boneta," 4–30. The beginnings of her mystical experiences began on Peter Olivi's feast day before his tomb. The result of her experience could have been a case study for budding inquisitors of why one might be wary of unapproved saints.

29. For the Olivi cult in particular, see Biget, "Pierre Déjean Olieu," 277–308. For a sympathetic portrayal of the Beguins, see Burnham, *So Great a Light*.

investigations of popular cults.[30] In response, Olivi's partisans among the friars took special pains to emphasize that they did not treat him as a canonized saint (though it is clear that they accorded him all the benefit of a local cult, including recording miracles and preaching on his feast day). Lay devotees did not have time for such fine theological distinctions. One Marie de Serra made it very clear that she cared little for a papal canonization decree: "She said she had heard a public sermon in Narbonne on the feast of brother Peter Iohannis, that the said brother Peter Iohannis was their father and not a canonized saint. She said it didn't matter if he was canonized by men, since God had canonized him in life and in death as they said, and she believed it to be true."[31] Thus Olivi's cult must be understood on several different levels: that of the official church, that of the Spiritual promoters, and that of the unlettered lay devotees.

In any case, several of Olivi's teachings were formally condemned at the Council of Vienne in 1312. Quickly Olivi's followers became vehemently suspected of heresy, since Olivi's tomb was the visible center of the controversy. Here was an excellent way to measure praxis against orthodoxy, according to the mind of the church. Canonization could only come from the pope, and Olivi's teachings had been condemned. This meant that veneration of Olivi's remains were heretical twice over. In 1318 Peter's tomb was utterly destroyed, and there is no satisfactory account of what happened to the body.[32] Pope John XXII (r. 1316–34) had gone on the offensive. He deeply irritated the Spirituals of the Franciscan order when he declared that Christ held property, so much so that they in turn declared the pope a heretic. John's public response to this was to destroy the epicenter of Olivi's nascent cult. The Spirituals were chagrined at the loss of their cultic center and in response began to put forth the idea that the pope was the antichrist. For its part, the inquisition began a campaign to uproot the followers of Olivi and opened widespread investigations into their activities. One of the most common beliefs of the Spirituals and Beguins (as they came to be called by the inquisition) is that those who were persecuted by the church

30. "In XLV capitulo ponuntur abiurationes errorum de usu paupere et vulnere Christi laterali *et defunctis non canonizatis non festivandis facte per omnes conventus fere et omnes fratres totius provincie Provincie*" (emphasis added). Raymondus de Fronciacho, *Sol Ortus*, 3:17.

31. Burr, *Spiritual Franciscans*, 228. "Item dixit se audivisse in sermone publico in Narbona quando fiebat festum de fratre P. Johannis quod dictus frater P. Iohannis erat pater eorum et sanctus non canonizatus, et non opportebat quod per hominem canonizaretur, quia Deus canonizaverat eum in vita et morte ut dicebant, et ipsa credidit ista esse vera." In Limborch, *Historia inquisitionis*, 319.

32. Burr, *Spiritual Franciscans*, 211–12.

and killed were holy martyrs.[33] Once again we see the theme of the secret, small, and persecuted church.

The issue really boiled over in 1318 when four Spiritual Franciscans were burned on the orders of the Franciscan inquisitor in Marseilles. These four came to be venerated as saints by their immediate brethren. Pierre Tort, whom we have already met, declared: "Concerning those others, however, whom he thought had died as faithful catholics and glorious martyrs, he believed that once the carnal church was destroyed—which would be in a short time—the spiritual church to reign after its destruction would recognize that those Friars Minor and Beguins had been condemned unjustly by the carnal church, consider them glorious martyrs, and accord them a feast day just as there is now a feast of the martyrs of Christ."[34] A Beguine named Alarassis Biasse confirms in her deposition that she had met many Beguins who shared a similar perspective, though she herself is ambiguous regarding whether she believed it.[35] Other Spirituals who had been persecuted by the church generated similar devotion. One Pons Bautugat was mentioned by two luminaries of the spiritual tradition: Ubertino da Casale and Angelo Clareno. For refusing to repudiate Olivi's writings, he was cast into prison, where he suffered bitterly but died with a "beatific vision" on his face and with the "odor of sanctity."[36] Such saints merited devotion among the Beguins, who began to create their own, parallel communion of holy men and women to be venerated. In 1322 Bernard Gui, the famous Dominican inquisitor, sentenced a Beguin named Peter Dominic. Bernard learned that Peter had composed a litany that mixed Christian saints with around seventy Beguin ones.[37] Here was a significant conventionalization of religious heresy. The parallel church had produced new saints, skillfully woven into the historical fabric of the litanies so popular among the laity.

Devotion did not stop merely at pious invocation and remembrance. Lay practice began to bleed over into heterodoxy. The Beguins began to collect

---

33. Burr calls this "a belief that was common currency among the Beguins." Ibid., 217.

34. Confession of Pierre Tort, quoted ibid., 224.

35. Ibid., 229.

36. Ibid., 90.

37. "Laudans illos quos prius condempnatos per ecclesie judicium tanquam hereticos audiverat et sciebat eorumque nomina memoriter retinebat ausus est conscribere in letania quam manu propria scripsit inter sanctos . . . more ecclesiastico, letaniam dicendo nunc alte nunc demisse, dampnatorum hominum oraciones et suffragia pluribus vicibus . . . et letaniam ipsam un qua prefatorum dampnatorum hominum nomina manu sua conscripserat numer circiter septuaginta." Limborch, *Historia inquisitionis*, 385–86. Referenced in Burr, *Spiritual Franciscans*, 246.

relics from the burned Franciscans and from others who had died under suspicion by the church or who had been persecuted in some way. The inquisitorial records bear witness that people had been accumulating bits of body parts or instruments of execution and had begun to create a system of paraliturgical devotion toward them. These people would do honor to the relics, kiss them, and keep them in primitive reliquaries that the depositions call pyxes. The inquisition record is careful to note that the suspects kept these relics "as if they were the relics of saints canonized by the Church."[38] A woman named Esclarmonde was executed in 1322 in Lunel. Some members of her family took back bits of her body after the sentence was carried out. This might be dismissed as merely familial devotion, but Esclarmonde became known as a Beguine saint, and devotees carried her relics from place to place for veneration. The reason for this—adduced by a Martin de Saint-Antoine—was that she was not seen as a sinner and was a good person. For this reason (much like Bompietro in Bologna in 1299) she had been killed unjustly, and in the minds of medieval laypeople, that made her a martyr.[39] More remarkable was the testimony of Berenger Roque. He, too, took home a piece of flesh from the Lunel executions, because he considered that the victims were saints. He kept the relic on a table, but after a while it began to corrupt. Disappointed that the relic did not give evidence of sanctity, he discarded it in his garden. Burr humorously refers to this as a "do-it-yourself home canonization process," but it relates something significant.[40] The laity still considered that it had a role to play in the discernment of sanctity, while, increasingly the institutional church saw dangerous possibilities in this perspective.

This new practice of heretics venerating relics indicates two things. The first is that the Beguins and the Fraticelli (the name of the Spiritual Franciscans in Italy) were untouched by the anti-incarnational theology of the Cathars.[41] Their concerns were totally different. The second is that lay piety really had begun to cross the lines of orthodoxy. The veneration of relics

---

38. "Recognovit se habuisse et recipisse et tenuisse de ossibus illorum beguinorum qui fuerunt condempnati . . . et reposuisse in quadam pixide parva ad conservandum in archa Bernarde uxoris sue et scivisse quod Bernarda uxor sua habuerat de ossibus quorundam beguinorum combustorum a Petro hosptialis beguino et reposuerat in eadem pixide et cum aliis conservabat pro reliquiis, tanquam si essent reliquie sanctorum canonizatorum per ecclesiam." Confession of Raymond d'Antusan, Limborch, *Historia inquisitionis*, 310. These are significant, specific, and unexpected details in the records. Far from being a stereotyped presentation of heresy, they have a ring of truth, even through the mediated layers of inquisition accounts.

39. Burr, *Spiritual Franciscans*, 254. See also Vauchez, *Sainthood*, 146–58.

40. Burr, *Spiritual Franciscans*, 255. Cf. Manselli, *Spirtuali e beghini in Provenza*, 310–11.

41. Well, perhaps they had a "glancing blow," but that is a topic for another study.

and the expectation of miracles were too deeply ingrained in the Christian soul. Partisans of these groups had grown up in a world of immemorial orthopraxis. Perhaps the devotees of various strains of heresy simply became more receptive to such seemingly natural practices. On the other hand, it is also possible that some of the criticisms of the Beguins toward the institutional church did come from the Waldensians. Perhaps they, too, thought of themselves as a "remnant church." The problem for the church and the inquisition this time was distinct from the one they had faced from Cathar theology. What happened here was no denial of the cult of the saints; rather, it was the wholesale co-option of the doctrine itself into the service of heterodoxy. Here was an example of where piety could become dangerously misplaced in the eyes of institutional Catholicism, and it reinforced the outlook of church officials that such manifestations of devotion had to be carefully monitored and managed. In the case of Cathar anti-incarnationalism or the challenge of a parallel communion set up by Spirituals or Waldensians, the church responded strongly. In each instance the doctrine of the veracity of papal canonizations was the critical linchpin in the church's response. Since the cult of saints was so established in the church, there was little further development needed there; only the innovation of solemn papal canonization needed elaboration. In the case of the creation of alternate communions, the uniqueness and gravity of papal canonization had to be emphasized. The heresies of the central Middle Ages, then, affected the development of papal infallibility in canonization from two directions. What emerged was a doctrine with clarity and precision, which could be used in heresy investigations to buttress the claims of the mendicant orders, to underscore the authority of Rome, and to secure the presentation of holiness toward the whole church.

John XXII was not simply content to attack heretics through the inquisition. He had a multipronged strategy for dealing with the recalcitrant, and it was during John's pontificate that the long-maturing doctrine of papal infallibility in canonization finally bore its ultimate fruit. Trained in the Thomistic tradition and very dedicated to the teachings of the Dominicans, John had a systematic and legal mind that enabled him to approach a problem from a variety of angles. Confronted with the rebellion of the Spirituals of France and their Italian allies, the Fraticelli, John wasted no time in enforcing and expanding on the decrees of the Council of Vienne (1311–12). He mounted an attack on the dissidents that included both local inquisitions and papal pronouncements, the most significant of which was "Cum inter nonnullos," which declared formally that Christ and the apostles had owned common property.[42] With this the church defined the most tenaciously held doctrine of the Spirituals as heresy, and the inquisitors had one more question to ask the accused. Yet John was not finished. He employed his power of canonization in such a way as to underscore the theological pronouncements he had made and the policies that he pursued. Of his three canonizations, two directly related to the Spiritual conflict. John first saw the *causa* of the Franciscan prince-bishop Louis of Toulouse as an excellent example of Franciscan purity that was at the same time loyal to Rome.[43] Louis's life and cult had already received long and detailed inquiry before John became pope. He received the dossier at the opportune time to use the canonization to strike at the Spirituals. John had known Louis personally and (much like Gregory IX and Francis) used this personal knowledge as a guarantee of the saint's orthodoxy. The canonization of St. Louis of Toulouse was one of the first acts of his long pontificate: a testimony to the thoroughness of the canonization inquiry, the certitude of John himself, and the holiness of Louis.[44] During this ceremony the pope uttered the by-then-standard prayer that God might not permit him to err in the undertaking.[45] This was followed by the invocation of the *Veni Creator* hymn to the Holy Spirit, begging for inspiration. Following the solemn canonization—whose formula had been set well before this time—the pope introduced the liturgical usage of the saint within the *Confiteor* prayer and offered several orations beseeching the intercession of the newly canonized. John XXII had standardized, with the highest possible ceremonial and language, the practice of canonization for all future generations. Louis's canonization did not have quite the effect on the Spirituals that John had intended. While personally above reproach, Louis had, as a very young man, written a missive to Peter Olivi, but no evidence exists that they ever actually met or that Olivi's writings had much of an effect on Louis.[46] Further, Louis was personally very pious and dedicated to poverty while at the same time being a loyal son of the church.

---

42. It is also significant that when John defined this as a heresy, he drew his language from canonization bulls, following the example of his predecessor Boniface VIII (r. 1294–1303), who, when he chose to define something as solemnly as he possibly could in his bull "Unam Sanctam," chose language that aped that of canonization announcements, i.e., "Declaramus, dicimus, definimus, et pronuntiamus . . ."

43. A still useful biography of Louis can be found in Toynbee, *Saint Louis of Toulouse*.

44. John XXII, "Sol oriens mundo" [April 7, 1317], Fontanini, 122–26.

45. After this point the prayer features in the papal *Ordo Romanus*. As we have seen, Hostiensis referred to a similar prayer in the 1270s, though it is not clear if it was yet an established insertion. See chap. 3, n34. It does not seem a casual insertion (and the identical prayer is still used today). Toynbee, *Saint Louis of Toulouse*, 204.

46. Toynbee, *Saint Louis of Toulouse*, 217–18, offers the suggestion that the two were friends but provides no evidence for this whatsoever. Burr, *Spiritual Franciscans*, 74, seems to dismiss the possibility.

In a certain sense, if everyone in the Franciscan order had behaved like Louis, there probably would never had been a schism. Because of Louis's personal poverty, the Spirituals were content enough with the canonization, choosing to emphasize those characteristics rather than seeing him through the pope's preferred lens of obedience. John would have to try again.

The Spirituals would not have to wait long to encounter a saint whom they especially despised. For a long time John had been devoted to the teachings of Thomas Aquinas; we still have manuscripts of the *Summa Theologiae* from Avignon with John's personal glosses.[47] John was determined to canonize the Dominican professor and in so doing to extend a halo of approval over his teachings. Unfortunately Thomas was a particular irritation to the Spirituals, something of which John was well aware by the year of his canonization, 1323. Unlike John's glorification of Louis, Thomas's elevation would illustrate the conflict in stark terms. John was careful to frame his first sallies against the Spirituals in 1317 using Thomas's own arguments. The Dominican professor, taking the standard line of his order, had stressed that the vow of obedience was superior to the vows of poverty and chastity, since the latter merely dealt with bodily issues while the obedience offered to God concerned the will itself.[48] Because of John's endorsement of Thomas's reasoning, throughout the Spiritual conflict the Dominican came to be regarded with John XXII as a traitor to evangelical life and one of the most prominent threats to the Spiritual path. When John canonized Thomas in 1323, the pope put an exclamation point on his earlier rulings. It was one of the most solemn canonization bulls to date, in which he inserted the liturgical invocation of the Trinity, "in the name of the Father, and of the Son, and of the Holy Spirit," in the midst of already elevated and solemn canonization language.[49] John wanted no mistake made: Thomas was a saint in heaven, and his teaching on poverty was correct. While little reference was made to Thomas's intellectual work (for a canonization, in the deep tradition of the church, was still about life and miracles), yet Thomas's teachings on poverty were in the air. John XXII himself gave a consistory sermon that celebrated Thomas's balanced approach to poverty. In eliding his thought with Thomas's, he declared that holding property in common is the true definition of the apostolic life.[50] In one of the most aggressive examples yet, orthodoxy and

---

47. Dondaine, "La Collection des oeuvres de saint Thomas," 127–28.

48. For Thomas's argument, see *Summa Theologiae* II–II, q. 186, a. 8.

49. John XXII, "Redemptionem misit Dominus" [July 18, 1323], Fontanini, 135–41.

50. "Ipse Dominus Papa predicavit . . . et mirabiles comendationes proposuit de Predicatorum ordine quam de sancto. Inter cetera, dixit quod iste sanctus in ordine sancto Predicatorum gessit vitam apostolicam, quum ordo nichil habet in proprio [et] in speciali, licet habeat in commune, addens 'et

orthopraxis had been heavily wedded in the canonization of the Angelic Doctor.

The Spirituals knew what was at stake and immediately began to accuse both Pope John and Thomas of being traitors to the Gospel. One Spiritual, Ubertino da Gubbio, confessed that he considered Thomas a heretic because he advanced the idea that poverty was a means to holiness and not an end in itself.[51] The problem became compounded when that same pope canonized Thomas. This turn of events enraged the Spirituals, for whom the canonization was an example of a heretic canonizing a heretic. The same Ubertino confessed that Thomas was not truly canonized and that God would permit no miracles by his intercession. Michele da Calco, a Spiritual leader, declared as much when he pronounced the canonization null and void.[52] Spiritual rhetoric heated up to a point where the Spirituals denounced previous saints en masse, especially those created since Gregory IX, the pope who had declared that Francis's last testament was not legally binding. The canonization of Thomas, then, in 1323 was another turning point. Heretics challenged both the authority of the pope and the sanctity of the subject and combined them into a unified critique of the canonization itself. The always colorful Na Prous Boneta confirmed that such sentiments had filtered down to the lay Beguins and Beguines. For her, Thomas Aquinas was Cain to Peter Olivi's Abel. This was because Thomas had attacked Olivi's ideas and so spiritually slew him (Prous Boneta was always a little hazy on chronology). In her mind John XXII and Thomas were of a piece, a heretic antichrist canonizing another heresiarch.[53] The Spirituals were eventually defeated, and Thomas was established as a canonized saint, further causing the church to insist on the prerogative of infallibility in saint creation.

☛ The Rearguard of Heresy

During the twilight of Catharism, fewer and fewer accounts of its particular beliefs and practices come down to us. What we are forced to do is to listen to the inquisitors, as they describe what remained of Catharism and the various other scattered heresies of the period. In the acts of the inquisition of

---

hanc vitam apostolicam reputamus.'" Anonymous account, *Fontes vitae S. Thomae Aquinatis*, 2:513–14.

51. Douie, *Heresy of the Fraticelli*, 188.

52. D'Alatri, *Eretici e inquisitori*, 36n57.

53. See Burr, *Spiritual Franciscans*, 231.

Carcassonne of 1308–9 (held just ten years after the anti-inquisitional reaction), we find, among the other recognized aspects of Cathar belief, "that blessed Francis or any other saint did no miracles at all."[54] Inquisitors themselves began to force the issue in their interrogations. Whereas earlier they asked simple questions about general topics, such as prayers for the saints or observance of feasts in general, now they began to get specific. Manuals now told them to ask particularly "whether Saint Dominic of the Friars Preachers and Saint Peter Martyr, and thus of other saints, whether they really were saints."[55] No questions about philosophy and theology here; instead, inquisitors got to the heart of the matter. This question implied a logical inference. The pope canonized Peter. The pope is infallible in canonization. Therefore Peter is in heaven. Does a suspect deny that Peter is in glory? Then he is a heretic. This is the articulation of a new heresy, drawn from both a developing doctrine and the historical contingencies generated by antiheretical saints. The doctrine of papal canonization had crystallized in its precision during the thirteenth century. To deny that a saint who had been solemnly canonized by the papacy is in heaven was to say that the pope and the Roman church had erred on a matter of doctrine. This was unacceptable. Usually such doctrinal definitions were not a problem. Benedict XII's determination of the immediacy of the Beatific Vision occasioned no protest (though it was indirectly addressed at the doctrine of soul sleep, espoused by some medieval heretics).[56] What we have witnessed here is the birth of a new heresy, identified but not created by the institutional church. Where it came from was not merely an assertion of power over marginalized subgroups; it proceeded from deep and mature reflection on the very practices of Christianity themselves. While this interpretation is assuredly open to debate, in reality the church did not just invent any of its doctrines; all of them matured and were defined in this way. While later such dogmas may have been used to enhance authority and to maintain power, they were not developed for those reasons.

Bernard Gui represents the final chapter in this development, so we will look at his analysis of the situation in his *Practica Inquisitionis*. He represents the culmination of doctrinal development, having completed his text around 1324, and his work is the summation of its application to actual lived religion

---

54. Döllinger, 2:40.

55. Questions to be posed to suspected Albanensees, ibid., 1:319. Later in the same manual Waldensians were to be directly asked about St. Sylvester. Similarly, Cathars were to be asked about John the Baptist.

56. While most trace the "soul sleep" doctrine to Calvin and the Anabaptist tradition, it is clear that they had some intellectual antecedents among the heretics of the late medieval world.

as well as a witness to heretical responses. His perspective, then, is representative of the normative attitude of the institutional church, and so his is a weighty indicative voice. Gui neatly summarizes and systematizes the inquisitorial practice and observations of belief of the century previous to his. He leaves us with a schema of heretical beliefs that are born from that experience as well as his own personal efforts as an inquisitor on the ground. He sums up Waldensian belief as follows:

> Also they say that there are no true miracles in the Church performed by the merits and prayers of the saints, because not one of them ever performed any miracle. Further, they say secretly that the saints in heaven do not hear the prayers of the faithful, neither do they care about the cult whereby they are honored on earth, and they say that the saints do not pray for us and so do not implore their suffrages. Wherefore they spurn the feasts wherein we celebrate the saints as well as avoiding other actions by which we honor and venerate them, and on feast days, when they are able to, they do manual labor. These three things they do not indifferently tell to all, but only to those perfected within their sect, namely of the miracles of the saints, that they are not true, and refusing to beg the help of their suffrages, and of not celebrating holy days outside of Sunday and the feasts of the blessed Virgin Mary, though some add those of the apostles and evangelists.[57]

Here we see the generally standard position of the Waldensians, repeated in confessions wherever they were haled before the inquisition. The prayers and invocations of the saints are nonscriptural, and they are to be rejected with all their attendant solemnities. In spite of that, there is a suggestion that there was some pressure to social conformity in the community, for given the popularity of the cult of the saints, they are very careful about whom to tell this to, and they find it difficult to avoid the celebration of such feasts in most places. Theirs was a wholesale rejection of the communion of the saints, as it had developed both in theology and in lived religion. Such a rejection had necessitated the refinement of the dogmas surrounding those issues in the previous century and a half.

As for the Cathars, they were close to being extinct by the time Bernard was writing. While he does not break them down into their component sects, as someone such as Rainerio Sacconi did, Bernard is able to distill the heart of the Cathar belief. "They deny the incarnation of the Lord Jesus Christ

---

57. Trans. from Bernard Gui, *Practica inquisitionis hereticae pravitatis*, 248; *SOP* 1.630.

through Mary, ever virgin."[58] All Cathar practices can be traced from this root belief rather than from their theoretical dualism. While Bernard does not provide any extended discussion of their attitude toward the cult of the saints, such things can be inferred by his description of their rejection of the veneration of the cross, in their denial of the authority of the Roman church, and about their exclusive salvation doctrines. All of those things, taken together, were a direct attack on the church's supervision of the cult of the saints. This anti-incarnational perspective was the second threat to the doctrine of the communion of saints and of canonization faced by the church.

The third and final threat—and of far more moment to Bernard—was the issue of the Beguins and the Fraticelli. He accurately sums up of the beliefs of these groups, many of which he had personally interrogated. "Those men [the four Franciscans executed in 1318] were not heretics, but Catholics, glorious martyrs whose prayers and good offices they entreat. . . . These men have no less merit in God's eyes than the martyr saints, Laurence and Vincent."[59] Bernard knew precisely how to investigate such claims. First he instructs inquisitors to ask whether any suspects believed that any executed Beguins were "Catholics and holy martyrs." This line of questioning was to be followed by the clincher: did the suspects have any relics of such "martyrs?" Did the suspect venerate them? Where had the suspect acquired them? Here was the third and final threat to the church's doctrine and practice. The Beguins did not deny the incarnation, nor did they dispute the particular doctrine of the communion of saints. Rather, they were attempting to co-opt the doctrine and turn it to their own purposes. In a certain sense the Beguins were the last of the lay traditionalists: the ones who were able to discern holiness and spontaneously recognize and venerate sanctity, independent of church approbation.[60] This was the last group that the church had to deal with.

We can see that it was the convergence of three heterodox challenges that forced the church to clarify what exactly it meant by the glorification and canonization of saints. First, it had to respond to the metathreat posed by theoretical Catharism, denying the goodness of the material world and the reality of the Incarnation, not to mention the cascade of Catholic religious

---

58. Ibid., 238.

59. "Dicunt ipsos non fuisse hereticos, set catholicos et esse martires gloriosos, ipsorumque implorant orationes et suffragia apud deum quam sanctos Laurentium et Vincentium martires." Ibid., 270.

60. While spontaneous recognition of sanctity remains a key aspect of Catholic doctrine, it is accompanied by and crowned with official church participation at every moment of the process. No more could there be celebration of sanctity without at least the indirect participation of the official church.

practices that flowed from those teachings. Second, it had to deal with the more particularized contentions of Waldensianism, which challenged the doctrine and practices of the communion of saints. Finally, it had to confront lived lay religion, so long accustomed to the spontaneous and local recognition of holiness and particularly manifested in the Spiritual Franciscan movement and its branches. In the end the church destroyed Catharism, marginalized the Waldensian position, and successfully placed a supervisory framework over lay piety. Here the doctrines of canonization and saint veneration touched the very core of the Christian faith. In saints the abstract doctrines of the creed became personalized. Saints, as it were, became living icons of the dogmas of Christianity. Taken in this sense, one could not easily dismiss them. To deny a saint was to deny the Christian faith. It was heresy. Though many heretics in the period challenged the doctrine, the denial of infallibility in these cases came to be particularly imputed to the Fraticelli, since by the end of the fourteenth century Nicholas of Eymerich lists it as the sixteenth of their particular heresies.[61] Papal infallibility in canonization had become cemented as a doctrine in the Catholic Church, and its denial had become heresy.

✏ The Church Closes Ranks

I have argued that the theories of Thomas and Bonaventure evolved in the context of the controversy over the mendicant saints. Their thoughts tended to buttress claims of papal infallibility corresponding roughly with the quickly developing practices of the Roman curia, but it appeared now that practice itself was outpacing theory. Papally created saints were being defended with enthusiasm, while the papal bulls and canonization liturgies had become exceptionally solemn. Still, these things were occurring while theologians and canonists were still considering the question. Around the year 1300 Augustinus Triumphus (d. 1328), usually a spirited advocate of papal claims, made only a halfhearted attempt to claim infallibility in canonization. Augustinus does not accept Thomas's three ways of judging—he perhaps did not know Quodlibet IX—and falls back on the canonists' two:

> Since it was said to Peter by Christ in Luke 22 "I have prayed for you Peter, that your faith might not fail" . . . therefore the faith of the successor of Peter is not able to fail. . . . Therefore the Pope in canoniz-

---

61. Nicholas Eymerich, *Directorium Inquisitorum*, 298, 302.

ing according to the present justice cannot err, since he believes a man to be a saint, so that he receives information which is sent and approved by him. As Blessed Augustine says in his letter to Abbot Severus . . . he who believes, what he speaks, even if he might speak falsely, speaks faithfully; he who does not believe those things he speaks, even if he speaks truly, speaks unfaithfully. Therefore as much as the Pope does not endorse the truth in canonizing or in approving some saint, from which he faithfully and truly approves according to the information given to him, he does not err.[62]

Augustinus begins with the standard proof text of the indefectibility of Peter's faith. Though it seems that at first he is going to reinforce the idea of infallibility, in reality he does nothing of the kind. He does not articulate any theology of canonization. Rather he is simply protecting the reputation and honor of the pope. The bulk of Augustinus's article is dedicated to showing that human testimony is enough for the pope to judge according to "present justice." The pope believes people who tell him a man is holy, so he canonizes on that basis, and so he believes what he is doing is true. Whether or not it is true in reality is quite another matter, one that Augustinus ignores.[63] It seems as if the Augustinian friar has missed the point on this. In his desire to answer those who impugn the honor of the pope, he has forgotten the question. Tierney is quite right in this instance: Augustinus Triumphus is concerned with the power of the pope, that is, with his sovereignty rather than with his infallibility. In the end he gives little support to formal infallibility, giving credence to Brian Tierney's claim that infallibility was a burden

---

62. "Quia dictus est Petro a Christo, Lucam 22, ego rogavi pro te Petre: ut non deficiat fides tua. . . . Fides ergo pape successoris Petri: non potest deficere. . . . Papa ergo canonizando aliquem secundum praesentem iustitiam non errat, quia sic credit eum sanctum esse, ut informationem recipit secundum allegata et probata sibi. Dicit autem Divus Augustinus in quadam epistola ad Palmatium commendantem eum de sanctitate et sciencia. Qui enim sic credit, ut loquitur, etiam si falsa loquatur, fideliter loquitur; qui autem non credit, quae loquitur, etiam si vera loquatur, infideliter loquitur. Quantumcumque igitur Papa non vera approbet canonizando vel approbando aliquem santum, ex quo fideliter et vere approbat secundum informationem sibi factam, non errat." Augustinus Triumphus, *Summa de Potestate Ecclesiae*, 58ᵛ. Wetzstein analyzes Augustinus's arguments in id., *Heilige vor Gericht*, 276–82.

63. Benedict XIV perceptively notes that while this argument was used by the tradition in ascribing infallibility of the pope, actually it does not. Perhaps the most salient thing was that the language of infallibility was in the air, and Augustinus's introduction of his argument as such indicates that he is a proponent of it and was received as such by subsequent thinkers. See Lambertini, vol. 1, c. 43, n3. "Huius scilicet gravissimi auctoris sententia, etsi prima facie favorabilis videatur infallibilitati Romani pontificis in canonizatione, revera tamen talis non est: cum ex ea ad summum deservum sanctorum fastis adscribit; cum quo utique stare potest, ut definiat de eo quod verum non est, ideoque materialiter mentiatur."

that the popes would rather have avoided. In reality it is simply a burden that Augustinus would rather have avoided.

It was not only theologians who stuck to the older teaching but canonists too. The Decretalist tradition continued the views of Innocent IV and Hostiensis, when Johannes Andreae substantially backed up their opinion in the first half of the 1300s. He is mostly content to repeat Hostiensis. "And if the Church might err in canonization (which is not to be believed, although it may happen, *De sent. Excomm. A Nobis*), nevertheless prayers in honor of such as these are acceptable and pleasing. Through the faith of Christ all are made clean. . . . And if it might be that the truth of canonization fails, the faith does not fail."[64] When Johannes commented on the *Liber Extra*, however, he was content to give an account of the ordinary process involved in a canonization. At the end he writes of the liturgical prayer that "God will not permit them [the Roman church] to err in this business."[65] One must ask, then, what was the motive force behind a doctrine that by the fifteenth century would become the common opinion of theologians down to the present day? It came from only one direction: the Dominican order.

Bonaventure had implicitly (and somewhat cavalierly) defended the pope's prerogative of infallibility in canonization, though by the time of the controversy of the Fraticelli, Franciscan thought had quieted significantly about his position.[66] It was rather the Dominicans who advanced the doctrine. The theologians of the Friars Preachers had been solidly behind Thomas's position since he articulated it. Thomas's successor in the Dominican regency at Paris, Hannibaldus di Hannibaldis, wrote a quodlibet on whether all canonized saints were in heaven. While we unfortunately do not have the content of this quodlibet, the question was in the air.[67] It was John of Naples, O.P. (d. 1336), who set the tone for the rest of the tradition. John had been one of the promoters of Thomas's cause at the curia, so he was intimately invested in the question. In his quodlibetal question 2, John deals with infallibility in canonization at length. Strangely, though, John ignores Thomas's

---

64. "Et si in ecclesia erraret (quod non est credendum licet accidere possit, *De Sent. Excomm. A Nobis*) nihilominus preces in honorem talis acceptae et grate sunt. Per fidem Christi omnia purgantur. . . . Et esto quod veritas canonizationis deficiat, non deficit fides." Giovanni d'Andrea (Johannes Andreae), *Novella super VI. Decretalium*, 3.22, *De reliquiis*. Cited from Schenk, *Die Unfehlbarkeit des Papstes*, 9n17.

65. "Deus non permittat eos errare in hoc negotio." Giovanni d'Andrea (Johannes Andreae), *In Tertium Decretalium Librum Novella Commentaria*, 230.

66. As Schenk notes, it was only in the seventeenth century that Bonaventure's position came to be well known.

67. Glorieux, *La littérature quodlibétique*, 2:129–30, Paris: Bibliothèque Nationale MS Lat. 13466, fos. 127[c-d].

solution and adopts the twofold manner of judgment used by the canonists. After speaking of human judgment concerning things such as benefices, promotions, and judicial sentences, whereby all agree that the pope can err, John continues:

> There are other things that the Pope does, which pertain to the Universal Church or to the Faith—those are determinations and declarations, which deal with articles of faith and the sacraments of the Church and all things contained in sacred Scripture, even about good morals— those are the statutes, decrees, and decretals, and in such it is said, that although absolutely, thinking about only the persons of the Popes and Cardinals, the Pope with them is able to err, nevertheless accounting for Divine providence, it is to be believed that the Pope cannot err, since Christ prayed for the Church in Luke 22, "I have prayed for you Peter, that your faith may not fail," and to say that in any matter the Pope is able to err, is heretical. Thomas says as much in Quodlibet 9.[68]

But Thomas does not say as much; Thomas says much more. John is not correctly relaying Thomas's sophisticated position but rather embraces Bonaventure's heavy-handed one. John's argument does not employ the elegant solution of the three ways of judging that Thomas developed, nor does he even really employ the canonists' two ways. Instead he makes a distinction between the pope and cardinals, and the pope alone (*ex sese et non ex consensu ecclesiae*, apparently). He makes really no clear argument to back this assertion up. It is not a position based on rational assessment but rather one that uses the papal blank check of Luke 22:32, which Augustinus appealed to and then backed away from. John apparently had no such reservations. Schenk traces the ironic history of this minor Dominican thinker in his book. St. Antoninus (1389–1459), Castellanus (fl. 1520), and Sylvester Prieras (fl. 1510) all cite John's quodlibet as evidence of infallibility in canonization, and all claim that John accurately relays Thomas's teaching. The considerable irony will be that the Dominicans adopted Bonaventure's ambitious but relatively underdeveloped position and not Thomas's sophisticated

---

68. "Quaedam alia sunt, quae facit Papa, pertinencia ad statum universalem totius Ecclesiae, vel quantum ad fidem—ut sunt determinationes et declarationes, quae spectant ad fidem et articulos et Ecclesiae sacramenta et omnia alia contenta in sacra Scriptura, sive quantum ad bonos mores— ut sunt statuta, decreta, et decretales, et in talibus dicendum est, quod licet absolute, pensatis solis personis Papae et Cardinalium, Papa cum ipsis potest errare, supposita tamen divina providentia, credendum est, papam errare non posse, quia Christus oravit pro Ecclesia, Luc. 22: Ego pro te rogavi, Petre, ut non deficiat fides tua, et dicere quod in huiusmodi Papa errare possit, esse haereticum. Id. in Thomas in quodlibeto." John of Naples, "Quodlibet 2"; cited from Schenk, *Die Unfehlbarkeit des Papstes*, 15.

one (though Thomas's insistence on pious belief over dogma will remain in Dominican thought).

A new doctrine had been discerned. Over the course of hundreds of years the church reflected on its own praxis, was challenged by dissident voices, and meditated deeply on the meanings of the material world, the communion of saints, the sense of the faithful, and the riches of the liturgy. In the end, what was achieved was a logical outworking of the Christian doctrine of the saints and of ecclesial ordering. The church had detected anti-incarnationalism among the Cathars and had defeated it. Likewise it rejected the idea of parallel communion of saints desired by the Beguins and Fraticelli. The church and her saints had emerged from the battle successfully, and the pantheon of orthodox holy men and women held the field, in a new form certainly but one deeply connected with the past. The papacy accrued immense prestige and significant power because of the struggle. Driven into hiding but not defeated were the Waldensians. Their critique of the doctrine of the communion would dissipate but not disappear. Within several hundred years, their teachings would arise again. The Middle Ages had seen the conflict fought on multiple fronts, and the orthodox saints, whose cults were supervised by the institutional church, had prevailed. During the Reformation the battle would recommence. The "War between the Saints" was over. The "War against the Saints" was about to begin.

Conclusion

In May of 2013 I had the good fortune of being present for the canonization of hundreds of saints by Pope Francis. Once again, I was forcefully struck by both the solemnity of the canonization language and the historical depth behind it. For something to remain that stable for nearly eight hundred years is surely extraordinary. It has been my intention in this book to trace how and why the doctrine of papal canonization developed in the church and to examine the manner in which it came to be considered an infallible pronouncement. In so doing I have hoped to do several things. In the first place I wanted to shift the debate about infallibility away from the later poverty controversies and move it back into the period of the debates about the place of the mendicants in the wider church. Further, I have tried to indicate how papal infallibility in canonization was a response to events on the ground. In responding to heresies, the papacy had to contend with generalized anti-incarnational sentiment, though as time went on these attacks became increasingly focused. In promoting the mendicant orders and in defending their saints, the popes were making radical new claims about the nature both of sanctity and of the papal office. Yet it was not a creation ex nihilo. The tools for the refinement of the doctrine had their roots in early Christianity and in the lived orthopraxis of the Christian church. The popes innovated, certainly, but they innovated in continuity with the past, uniting themselves to one of the strongest living streams of

lay piety to defeat heresy, safeguard the orthodoxy of the church, and solidify their own position as the Vicars of Christ. Finally I wanted to bring
together intellectual, social, and cultural history in such a way as to make
them mutually revealing. By situating intellectual developments against
actions by the mendicants, the laity, and various heretics, I hoped to throw light
on the evolution of some of the central doctrines of the Catholic Church.
The further history of that evolution is also exceptionally interesting, and a
brief overview is merited here.

Having defeated the heretics, the papacy clarified orthodox doctrine regarding saints, and the Dominicans promoted it. The Preachers did this for
a number of reasons. First, they wanted to defend the authenticity of their
saints, who had been so directly assaulted in their first century of existence.
Second, they wanted to maintain the prestige of the papacy that had done so
much for them. Third, they saw it as a correct theological deduction, necessary to a full appropriation of Thomas's thought. Fourth, they were forced
to defend and articulate the doctrine because of continual harassment on
the ground, both from the laity and from the few remaining heretics. In this
sense the doctrine had a certain "trickle-up" effect, for intellectual development flowed from practical experiences in everyday preaching and inquisitional experience. They knew that their saints were under attack. They
knew that people echoed the eloquent Waldensian deacon Raymond de la
Costa, who in 1319 stated "that he did not believe anyone was a saint—even
if the Roman Church might have canonized him—unless that one believed
the faith of his church and underwent persecution by them [the Roman
church]."[1]

Though the Dominicans (or perhaps the Bonaventurians) eventually triumphed, it was not at all clear that the rest of the church always shared their
sentiments. The developing doctrine did not prevent Bridget of Sweden from
attacking St. Eric at the end of the fourteenth century. She did not know
where he was, but it certainly was not heaven.[2] Bridget herself was canonized after her death, and if canonized saints could not be expected to believe
it, who could? Certainly not the Piedmontese Waldensian, Giacomo Risto-

---

1. "Quod non credit aliquem fuisse sanctum, licet ecclesia Romana eum canonizasset pro sancto,
qui non crederet illud, quod eorum ecclesia credit, et qui eos persequtus [*sic*] fuisset." Errors of
Raymundus da Costa, Waldensian Deacon, in *Le Registre d'inquisition de Jacques Fournier*, ed. Duvernoy, 1:108. The error imputed to Raymond agrees with his own comments in his later depositions,
though earlier, on p. 66, he maintained that it truly was the pope's sole right to canonize. By that
time, however, Fournier had teased out more explicit descriptions from Raymond.

2. Bridget of Sweden, *Revelaciones*, II, cited from Vauchez, *Sainthood*, 172n51. It is also important to
note that Eric never did receive formal, papal canonization, though his cult was tolerated and even
encouraged.

lassio di Carmagnola. In 1395 he declared to the inquisition that Peter of Verona was no saint and was damned, since Peter had persecuted the servants of Christ.[3] Peter became an object of heretical hatred twice over, once when the pope made him an inquisitor and again when the pope canonized him. But Peter was the axis of the development, for in his cult one sees both the crystallization of opposition and the orthodox doctrine coming into focus. The formation of this doctrine was the result of a dialogic process, which had its roots in the papal reserve, took its material from the debate against heterodox beliefs, had its catalyst in the canonizations of the mendicants, and found its end result in the articulation of a new heresy—a heresy whose conditions the church itself discerned. Theology and practice fed each other in this case, two streams that ultimately crossed to make a turbulent doctrinal maelstrom. Conventionalization of belief took place on both sides. The papal reserve became the defense of particular saints on the ground, while theoretical heterodoxies about the communion of saints turned into parallel hierarchies and vicious denunciations of papal and mendicant models of holiness.

By the fifteenth century the doctrine had coalesced. John de Torquemada (Johannes de Turrecremata, 1388–1468), the powerful Dominican cardinal and author of one of the first formal ecclesiological summae, was clear that the pope was absolutely infallible in canonization. Ironically the specific teaching became less important in the Reformation debates, as the reformers wanted to attack the whole Catholic system of veneration and intercession rather than critiquing individual papal canonizations. Nonetheless, papal infallibility in canonization became the most commonly accepted of teachings. Max Schenk has an impressive list of theologians who accepted the doctrine of infallibility. Most accepted it unconditionally, including Prospero Lambertini, who became Pope Benedict XIV (r. 1740–58) and who outlines his discussion of infallibility in volume one of his exhaustive work on the canonization of saints. Others, following St. Thomas, accept infallibility as a pious belief but maintain that to reject a canonized saint is heresy. At the time Schenk wrote in 1965, no Catholic thinker of stature had denied infallibility to the pope in canonization since the 1600s. The teaching of the canonists, with their circumspection regarding human testimony, was entirely dispensed with after Johannes Andreae (d. 1348), and the theological perspective came to dominate.

The popes themselves began to take this infallibility for granted. Significantly, in his canonization of St. Bonaventure in 1482, Sixtus IV declared,

3. Merlo, "S. Pietro Martire," 473–74.

"We are confident that in this canonization God does not permit us to err."[4] He had perhaps been reading Bonaventure's *opera*. Sixtus V (r. 1585–90), in his allocution before the canonization of St. Didacus, delivered a long excursus about how the Roman pontiff was infallible in the canonization of saints. Clement VIII, in his 1594 canonization of St. Hyacinth, taught that the numerous invocations of the Holy Spirit in the act of canonization demonstrated that the church could not commit any error.[5] The popes clearly believed that they were exercising personal infallibility in their decrees of canonization.

Given the foregoing work, one can see where they might have acquired this idea. For a millennium, the papacy and episcopate had developed and tended the ancient cults of the saints. This encouraged meditation on what the church did and what it ought to be doing regarding the veneration of its holy ones. In addition, the church had been struggling against dualism since its very foundation. The discovery of medieval dualisms provoked a vigorous defense of the goodness of the material world and of the Incarnation of God. These responses created new theological considerations and led to improved bureaucratic and legal processes. A desire to exercise solicitude and protection over the Christian people ushered in the creation of a machinery of investigation. The challenge of heresy brought precision, and the church's response was sharpened by the encounter with heterodoxy. The power to shape the direction of holiness for the Christian world was also at stake, as the universalizing claims of Rome and the mendicant orders eventually triumphed over local, more homely forms of cultic devotion. The age saw one of the most successful of the Roman Catholic Church's efforts at defending and promoting holiness as well as marking the ascendancy of the papacy, law, and orthodoxy over the Christian world. So successful was this transformation that it remains almost entirely unchanged in the present day. The principles and practices forged in medieval combat still serve in the creation and recognition of holiness. Most pertinent to this work, though, the ground for the eventual definition of the personal infallibility of the pope was tilled and planted during this period. The doctrine did not have its origins, then, in the debate over the binding force of papal decrees in the Spiritual Franciscan controversy. Rather, it transpired at the core of the Catholic faith itself: in the struggle over the bodies and at the tombs of its saints,

---

4. "Confidentes, quod in hac canonizatione non permittat nos Deus errare." Cf. Lambertini, vol. 1, chap. 43, n2.

5. For these cases, see Keida, "Infallibility of the Pope," 408–9.

which were doorways between heaven and earth, present testimonies of the goodness of the material world and of the pervasiveness of the Incarnation, and monuments to the continuity of the church with its own tradition. In maintaining all these things, the Roman church, in new ways and with new forms, sought to keep that faith "once for all delivered to the saints."

☙ APPENDIX

Thomas Aquinas, Quodlibet IX, q. 8

☙ Title 1

Whether all saints who are canonized by the Church are in glory or whether some are in hell.

☙ Title 2

And it seems that some are able to be in hell among those who are canonized by the Church.

☙ Argument 1

No one is able to be certain about the condition of anyone, as one is of himself, "For who among men knows the things of a man save the spirit of man which is in him?" as 1 Corinthians 2:11 has it. But man is not able to be certain about his own condition, as to whether he be in a state of salvation for as Sirach 9:1 says, "Love from hatred man cannot tell." Therefore how much less can the Pope know, therefore he is able to err in canonization.

✒ Argument 2

Furthermore, whoever relies upon a fallible medium in judging is able to err. But the church in canonizing saints relies upon human testimony, when she inquires of witnesses regarding life and miracles. Therefore, since the testimony of humans may be fallible, it seems that the church is able to err in canonizing saints.

✒ Contra 1

On the contrary, in the church there is not able to be a damnable error. But it would be a damnable error if she would venerate a saint who was a sinner, because anyone knowing their sin might believe the church to be false and if this were to happen, they might be led into error. Therefore the church is not able to err in such things.

✒ Contra 2

Further, Augustine says in a letter to Jerome that if there is admitted to be any lie in canonical scripture our faith will waver, since it depends on canonical scripture. But we are bound to believe that which is in holy scripture, so also that which is commonly determined by the church; wherefore heretics are judged who believe things contrary to the determinations of the Councils. Therefore the universal judgment of the church is not able to err, and thus the same result as above.

✒ Response

It must be said, that something can be judged to be possible when considered in itself, which in relation to something outside itself is found to be impossible. Therefore I say that the judgment of those who rule the church is able to err in anything, if they are considered in their persons. If, in truth, divine providence is considered—by which the Holy Spirit directs his Church so that she might not err, as He Himself promised in John 10, that the Spirit was coming to teach them all truth, namely about those things necessary for salvation—then it is certain that it is impossible for the judgment of the universal church to err in those things which pertain to the faith. Wherefore how much more certain is the determination of the Pope, to whom it pertains to pronounce on faith, than in the wisdom of any other man in their scriptural opinions; it is read when Caiaphas—though wicked— nevertheless prophesied because he was high priest, though he did not know it (that is, he did not know it himself) as John 11:51 has it. Truly in other determinations which pertain to particular facts, as is done with property, or crimes, or other such things, it is possible for the church to err on account of false testimony. But truly the canonization of saints is between these two things. Since the honor we pay the saints is in a certain way a profession of faith, i.e., a belief in the glory of the Saints, we must piously believe that in this matter also the judgment of the Church is not liable to error.

✎ Ad 1

To the first is therefore to be said, that the Pontiff—to whom it belongs to canonize saints—is able to certify the condition of any by means of an inquiry into their life and by witnesses to their miracles; and especially by the inspiration of the Holy Spirit, who searches all things, even unto the profundity of God.

✎ Ad 2

To the second is to be said, that Divine Providence preserves the Church assuredly in such things as may be deceived by fallible human testimony.

✒ BIBLIOGRAPHY

Manuscripts

Dublin: Trinity College MS 267, *Waldensian Calendar.*
——: Trinity College MS 606, *Sarum Calendar.*
——: Trinity College MS 1765, *Diurnal for Dominican Nuns.*
Florence: Biblioteca Nazionale MS Conv. Sopp. A. 9. 1738, Peter of Verona, *Summa contra Hereticos.*
——: Biblioteca Nazionale MS Conv. Sopp. J. 7. 30, Tommaso Agni, *Legenda S. Petri Martyris.*
Milan: Biblioteca Ambrosiana MS A 189 inf, *Manuale Ambrosianum cum Calendario.*
——: Biblioteca Ambrosiana MS A 227 inf, "[Process against Stefano Confalonieri, 1293]."
Munich: Bayerische Staatsbibliothek CLM 2951a, Bertholdus of Ratisbon, *Sermones.*
——: Bayerische Staatsbibliothek CLM 14620, Moneta of Cremona, *Summa contra Hereticos.*
Novara: Biblioteca Comunale MS 10, Tommaso Agni, *Legenda S. Petri Martyris.*
Nuremberg: Stadtbibliothek MS Cent. 2: 17, Humbert of Romans, *De modo prompte cudendi sermones,* pts. 2 and 3.
Paris: Bibliothèque Nationale MS Lat. 3285A, Jacobus of Voragine, *Sermones de Sanctis.*
——: Bibliothèque Nationale MS Lat. 13466, Hannibaldus de Hannibaldis, *Quodlibeta.*
Perugia: Biblioteca Comunale Augusta MS 1065, Peter of Verona, *Summa contra Hereticos.*
Rome: Archives of the Dominican Order: MS Series XIV, 1, "Officium Ecclesiasticum secundum Ord. FF. Praed."
——: Archives of the Dominican Order: MS Series XIV, 54, Ambrosius Taegio, O.P., *Legenda Beatissimi Petri Martiris.*
Toulouse: Bibliothèque Municipale MS 82, Dominican Lectionary (1297–1323).
——: Bibliothèque Municipale MS 481, Tommaso Agni, *Legenda S. Petri Martyris.*
Trier: Stadtbibliothek MS 1168 (ex 231), Berengarius de Landora, O.P., *Miracula Collecta de Mandato Berengarii Magistri Ordinis.*
Vatican: Biblioteca Apostolica MS Borgh. 272, Huguccio of Pisa, *Summa.*
——: Biblioteca Apostolica MS Borgh. 2280, Huguccio of Pisa, *Summa.*

——: Biblioteca Apostolica MS Vat. Lat. 1291, Praepostinus of Cremona, *Summa contra Catharos.*

——: Biblioteca Apostolica MS Vat. Lat. 7592, "Miraculi S. Antonii."

——: Biblioteca Apostolica MS Reginensis Lat. 428, Moneta of Cremona, *Summa contra Catharos.*

——: Biblioteca Apostolica MS Reginensis Lat. 584, Gérard de Frachet, *Vitae Fratrum.*

Venice: Biblioteca Marciana MS Lat. IX. 17, Pietro Calo, *Magnum Legendarium.*

Printed Primary Sources

Acta Capitulorum Generalium Ordinis Praedicatorum, Vol. 1: 1220–1303. Edited by Benedict M. Reichert, O.P. MOPH 3. Rome: In domo generalitia, 1898.

Acta Capitulorum Provincialium: Provinciae Romanae 1243–1344. Edited by Thomas Kaeppeli and Antoine Dondaine. MOPH 20. Rome: In domo generalitia, 1920.

Acta Sancti Officii Bononie ab anno 1291 usque ad annum 1310. Edited by Lorenzo Paolini and Raniero Orioli. Fonti per la storia d'Italia. Rome: Istituto Palazzo Borromini, 1982.

"Acta Sancti Officii Bononiae." *Atti e memorie: Deputazioni di storia patria per le provincie dell'Emilia, Deputazione di storia patria per l'Emilia e la Romagna* 14 (1896): 235–300.

Acta Sanctorum quotquot Toto Orbe Coluntur vel a Catholicis Scriptoribus Celebrantur ex Latinis et Graecis Aliarumque Gentium Antiquis Monumentis Collecta, Digesta, Illustrata, 2nd ed., ed. Godefridus Henschenius et al., 60 vols. in 70. Paris: Palme, etc., 1867–1940.

Acta synodi Atrebatensi a Gerardo Cameracensi et Atrebatensi inquisitionis haereticae pravitatis Neederlandicae. 5 vols. Ghent: J. Vuylsteke, 1889–1906.

Andreas Florentinus. *Summa contra hereticos.* Edited by Gerhard Rottenwöhrer. Quellen zur Geistesgeschichte des Mittelalters 23, MGH. Hannover: Hahnsche Buchhandlung, 2008.

Angela of Foligno. *Le livre de l'expérience des vrais fidèles.* Edited by M. J. Ferre and L. Baudry. Paris: Editions E. Droz, 1927.

Antonino Pierozzi [St. Antoninus of Florence]. *Chronicon seu Opus Historiarum.* Nurenburg: Koberger, 1484.

Arcangelo, Giani. *Annalium Sacri Ord. Fratr. Servorum B. M. V. Centuriae Quattuor.* Lucca: Marescandoli, 1719.

Augustinus Triumphus. *Summa de Potestate Ecclesiae.* Rome, 1479.

Bartolomeo da Pisa. *De Conformitate Vitae B. Francisci ad Vitam Domini Iesu, auctore Fr. Bartholomaeo de Pisa.* Analecta Franciscana 4–5. Rome: Quaracchi, 1906.

Bartolomeo da Trento. "Epilogus in Gesta Sanctorum." Edited by Domenico Gobbi. *Bartolomeo da Trento: Domenicano e agiografo medievale.* Trent: Grafiche Artigianelli, 1990.

Beiträge zur Sektengeschichte des Mittelalters. Edited by Ignaz von Döllinger. 2 vols. 1890; repr. New York: B. Franklin, 1960.

Benedict XIV (Prosper Lambertini). *De Servorum Dei Beatificatione et Beatorum Canonizatione.* 4 vols. Prati: Alberghetus, in Typographia Aldina, 1839–1847.

Berengarius of Landora. *Miracula Sancti Dominici Mandato Magistri Berengarii Collecta, Petri Calo Legendae Sancti Dominici.* Edited by Simon Tugwell. MOPH 26. Rome: Dominican Historical Institute, 1997.

Bernard Gui. *De Fundatione et Prioribus Conventuum Provinciarum Tolosanae et Provinciae Ordinis Praedicatorum.* Edited by P. Amargier. MOPH 24. Rome: Institutum Historicum Ordinis Fratrum Praedicatorum, 1961.

———. *Practica inquisitionis hereticae pravitatis.* Edited by Celestin Douais. Paris: Picard, 1886.

Bonaventure da Bagnoregio. *Doctoris seraphici S. Bonaventurae Opera omnia.* 10 vols. Rome: Quaracchi, 1882–1902.

———. *Opera Omnia.* Edited by Adolphe Peltier. 15 vols. Paris: L. Vives, 1864–1871.

Boso. *Boso's Life of Alexander III.* Translated by G. M. Ellis. Totowa, NJ: Rowman and Littlefield, 1973.

Brevis Summula contra herrores notatos hereticorum. Edited by Célestin Douais. In *La Somme des autorités à l'usage des prédicateurs méridonaux au XIIIe siècle.* Paris: Picard, 1896.

Bridget of Sweden. *Revelaciones.* Edited by Birger Bergh. 7 vols. Uppsala: Almqvist and Wiksell, 1967.

Bullarium Franciscanum Romanorum Pontificum: Constitutiones, epistolas, ac diplomata continens Tribus Ordinibus Minorum, Clarissarum, et Poenitentium a seraphico patriarcha Sancto Francisco institutis concessa ab illorum exordio ad nostra usque tempora. Edited by G. G. Sbaralea. 4 vols. 1759; Assisi: Edizioni Porziuncola, 1983.

Bullarium Ordinis Fratrum Praedicatorum. Edited by Thomas Ripoll. 7 vols. Rome: Ex Typographia Hieronymi Mainardi, 1759.

Caesarius of Heisterbach. *Caesarii Heisterbacensis monachi ordinis Cistercensis: Dialogus Miraculorum.* Edited by Joseph Strange. 3 vols. Cologne: J. M. Heberle, 1851.

"Cartulaire de l'abbaye de Saint-Père de Chartres," *Collection des cartulaires de France* 1, in Collection de documents inédits sur l'histoire de France, ser. 1: Histoire politique, Paris: 1840.

Chartularium Universitatis Parisiensis. Edited by Heinrich Denifle, O.P. Paris: Ex typis fratrum Delalain, 1899.

Codex constitutionum quas summi. pontifices ediderunt in solemni canonizatione sanctorum a Johanne XV. ad Benedictum XIII sive ab A.D. 993. ad A.D. 1729. Edited by Giusto Fontanini. Rome: Ex typographia Rev. Camerae apostolicae, 1729.

"Codex Diplomaticus: Monasterii Sancti Petri Carnotensis." In *Collection des Cartulaires de France, Tome 1: Cartulaire de l'Abbaye de Saint-Père de Chartres,* edited by M. Guérard. Paris: Crapelet, 1840.

Constitutiones Antiquae Ord. Frat. Praedicatorum. Edited by H. C. Scheeben. Analecta sacri ordinis fratrum Praedicatorum 2. Rome: In domo generalitia, 1895.

Corpus Documentorum Inquisitionis Hereticae Pravitatis Neerlandicae. Edited by P. Fredericq. Ghent: J. Vuylsteke, 1889.

Corpus Iuris Canonici II *(Liber Extra).* Edited by Emil Friedberg. Leipzig, 1881; repr. Graz: Akademische druck u. Verlagsanstalt, 1956.

Davril, A., and T. M. Thibodeau. Corpus Christianorum: Continuatio Mediaevalis 140. Turnhout: Brepols, 1995.

Decretum Magistri Gratiani. 2nd ed. Edited by E. Friedberg. Corpus Iuris Canonici, vol. 1. Leipzig: Tauschnitz, 1879.

de Frachet, Gérard, O.P. *Lives of the Brethren of the Order of Preachers, 1206–1259*. Translated by Placid Conway, O.P. London: Burns, Oates and Washbourne, 1924.

———. *Vitae Fratrum Ordinis Praedicatorum*. Edited by Benedict Maria Reichert, O.P. MOPH 1. Louvain: Charpentier, 1896.

de Mailly, Jean. *Abbrevatio in Gestis et Miraculis Sanctorum*. Edited by Antoine Dondaine, O.P. Bibiotheque d'histoire Dominicaine 1. Paris: Cerf, 1947.

Fiamma, Galvano, O.P. *Cronica ab Anno 1170 Usque ad 1333*. Edited by Benedict M. Reichert, O.P. MOPH 2. Rome: In domo generalitia, 1897.

Fontes Francescani. Edited by Enrico Menestó, Stefano Brufani, Giuseppe Cremascoli, Emore Paoli, Luigi Pellegrini, and Stanislao de Campagno. Sta. Maria degli Angeli, Assisi: Edizioni Porziuncula, 1995.

Fontes vitae S. Thomae Aquinatis: Notis historicis et criticis illustrat. Edited by Dominic Prümmer and M. H. Laurent. 2 vols. Toulouse: Privat, 1912–37.

Francis of Assisi: Early Documents. Edited by Regis J. Armstrong, O.F.M. Cap., J. A. Wayne Hellmann, O.F.M. Conv., and William J. Short, O.F.M. 4 vols. New York: New City Press, 2000.

Gregory IX. *Les Registres de Gregoire IX*. Edited by L. Auvray. 2 vols. Paris: A. Fontemoing, 1896.

———. *Scripta de Sancto Domenico*. Edited by Simon Tugwell. MOPH 27. Rome: Institutum Historicum Ordinis Fratrum Praedicatorum, 1998.

———, and Stephan de Salaniaco. *De Quattor in Quibus Deus Praedicatorum Ordinem Insignavit*. Edited by Thomas Kaeppeli. MOPH 22. Rome: Institutum Historicum Ordinis Fratrum Praedicatorum, 1949.

Hostiensis (Henry of Segusio). *In Tertium Decretalium Librum Commentaria*. Venice: Divinitas, 1581.

Hugh of St. Cher. *Hugonis de Sancto Charo Opera Omnia in Universum Vetus et Novum Testamentum*. 8 vols. Venice: Apud Nicolaum Pezzana, 1732.

Humbert of Romans. *Opera de Vita Regulari*. Edited by J. J. Berthier. 2 vols. Rome: Typis A. Befani, 1888.

Jacobus of Voragine. *The Golden Legend: Selections*. Translated by Christopher Stace. London: Penguin, 1998.

———. *The Golden Legend*. Translated by Ryan Granger and Helmut Ripperger. New York: Arno, 1969.

———. *Legenda Aurea*. Edited by Giovanni Paolo Maggioni. 2 vols. Florence: Tavarnuzze, 1998.

———. *Sermones Aurei de Praceipuis Sanctorum Festis Quae in Ecclesia Celebrantur, a Vetustate et in Numeris Prope Mendis Repurgati*. Mainz: Petrus Cholinus, 1616.

———. *Sermones Quadragesimales Eximii Doctoris, Fratris Iacobi de Voragine, Ordinis Praedicatorum, Quondam Archiepiscopi Ianuensis*. Venice: Iohannes Baptista Somaschus, 1571.

Johannes Andreae. *In Tertium Decretalium Librum Novella Commentaria.* Venice: Franciscum Franciscium, 1581.

———. *Novella super VI. Decretalium.* Venice: Pincius, 1499.

Jordan of Saxony. *Libellus de Principiis Ordinis Praedicatorum.* Edited by H. C. Scheeben. MOPH 16. Rome: Institutum Historicum Ordinis Fratrum Praedicatorum, 1935.

———. *On the Beginnings of the Order of Preachers.* Translated by Simon Tugwell. Dublin: Dominican Publications, 1982.

Le Registre D'inquisition de Jaques Fournier, Évêque de Pamiers (1318–1325). Edited by Jean Duvernoy. 3 vols. Toulouse: Privat, 1965.

Liber de duobus principiis. Livre des deux principes: Introduction, texte critique, traduction, notes et index. Edited by Christine Thouzellier. Paris: Éditions du Cerf, 1973.

Litterae Encyclicae Magistrorum ab Anno 1233 Usque ad Annum 1376. Edited by Benedict M. Reichert, O.P. MOPH 5. Rome: Institutum Historicum Ordinis Fratrum Praedicatorum, 1900.

Materials for the History of Thomas Becket, Archbishop of Canterbury. Edited by James Cragie Robinson. Vols. 1–2. London: Her Majesty's Stationary Office, 1875.

Matthaei Parisiensis. *Historia Anglorum, Sive, ut Vulgo Dicitur, Historio Minor, Vol. III, A.D. 1246–1253.* Edited by Sir Frederic Madden. London: Her Majesty's Stationery Office, 1869.

Meyer, Johannes, O.P. *Chronica Brevis Ordinis Praedicatorum.* Edited by Heribert Scheeben. Quellen und Forschungen zur Geschichten des Dominikanerordens in Deutschland. Leipzig: Albertus-Magnus-Verlag, 1933.

"Miracula Sancti Francisci." *Archivum franciscanum historicum* 12 (1919): 321–401.

Moneta of Cremona, O.P. *Venerabilis patris Monetæ Cremonensis ordinis prædicatorum s. p. dominico æqualis Adversus Catharos et Valdenses libri quinque.* Edited by Tommaso Agostino Ricchini. Rome: Ex Typographia Palladis, 1743.

Nicholas Eymerich, O.P. *Directorium Inquisitorum.* Venice: Apud Marcum Antonium Zalterium, 1595.

Patrologiae Cursus Completus: Ser. Lat. Edited by J. P. Migne. Paris: In via dicta d'Amboise, près la Barrièr d'Enfer, ou Petit-Montrouge, 1845.

Peregrinus of Opole. *Sermones de Tempore et de Sanctis.* Edited by Richardus Tatarzynski. Studia "Przegladu Tomistycznego." Warsaw: Institutum Thomisticum, 1997.

Praepositinus of Cremona. *The Summa Contra Haereticos Ascribed to Praepositinus of Cremona.* Edited by Joseph N. Garvin and James A. Corbett. Publications in Mediaeval Studies 15. Notre Dame, IN: University of Notre Dame Press, 1958.

Processus Apostolici Auctoritate Innocentii Papae IV Annis 1251, 1253, et 1254 Constructi de Vita, Virtutibus et Miraculis B. Johannis Boni Mantuani. AS 51 (October, 9): 778–885.

Processus canonizationis sancti Dominici apud Bononiam et Tholosam. Edited by A. Walz. MOPH 16. Rome: Dominican Historical Institute, 1935.

Ralph of Coggeshale. *Chronicon Anglicanum*. Rolls Series, 66. Edited by Joseph Stevenson. London: Her Majesty's Stationery Office, 1875.

Raymondus de Fronciacho. "Sol Ortus." *Archiv für Literatur- und Kirchengeschichte des Mittelalters*. Edited by Heinrich Denifle and Franz Ehrle. Berlin: Wiedmannsche Buchhandlung, 1887.

Raynerius Sacconi, O.P. *Summa de Catharis*. Edited by François Šanjek. *AFP* 44 (1974): 31–60.

Rituale Romanum: Iuxta Typicam Vaticanam. New York: Benzinger Brothers, 1953.

Saint Dominic: Biographical Documents. Edited by Francis C. Lehner, O.P. Washington, DC: Thomist Press, 1964.

Salimbene da Adam. *The Chronicle of Salimbene de Adam*. Translated by Joseph. L. Baird. Binghamton, NY: Medieval and Renaissance Texts and Studies, 1986.

———. *Cronica*. Edited by Guiseppe Scalia. 2 vols. Corpus Christianorum: Continuatio Mediaevalis 125. Turnholt, Belgium: Brepols, 1998–99.

Sinibaldo dei Fieschi (Innocent IV). *Commentaria: Apparatus in Quinque Libros Decretalium*. Frankfurt, 1570; repr. Frankfurt am Main: Minerva, 1968.

———. *Les Registres d'Innocent IV: Publiés ou analysés d'après les manuscrits originaux du Vatican et de la Bibliothèque Nationale*. Edited by Élie Berger. 4 vols. Paris: E. Thorin, 1884–1920.

Stephen of Bourbon, O.P. *Traité sur les sept dons du Saint Esprit*. Edited by A. Lecoy de la Marche. Paris: Librairie Renouard, 1877.

Thomas Aquinas. *Sancti Thomae de Aquino Opera omnia: Iussu impensaque, Leonis XIII. P.M. edita*. Romae: Ex Typographia Polyglotta S.C. de Propaganda Fide, 1882–.

Thomas Becket. *The Correspondence of Thomas Becket: Archbishop of Canterbury 1162–1170*. Edited and translated by Anne Duggan. Oxford Medieval Texts. 2 vols. Oxford: Oxford University Press, 2000.

Victor III. *Libelli de lite (Dialogi de miraculis Sancti Benedicti Liber Tertius auctore Desiderio abbate Casinensis ed.)* MGH, Scriptores 30.2. Hannover: Deutsches Institut für Erforschung des Mittelalters, 1934.

Vita prima di S. Antonio, o, Assidua. Edited by Vergilio Gamboso. Padua: Edizioni Messagero, 1981.

Wadding, Luke. *Annales Minorum Seu Trium Ordinum*. Vol. 5 (1276–1300). Florence: Quaracchi, 1931.

———. *Scriptores Ordinis Minorum*. Frankfurt am Main: Minerva, 1967.

William of Puylaurens. *Chronica*. Edited by J. Beyssier. *Bibliothèque de la Faculté des Lettres de l'Université de Paris* 18 (1904): 119–75.

William of Saint-Amour. *The Opuscula of William of Saint-Amour*. Edited by Andrew Traver. Münster: Aschendorff, 2003.

———. *William of Saint-Amour: De periculis novissimorum temporum*. Edited by G. Geltner. Dallas Medieval Texts and Translations 8. Louvain, 2008.

Secondary Works

Abulafia, David. *Frederick II: A Medieval Emperor.* New York: Oxford University Press, 1992.

Alberigo, Giuseppe. *Cardinalato e collegialità: Studi sull'ecclesiologia tra l'XI e il XIV secolo.* Florence: Vallecchi, 1969.

Ames, Christine Caldwell. "Does Inquisition Belong to Religious History?" *American Historical Review* 110, no. 1 (February 2005): 11–37.

——. "Peter Martyr: The Inquisitor as Saint." *Comitatus* 31 (2000): 137–73.

——. *Righteous Persecution: Inquisition, Dominicans, and Christianity in the Middle Ages.* Philadelphia: University of Pennsylvania Press, 2008.

Amore, Agostino. "La canonizazzione vescovile." *Antonianum* 52 (1977): 231–66.

Arnold, John H. "Inquisition, Texts and Discourse." In *Texts and the Repression of Medieval Heresy*, edited by Caterina Bruschi and Peter Biller, 63–80. York Studies in Medieval Theology 4. York: York Medieval Press, 2003.

Audisio, Gabriel. *The Waldensian Dissent: Persecution and Survival, ca. 1170–1570.* Cambridge: Cambridge University Press, 1999.

Balet, Jean-Daniel. "La liturgie dominicaine au XIIIe siècle." In *Lector et compilator: Vincent de Beauvais, frère prêcheur, un intellectuel et son milieu au XIIIe siècle*, edited by Serge Lusignan and Monique Paulmier-Foucart, 333–41. Rencontres à Royaumont 9. Grâne: Editions Créaphis, 1997.

Barber, Malcom. "Moving Cathars: The Italian Connection in the Thirteenth Century." *Journal of Mediterranean Studies* 10, no. 1–2 (2000): 5–19.

Barlow, Frank. *Thomas Becket.* Berkeley: University of California Press, 1986.

Batallion, Louis-Jaques. "La predicazione dei religiosi mendicanti del secolo XIII nell'Italia centrale." *Mélanges de l'école française de Rome: Moyen âge—temps modernes* 89 (1977): 691–94.

Beaudoin, Yvon, O.M.I. "History of Canonizations." In *Canonization: Theology, History, Process*, edited by William H. Woestman, O.M.I., 20–33. Ottawa: Faculty of Canon Law–Saint Paul University, 2002.

Beissel, Stephan. *Die Verehrung der Heiligen und ihrer Reliquien in Deutschland im Mittelater.* Darmstadt: Wissenschaftliche Buchgesellschaft, 1890.

Benedetti, Marina. *Io non sono Dio: Guglielma di Milano e i Figli dello Spirito santo.* Milan: Edizioni Biblioteca Francescana, 1998.

——. *Milano 1300: I processi inquisitoriali contro le devote e i devoti di santa Guglielma.* Milan: Libri Scheiwiller, 1999.

Bennett, R. F. *The Early Dominicans: Studies in Thirteenth Century Dominican History.* Cambridge: Cambridge University Press, 1937.

Berresheim, Heinrich. *Christus als Haupt der Kirche nach dem heilgen Bonaventura: Ein Beitrag zur Theologie der Kirche.* Münster: Antiquariat Th. Stenderhoff, 1983.

Betti, M. "Il magistero infallibile del Romano Pontefice." *Divinitas* 3 (1961): 581–606.

Biget, Jean-Louis. "Culte et rayonnement de Pierre Déjean Olieu en Languedoc au début du XIVe siècle." In *Piette de Jean Olivi (1248–1298)*, edited by Alain Boureau and Sylvain Piron, 277–308. Paris: J. Vrin, 1999.

Biller, Peter. *Through a Glass Darkly: Seeing Medieval Heresy.* London: Routledge, 2001.

Blumenthal, Uta-Renate. *The Investiture Controversy: Church and Monarchy from the Ninth to the Twelfth Century*. Philadelphia: University of Pennsylvania Press, 1988.

———. *Papal Reform and Canon Law in the 11th and 12th Centuries*. Aldershot: Ashgate, 1998.

Bonniwell, William. *A History of the Dominican Liturgy*. New York: Wagner, 1944.

Bonser, Wilfred. "The Cult of Relics in the Middle Ages." *Folk-Lore* 73–74 (1962–63): 234–56.

Borst, Arno. *Die Katharer*. Stuttgart: Hiersemann, 1953.

Boureau, Alain. *La Légende dorée: Le système narratif de Jacques de Voragine (†1298)*. Paris: Éditions du Cerf, 1984.

———."Saints et démons dans les procès de canonisation du début du XIVe siècle." In *Procès de canonisation au moyen âge: Medieval Canonization Processes*, edited by Gábor Klaniczay, 199–221. Collection de l'école Française de Rome, 340. Rome: École Française de Rome, 2004.

———. "Vitae fratrum, Vitae patrum: L'ordre dominicain et le modèle des pères du désert au XIIIe s." *Mélanges de l'ecole française de Rome: Moyen âge–temps modernes* 99, no. 1 (1987): 79–100.

Brackmann, A. "Zur Kanonisation des Erzbischofs Anno von Köln." *Neues Archiv für ältere deutsche Geschichtskunde* 32 (1906–1907): 157–70.

Bredero, Adrian. *Bernard of Clairvaux: Between Cult and History*. Grand Rapids, MI: Eerdmans, 1996.

———. *Christendom and Christianity in the Middle Ages*. Grand Rapids, MI: Eerdmans, 1994.

Brett, Edward Tracy. *Humbert of Romans: His Life and Views of Thirteenth-Century Society*. Toronto: Pontifical Institute of Medieval Studies, 1984.

Broderick, John. "A Census of the Saints (993–1955)." *American Ecclesiastical Review* 135 (1956): 87–115.

Brown, Peter. *The Cult of the Saints: Its Rise and Function in Latin Christianity*. Chicago: University of Chicago Press, 1981.

———. "The Rise and Function of the Holy Man in Late Antiquity." *Journal of Roman Studies* 61 (1971): 80–101.

———. *Society and the Holy in Late Antiquity*. Berkeley: University of California Press, 1982.

Brundage, James. *Medieval Canon Law*. London: Longman, 1995.

Burnham, Louisa. *So Great a Light, So Great a Smoke: The Beguin Heretics of Languedoc*. Ithaca, NY: Cornell University Press, 2008.

Burr, David. *Olivi's Peaceable Kingdom*. Philadelphia: University of Pennsylvania Press, 1993.

———. *The Spiritual Franciscans from Protest to Persecution in the Century after Saint Francis*. University Park: Pennsylvania State University Press, 2001.

Bynum, Caroline Walker. *Holy Feast and Holy Fast: The Religious Significance of Food to Medieval Women*. Berkeley: University of California Press, 1987.

———. "Miracles and Marvels: The Limits of Alterity." In *Vita Religiosa im Mittelalter: Festschrift für Kaspar Elm zum 70. Geburtstag*, edited by Franz J. Felten and

Nikolas Jaspert, 799–817. Berliner historische Studien 31. Berlin: Duncker and Humblot, 1999.

——. *The Resurrection of the Body in Western Christianity, 200–1336.* New York: Columbia University Press, 1995.

——. "Wonder." *American Historical Review* 102, no. 1 (1997): 1–26.

Callaghan, Daniel. "The Sermons of Ademar of Chabannes and the Cult of St. Martial of Limoges." *Revue Bénédictine* 86 (1976): 251–95.

Cameron, Euan. *Waldensees: Rejections of Holy Church in Medieval Europe.* Oxford: Blackwell, 2000.

Cannon, Joanna. "Dominic Alter Christus? Representations of the Founder in and After the Arca di San Domenico." In *Christ among the Medieval Dominicans: Representations of Christ in the Texts and Images of the Order of Preachers,* edited by Kent Emery Jr. and Joseph Wawrykow, 26–48. Notre Dame, IN: University of Notre Dame Press, 1998.

——. "Dominican Patronage of the Arts in Central Italy: The Provincia Romana, c. 1220–1320." PhD diss., Courtauld Institute of Art, University of London, 1980.

Cappelli, Adriano. *Cronologia: Cronografia e calendario perpetuo.* Milan: Hoepli, 1988.

Cipolla, C. "Appunti eccelliniani: Sul processo di canonizzazione del B. Giovanni Buono." *Atti del R. Istituto Veneto di Scienze, Lettere ed Arti* 70 (1910): 401–8.

Clarke, Peter D., and Anne Duggan, eds. *Pope Alexander III (1159–1181): The Art of Survival.* Aldershot: Ashgate, 2012.

Cobban, Alan B. *The Medieval Universities: Their Development and Organization.* New York: Harper and Row, 1975.

Collomb, Pascal. "Les éléments liturgiques de la Légende dorée: Tradition et innovations." In *De la sainteté à l'hagiographie: Genèse et usage de la Légende dorée,* edited by Barbara Fleith and Franco Morenzoni, 97–122. Publications romanes et françaises 229. Geneva: Droz, 2001.

The Concept of Heresy in the Middle Ages (11th–13th c.). Edited by W. Lordaux and D. Verhelst, 211–224. Leuven: Leuven University Press, 1976.

Congar, Yves, O.P. *L'église de Saint Augustin à l'époque moderne.* Paris: Éditions du Cerf, 1970.

Cormack, Margaret. *The Saints in Iceland: From the Conversion to 1400.* Subsidia Hagiographica 78. Brussels: Société des Bollandistes, 1994.

Corsi, Dinora. "Aspetti dell'inquisizione fiorentina nel '200." In *Eretici e ribelli del XIII e XIV secolo,* edited by Domenico Maselli, 65–91. Pistoia: Tellini, 1974.

Corvino, Francesco. *Bonaventura da Bagnoregio francescano e pensatore.* Bari: Dedalo libri, 1980.

Creytens, R., O.P. "Le Manuel de conversation de Philippe de Ferrare, O.P." *AFP* 16 (1946): 107–35.

——. "Barthelemy de Ferrare, O.P., et Barthelemy de Modene, O.P.: Deux ecrivants du XVe siècle." *AFP* 25 (1955): 345–416.

Crook, John. *The Architectural Setting of the Cult of Saints in the Early Christian West, c. 300–1200.* Oxford: Clarendon, 2000.

Cullen, Christopher. *Bonaventure.* Oxford: Oxford University Press, 2006.

Dalarun, Jacques. *La malavventura di Francesco: Per uno storico dell leggende francescane* Milan: Edizione Francescana, 1996.

———, ed. *François d'Assise: Écrits, vies, témoignages*. Paris: Éditions du Cerf, 2010.

d'Alatri, Mariano. "Culto dei santi ed eretici in Italia nei secoli XII e XIII." *Collectanea Franciscana* 45 (1975): 85–104.

———. "'Eresie' persequite dall'inquisizione in Italia nel corso del duecento." In *The Concept of Heresy in the Middle Ages (11th–13th c.)*, edited by W. Lordaux and D. Verhelst, 211–224. Leuven: Leuven University Press, 1976.

———. *Eretici e inquisitori in Italia: Studi e documenti*. 2 vols. Biblioteca Seraphico-Cappucina 31. Rome: Collegio San Lorenzo da Brindisi, 1986.

———. *L'inquisizione francescana nell'Italia centrale del duecento*. Rome: Istituto storico dei Cappuccini, 1996.

da Milano, Ilarino. *L'Eresia di Ugo Speroni nella confutazione del Maestro Vacario: Testo inedito del secolo XII con studio storico e dottrinale*. Studi e testi 115. Vatican City: Biblioteca apostolica vaticana, 1945.

———. "La 'Manifestatio heresis catarorum.'" *Aevum* 12 (1938): 281–333.

de Gaiffier, Baudouin. "Les revindications de biens dans quelques documents hagiographiques du XIe siècle." *AB* 50 (1932): 123–38.

Delaruelle, Etienne. *La piété populaire au moyen âge*. Bologna: Bottega d'Erasmo, 1980.

Delcorno, Carlo. "La predicazione duecentesca su san Pietro Martire." In *Chiesa, vita religiosa, società nel medioevo italiano*, edited by Mariaclara Rossi and Gian Maria Varanini, 305–18. Rome: Herder, 2005.

———. *La predicazione nell'eta communale*. Florence: Sansoni, 1974.

Delehaye, Hippolyte. *The Legends of the Saints: An Introduction to Hagiography*. Translated by V. M. Crawford. Notre Dame, IN: University of Notre Dame Press, 1961.

Delooz, Pierre. "Towards a Sociological Study of Canonized Sainthood in the Catholic Church." In *Saints and Their Cults: Studies in Religious Sociology, Folklore and History*, edited by Stephen Wilson, 189–216. New York: Cambridge University Press, 1983.

Denifle, Heinrich. *Die Universitäten des Mittelalters bis 1400*. Berlin: Weidmannsche Buchhandlung, 1885.

Desbonnets, Théophile. "La diffusion du culte de saint François d'après les bréviaires manuscrits étrangers à l'Ordre." *Archivium Franciscanum Historicum* 75 (1982): 155–215.

Dinzelbacher, Peter. *Heilige oder Hexen? Schicksale auffälliger Frauen in Mittelalter und Frühneuzeit*. Munich: Artemis and Winkler, 1995.

Dolciami, Francesco. "Francesco d'Assisi tra devozione, culto e liturgia." *Collectanea Franciscana* 71, no. 1–2 (2001): 5–45.

Dondaine, Antoine. "La Collection des oeuvres de saint Thomas dite de Jean XXII et Jaquet Maci." *Scriptorium* 29 (1975): 127–52.

———. "Durand de Huesca et la polémique anti-cathare." *AFP* 29 (1959): 268–71.

———. "La Hierarchie Cathare in Italie." *AFP* 19 (1949): 280–312.

———. "Le Manual de l'Inquisiteur." *AFP* 27 (1947): 85–194.

———. "Saint Pierre Martyr." *AFP* 23 (1953): 67–150.

———. *Un Traité néo-manichéen du XIIIe siècle: Le* Liber du duobus principiis, *suivi d'un frangment de rituel cathare.* Edited by Antoine Dondaine. Rome: Dominican Historical Institute, 1939.

Douie, Decima L. *The Conflict between the Seculars and Mendicants at the University of Paris in the Thirteenth Century.* London: Blackfriars, 1954.

———. *The Nature and the Effect of the Heresy of the Fraticelli.* Manchester: Manchester University Press, 1932.

DuBois, Thomas A. *Sanctity in the North: Saints, Lives, and Cults in Medieval Scandinavia.* Toronto: University of Toronto Press, 2008.

Dufeil, Michel-Marie. *Guillaume de Saint-Amour et la polémique universitaire parisienne 1250–1259.* Paris: Picard, 1972.

Duffy, Eamon. "Finding St Francis: Early Images, Early Lives." In *Medieval Theology and the Natural Body,* edited by Peter Biller and A. J. Minnis, 193–236. York Studies in Medieval Theology 1. York: York Medieval Press, 1997.

———. *The Stripping of the Altars: Traditional Religion in England, c. 1400–c. 1580.* New Haven, CT: Yale University Press, 1992.

Duggan, Anne J. "The Cult of St. Thomas Becket in the Thirteenth Century." In *St. Thomas Cantilupe, Bishop of Hereford: Essays in His Honour,* edited by Meryl Jancey, 21–44. Hereford: Friends of Hereford Cathedral, 1982.

Dupront, A. "Pèlerinages et lieux sacrés." In *Mélanges F. Braudel, II.* Edited by R. Aron, E Bauer, M. Baulant, and I. Berend, 189–206. Toulouse: Privat, 1973.

Duvernoy, Jean, and Raoul Manselli. *Spirituels et béguins du Midi.* Toulouse: Privat, 1989.

Echard, Jaques, and Jaques Quietif. *Scriptores Ordinis Praedicatorum.* New York: B. Franklin, 1959.

Evans, Suzanne. "The Scent of a Martyr." *Numen: International Review for the History of Religions* 49, no. 2 (2002): 193–211.

Faloci-Pulignani, M. "Il Beato Simone da Collazzone e il suo processo nel 1252." *Miscellanea Francescana* 12 (1910): 117–32.

Farmer, David Hugh. "The Cult and Canonization of St Hugh." In *St Hugh of Lincoln: Lectures Delivered at Oxford and Lincoln to Celebrate the Eighth Centenary of St Hugh's Consecration as Bishop of Lincoln,* edited by Henry Mayr-Harting, 75–87. Oxford: Clarendon, 1987.

Fernandez-Gallardo Jimenez, Gonzalo. "A Propósito de los Milagros de San Antonio." *Estudios Franciscanos: Revista Cuatrimestral de Ciencias Eclesiásticas de las Provincias Capuchinas Ibéricas* 97, no. 416–17 (1996): 405–18.

Fichtenau, Heinrich. "Zum Reliquien wesen in früheren Mittelalter." *Mitteilungen des Instituts für Österreichische Geschichtsforschung* 60 (1952): 60–89.

Finucane, R. C. "The Use and Abuse of Medieval Miracles." *History* 60 (1975): 1–10.

Fleury, Claude. *Histoire ecclésiastique.* Paris: Didier, 1840.

Folghera, J. D. "Le Bienheureux Humbert de Romans: Maître de prédication." *L'Année Dominicaine* 65 (1929): 49–54, 84–87, 115–20, 149–54, 177–81, 229–33.

Folz, Robert. *Le Souvenir et la légende de Charlemagne dans l'Empire germanique médiéval.* Paris: Société d'Édition Les Belles Lettres, 1950.

Foreville, Raymonde. "La diffusion du culte de Thomas Becket dans la France de l'Ouest avant la fin du XIIe siècle." From *Cahiers du civilisation médiévale XIX: Poitiers, 1976*. London: Variorum Reprints, 1981.

Frassetto, Michael, ed. *Heresy and the Persecuting Society in the Middle Ages: Essays on the Work of R. I. Moore*. Leiden: Brill, 2006.

Freeman, Charles. *Holy Bones, Holy Dust: How Relics Shaped the History of Medieval Europe*. New Haven, CT: Yale University Press, 2011.

Friedlander, Alan. *The Hammer of the Inquisitors: Brother Bernard Délicieux and the Struggle Against the Inquisition in Fourteenth-Century France*. Leiden: Brill, 2000.

Frojmark, Anders. "The Canonization Process of Brynolf Algotsson." In *Procès de canonisation au moyen âge—Medieval Canonization Processes*, edited by Gábor Klaniczay, 87–100. Collection de l'école Française de Rome, 340. Rome: École Française de Rome, 2004.

Frugoni, Chiara. "The Cities and the 'New' Saints." In *City-States in Classical Antiquity and Medieval Italy*, edited by Anthony Molho, Kurt Raaflaub, and Julia Emlen, 71–91. Ann Arbor: University of Michigan Press, 1993.

——. *Francesco e l'invenzione delle stimmate: Una storia per parole e immagini fino a Bonaventura e Giotto*. Turin: G. Einaudi, 1993.

Frutaz, Amato Pietro. "Auctoritate beatorum apostolorum Petri et Pauli: Saggio sulle formule dei canonizzazione." *Antonianum* 42 (1967): 435–501.

Fumi, Luigi. "I Paterini in Orvieto." *Archivio storico italiano*. Ser. 3, vol. 22 (1892): 62–64.

Galbraith, G. R. *The Constitution of the Dominican Order: 1216–1360*. New Lork: Longman's, 1925.

García y García, Antonio. "La canonización de San Rosendo de Dumio." In *Estudios sobre la canonística portuguesa medieval*, edited by Antonio García y García, 157–72. Madrid: Fundación Universitaria Española, 1976.

Geary, Patrick. *Furta Sacra: Thefts of Relics in the Central Middle Ages*. Princeton, NJ: Princeton University Press, 1978.

——. *Living with the Dead in the Middle Ages*. Ithaca, NY: Cornell University Press, 1994.

——. "Saints, Scholars, and Society: The Elusive Goal." In *Saints: Studies in Hagiography*, edited by Sandro Sticca, 1–22. Medieval and Renaissance Texts and Studies 141. Binghamton, NY: Medieval and Renaissance Texts and Studies, 1996.

George, Philippe. "Les reliques des saints: Publications récentes et perspectives nouvelles." *Revue belge de philologie et d'histoire* 80, no. 2 (2002): 563–91.

Gilchrist, J. T. *Canon Law in the Age of Reform, 11th–12th Centuries*. Aldershot: Ashgate, 1993.

Gilliat-Smith, Ernest. *Saint Anthony of Padua according to His Contemporaries*. London: Dent, 1926.

Giraud, Jean. *Histoire de l'inquisition au moyen âge*. 3 vols. Paris: Auguste Picard, 1938.

Given, James B. *Inquisition and Medieval Society: Power, Discipline, and Resistance in Languedoc*. Ithaca, NY: Cornell University Press, 1997.

Glorieux, Palemon. *La littérature quodlibétique*. 2 vols. Paris: Vrin, 1925.

———. "Le plus beau Quodlibet de Saint Thomas est-il de lui?" *Mélanges de science religieuse III* (1946): 235–68.

Golinelli, Paolo. "Antichi e nuovi culti cittadini al sorgere dei communi nel nord-Italia." *Hagiographica* 1 (1994): 159–80.

———. *Città e culto dei santi nel medioevo Italiano.* Bologna: Clueb, 1996.

———. "Il comune italiano e il culto del santo cittadino." In *Politik und Heiligenverehrung im Hochmittelalter,* edited by Jürgen Petersohn, 573–93. Vorträge und Forschungen 42. Sigmaringen: Thorbecke, 1994.

———. "Il santo gabbato: Forme di incredulità nel mondo cittadino italiano." In *Progetti e dinamiche nella società comunale italiana,* edited by R. Bordone and G. Sergi, 389–414. Naples: Europa Mediterranea, 1995.

———. "Social Aspects in Some Italian Canonization Trials: The Choice of Witnesses." In *Procès de canonisation au moyen âge—Medieval Canonization Processes,* edited by Gábor Klaniczay, 165–80. Collection de l'école Française de Rome, 340. Rome: École Française de Rome, 2004.

Goodich, Michael. "The Canonization Policy of Celestine III." In *Pope Celestine III (1191–1198) Diplomat and Pastor,* edited by John Doran and Damian J. Smith, 305–17. Aldershot: Ashgate, 2008.

———. "Il fanciullo come fulcro di miracli e potere spirituale (XIII e XIV secolo)." In *Potere carismatici e infomali,* edited by A. Paravicini-Bagliani and A. Vauchez, 38–57. Palermo: Europa Mediterranea, 1992.

———. "Liturgy and the Foundation of Cults in the Thirteenth and Fourteenth Centuries." In *De Sion Exibit Lex et Verbum Domini de Hierusalem: Essays on Medieval Law, Liturgy, and Literature in Honour of Amnon Linder,* edited by Yitzhak Hen, 145–57. Cultural Encounters in Late Antiquity and the Middle Ages 1. Turnhout, Belgium: Brepols, 2001.

———. "*Mirabilius Deus in sanctis suis*: Social History and Medieval Miracles." In *Signs, Wonders, Miracles: Representations of Divine Power in the Life of the Church,* edited by Kate Cooper and Jeremy Gregory, 135–56. Woodbridge: Boydell, 2005.

———. "Miracles and Disbelief in the Late Middle Ages." *Mediaevistik* 1 (1988): 23–38.

———. *Miracles and Wonders.* Aldershot: Ashgate, 2007.

———. "The Politics of Canonization in the Thirteenth Century." *Church History* 44 (1975): 294–307.

———. "A Profile of Thirteenth-Century Sainthood." *Comparative Studies in Society and History* 18 (1976): 429–37.

———. "Reason or Revelation? The Criteria for the Proof and Credibility of Miracles in Canonization Processes." In *Procès de canonisation au moyen âge—Medieval Canonization Processes,* edited by Gábor Klaniczay, 181–97. Collection de l'école Française de Rome, 340. Rome: École Française de Rome, 2004.

———. "Vision, Dream, and Canonization Policy under Pope Innocent III." In *Pope Innocent III (1160/61–1216): To Root Up and To Plant,* edited by John C. Moore, 151–164. Leiden: Brill, 2003.

———. *Vita Perfecta: The Ideal of Sainthood in the Thirteenth Century,* Monographien zur Geschichte des Mittelalters 25. Stuttgart: Hiersemann, 1982.

Gregory, Brad S. *Salvation at Stake: Christian Martyrdom in Early Modern Europe.* Cambridge, MA: Harvard University Press, 1999.

Grieco, Holly. "The Boy Bishop and the 'Uncanonized Saint': St. Louis of Anjou and Peter John Olivi as Models of Franciscan Spirituality in the Fourteenth Century." *Franciscan Studies* 70 (2012): 247–82.

Grundmann, Herbert. *Religious Movements in the Middle Ages.* Translated by Steven Rowan. Notre Dame, IN: University of Notre Dame Press, 1995.

Guiraud, Jean. *Histoire de l'inquisition au moyen âge.* 3 vols. Paris: Auguste Picard, 1938.

Hamilton, Bernard. *The Medieval Inquisition.* New York: Holmes and Meier, 1981.

Hardon, J. A. "The Concept of Miracle from St. Augustine to Modern Apologetics." *Theological Studies* 15 (1954): 229–57.

Haseldine, David. "Early Dominican Hagiography." *New Blackfriars* 75, no. 885 (1994): 400–415.

Hasler, August Bernhard. *How the Pope Became Infallible.* Translated by Peter Heinegg. Garden City, NY: Doubleday, 1981.

Hayward, Paul Antony. "Demystifying the Role of Sanctity in Western Christendom." In *The Cult of Saints in Late Antiquity and the Middle Ages: Essays on the Contribution of Peter Brown,* edited by James Howard-Johnston and Paul Antony Hayward, 115–42. Oxford: Oxford University Press, 1999.

Heffernan, Thomas J. *Sacred Biography.* Oxford: Oxford University Press, 1988.

Heft, James. *John XXII and Papal Teaching Authority.* Texts and Studies in Religion 27. Lewiston, NY: E. Mellen, 1986.

Heintz, A. "Der Heilige Simeon von Trier, seine Kanonisation und seine Reliquien." In *Festschrift für Alois Thomas.* Edited by Albert Heintz, 163–73. Trier: Bistumsarchiv, 1967.

Herrmann-Mascard, Nicole. *Les reliques des saints: Formation coutumière d'un droit.* Paris: Klincksieck, 1975.

Hertling, Ludwig, S.J. "Materiali per la storia del processo di Canonizzazione." *Gregorianum* 16 (1935): 170–95.

Hinnebusch, William A. *The History of the Dominican Order.* 2 vols. Staten Island, NY: Alba House, 1966–1973.

Horst, Ulrich, O.P. *The Dominicans and the Pope: Papal Teaching Authority in the Medieval and Early Modern Tradition.* Translated by James D. Mixson. Notre Dame, IN: University of Notre Dame Press, 2006.

———. *Unfehlbarkeit und geschichte.* Mainz: Matthias Grünewald Verlag, 1982.

Housley, N. J. "Politics and Heresy in Italy: Anti-Heretical Crusades, Orders and Confraternities, 1200–1500." *Journal of Ecclesiastical History* 3, no. 2 (April 1982): 193–208.

Huber, Raphael M. *Saint Anthony of Padua: Doctor of the Church Universal; A Critical Study of the Life, Sanctity, Learning, and Miracles of the Saint of Padua and Lisbon.* Milwaukee, WI: Bruce, 1948.

Hull, Geoffrey. *The Banished Heart: Origins of Heteropraxis in the Catholic Church.* London: T and T Clark, 1995; 2010.

Huyskens, Albert, ed. *Quellenstudien zur Geschichte der hl. Elizabeth.* Marburg: Elwert, 1908.

Hyde, J. K. *Society and Politics in Medieval Italy: The Evolution of the City Life, 1000–1350.* London: Macmillan, 1973.

Jansen, Katherine Ludwig. *The Making of the Magdalen: Preaching and Popular Devotion in the Later Middle Ages.* Princeton, NJ: Princeton University Press, 2000.

Jensen, Brian Møller. "'In Placentia': A Study of Patron and Local Saints in Piacenza." *Ecclesia Orans* 13, no. 3 (1996): 439–61.

Jones, Philip. *The Italian City-State: From Commune to Signoria.* Oxford: Clarendon, 1997.

Jongen, Ludo. "Der blutende Faden in der Legenda de Sancto Petro Martyre." *Amsterdamer Beiträge zur Älteren Germanistik* 48 (1997): 41–55.

Kaeppeli, Thomas, O.P. "Kurse Mitteilungen über Mittelalterliche Dominikanerschriftsteller." *AFP* 10 (1940): 291–92.

———. "La Bibliotheque de Saint-Eustorge a Milan a la fin du XVe siècle." *AFP* 25 (1955): 5–74.

———. *Scriptores Ordinis Praedicatorum Medii Aevi.* 4 vols. Rome: Polyglottis Vaticanis, 1970.

———. "Une somme contre les heretiques de s. Pierre Martyr (?)." *AFP* 17 (1947): 295–335.

Kantorowicz, Ernst. *Frederick the Second, 1194–1250.* 1931. New York: L. F. Ungar, 1957.

Karlsson, Gunnar. *The History of Iceland.* Minneapolis: University of Minnesota Press, 2009.

Kee, Howard Clark. *Miracle in the Early Christian World.* New Haven, CT: Yale University Press, 1983.

Keida, Francis J. "The Infallibility of the Pope in His Decree of Canonization." *The Jurist* 6 (1946): 401–15.

Kemp, Eric. *Canonization and Authority in the Western Church.* Oxford: Oxford University Press, 1948.

Kieckhefer, Richard. "The Office of Inquisition and Medieval Heresy: The Transition from Personal to Institutional Jurisdiction." *Journal of Ecclesiastical History* 46 (1995): 36–61.

Klaniczay, Gábor. *Holy Rulers and Blessed Princesses: Dynastic Cults in Medieval Central Europe.* Cambridge: Cambridge University Press, 2002.

———. "Proving Sanctity in the Canonization Processes (Saint Elizabeth and Saint Margaret of Hungary)." In *Procès de canonisation au moyen âge—Medieval Canonization Processes,* edited by Gábor Klaniczay, 117–48. Collection de l'école Française de Rome, 340. Rome: École Française de Rome, 2004.

Klauser, Theodor. "Die Liturgie der Heiligsprechung." In *Heilige Überlieferung,* edited by Idelfons Hewegen, 212–33. Münster: Aschendorffsche Verlagsbuchhandlung, 1938.

Kleinberg, Aviad. "Canonization without a Canon." In *Procès de canonisation au moyen âge—Medieval Canonization Processes,* edited by Gábor Klaniczay, 7–18. Collection de l'école Française de Rome, 340. Rome: École Française de Rome, 2004.

———. *Prophets in Their Own Country: Living Saints and the Making of Sainthood in the Later Middle Ages.* Chicago: University of Chicago Press, 1992.

Knowles, David. *Thomas Becket.* Stanford, CA: Stanford University Press, 1970.

Koopmans, Rachel. *Wonderful to Relate: Miracle Stories and Miracle Collecting in High Medieval England.* Philadelphia: University of Pennsylvania Press, 2011.

Krafft, Otfried. *Papsturkunde und Heiligsprechung: Die päpstlichen Kanosisationen vom Mittelalter bis zur Reformation: ein Handbuch.* Koln: Böhlau, 2005.

Kristeller, Paul Oskar. "The Curriculum of the Italian Universities in the Middle Ages to the Renaissance." In *Proceedings of the PMR Conference* 9, edited by Joseph C. Schaubelt, Joseph Reino, and Phillip Pulsiano, 1–16. Villanova, PA: Villanova University Press, 1986.

Krötzl, Christian. "'Fama Sanctitatis' Die Akten der spätmittelalterlichen Kanonisationsprozesse als Quelle zu Kommunikation und Informationsvermittung in der mitelalterlichen Gesellschaft." In *Procès de canonisation au moyen âge— Medieval Canonization Processes,* edited by Gábor Klaniczay, 223–43. Collection de l'école Française de Rome, 340. Rome: École Française de Rome, 2004.

Kurze, Dietrich. "Anfänge der Inquisition in Deutschland." In *Die Anfänge der Inquisition im Mittelalter. Mit einem Ausblick auf das 20. Jahrhundert und einem Beitrag über religiöse Intoleranz im nichtchristlichen Bereich,* edited by Peter Segl, 131–93. Bayreuther Historische Kolloquien 7. Cologne: Böhlau, 1993.

———. *Quellen zur Ketzergeschichte Brandenburgs und Pommerns.* Berlin: De Gruyter, 1975.

Kuttner, Stephan. *The History of Ideas and Doctrines of Canon Law in the Middle Ages.* London: Variorum Reprints, 1980.

———. "La réserve papale du droit de canonisation." *Revue d'histoire de droit français et étranger* 17 (1938): 172–228.

Ladner, R. "L'Ordo praedicatorum avant l'ordre des Prêcheurs." In *S. Dominique: L'idée, l'homme, et l'oeuvre,* edited by P. Mandonnet and M. H. Vicaire, 1:11–68. 2 vols. Paris: Desclée, 1938.

La Grasta, Giovanna. "La canonizzazione di Chiara." In *Chiara di Assisi: Atti del XX convegno internazionale, Assisi, 15–17 ottobre 1992,* edited by Enrico Menestò, 299–324. Atti dei Convegni della società internazionale di studi francescani e del centro interuniversitario di studi francescani, nuova serie 3. Spoleto: Centro italiano di studi sull'alto medioevo, 1993.

Lambert, Malcolm. *The Cathars.* Oxford: Blackwell, 1998.

———. *Medieval Heresy.* Oxford: Blackwell, 1992.

Lansing, Carol. *Power and Purity: The Cathar Heresy in Medieval Italy.* Oxford: Oxford University Press, 1998.

Lappin, Anthony. "From Osma to Bologna, from Canons to Friars, from the Preaching to the Preachers: The Dominican Path towards Mendicancy." In *The Origin, Development, and Refinement of Medieval Religious Mendicancies,* edited by Donald S. Prudlo, 31–58. Leiden: Brill, 2011.

Lea, Henry Charles. *A History of the Inquisition in the Middle Ages.* 3 vols. New York: Harper and Brothers, 1887.

Leclercq, Jean. *A Second Look at Bernard of Clairvaux.* Kalamazoo, MI: Cistercian Publications, 1990.

Le Goff, Jacques. *The Birth of Europe.* Oxford: Blackwell, 2005.

———. "Le vocabulaire des catégories sociales chez saint François d'Assise et ses biographes du XIIIe siècle." In *Ordres et Classes: Colloque d'histoire sociale, Saint-Cloud, 24–25 mai 1967,* edited by D. Roche, 93–123. Paris: Mouton, 1973.

Leveleux, Corinne, and Albert Rigaudière. *La parole interdite: Le blasphème dans la France médiévale, XIIIe–XVIe siècles; Du péché au crime.* Paris: De Boccard, 2001.

Limborch, Philippus. *Historia inquisitionis cui subjungitur Liber sententiarum inquisitionis tholosanae.* Amsterdam: Henricus Wetstenius, 1692.

Loud, Graham A. "The Case of the Missing Martyrs: Frederick II's War with the Church 1239–1250." *Studies in Church History* 30 (1993): 141–52.

Luck, Georg. *Arcana Mundi: Magic and the Occult in the Greek and Roman Worlds.* Baltimore, MD: Johns Hopkins University Press, 1985.

Maierù, Alfonso. *University Training in Medieval Europe.* Translated by Darleen Pryds. New York: Brill, 1994.

Manselli, Raoul. "Les hérétiques dans la société Italienne du 13e siècle." In *Hérésies et sociétés dans l'Europe pré-industrielle, 11e–18e siècles,* edited by Jacques Le Goff, 199–202. Paris: Mouton, 1968.

——. "Per la storia dell'eresia nel secolo XII, Studi minori." *Bullettino dell'Istituto storico italiano per il Medio Evo e Archivio Muratoriano* 67 (1955): 189–264.

——. *La religion populaire au moyen âge: Problèmes de méthode et d'histoire.* Paris: Vrin, 1975.

——. *Spirtuali e beghini in Provenza.* Rome: Istituto storico Italiano per il medio evo, 1959.

——. *Studi sulle eresi del secolo XII.* Rome: Istituto storico per il Medio Evo, 1953.

May, William. "The Confession of Na Prous Boneta, Heretic and Heresiarch." In *Essays in Medieval Life and Thought,* edited by John Hine Mundy, 3–30. New York: Biblio and Tannen, 1965.

McHam, Sarah Blake. "The Cult of St. Anthony of Padua." In *Saints: Studies in Hagiography,* edited by Sandro Sticca, 216–32. Medieval and Renaissance Texts and Studies 141. Binghamton, NY: Medieval and Renaissance Texts and Studies, 1996.

Meersseman, Gilles-Gérard. "Les Confréries de Saint-Pierre Martyr." *AFP* 21 (1951): 51–196.

——. *Ordo Fraternitatis confraternite e pietà dei laici nel medioevo.* 3 vols. Rome: Herder, 1977.

Merlo, Grado. *Eretici ed eresie medievali.* Bologna: Il Mulino, 1989.

——. "Federico II, gli eretici, i frati." In *Federico II e le nuove culture: Atti del XXXI convegno storico internazionale, Todi, 9–12 ottobre 1994,* 45–67. Spoleto: Centro Italiano di studi sull'alto Medioevo, 1994.

——. "Il limite della diversità: Frati Predicatori ed eretici." In *Vita Religiosa im Mittelalter: Festschrift für Kaspar Elm zum 70. Geburtstag,* edited by Franz J. Felten and Nikolas Jaspert, 393–404. Berliner historische Studien 31; Ordensstudien 13. Berlin: Duncker and Humblot, 1999.

——. "Pietro di Verona, Difficoltà e proposte per lo studio di un inquisitore beatificato." In *Culto dei santi, istituzioni e classi sociali in età preindustriale,* edited by Sofia Boesch Gajano and Lucia Sebastiani, 471–88. L'Aquila, Italy: L. U. Japadre Editore, 1984.

——. *Valdesi e valdismi medievali: Itinerari e proposte di ricerca.* Turin: Claudiana, 1984.

Miller, Maureen C. *The Formation of a Medieval Church Ecclesiastical Change in Verona, 950–1150.* Ithaca, NY: Cornell University Press, 1993.

Moore, John C., and Brenda Bolton, eds. *Pope Innocent III and His World.* Aldershot: Ashgate, 1999.

Moore, R. I. "Between Sanctity and Superstition: Saints and Their Miracles in the Age of Revolution." In *The Work of Jacques Le Goff and the Challenges of Medieval History,* edited by Miri Rubin, 55–67. Woodbridge, Suffolk: Boydell and Brewer, 1997.

———. *The Formation of a Persecuting Society: Power and Deviance in Western Europe, 950–1250.* New York: Blackwell, 1987.

———. *Origins of European Dissent.* Toronto: University of Toronto Press, 1994; 1977.

———. *The War on Heresy: The Battle for Faith and Power in Medieval Europe.* London: Profile, 2012.

Moorman, John R. H. *A History of the Franciscan Order from Its Origins to the Year 1517.* Oxford: Clarendon, 1969.

Morris, Colin. *The Discovery of the Individual, 1050–1200.* New York: Harper and Row, 1972.

———. *The Papal Monarchy: The Western Church from 1050 to 1250.* Oxford History of the Christian Church. Edited by Henry and Owen Chadwick. Oxford: Clarendon, 1991.

———. "San Ranieri of Pisa: The Power and Limitations of Sanctity in Twelfth-Century Italy." *Journal of Ecclesiastical History* 45 (1994): 588–99.

Mortier, Daniel Antonin. *Histoire des maîtres généraux de l'Ordre des frères prêcheurs.* 8 vols. Paris: A. Picara, 1902–1920.

Mueller, Joan. *A Companion to Clare of Assisi.* Leiden: Brill, 2010.

———. *The Privilege of Poverty: Clare of Assisi, Agnes of Prague, and the Struggle for a Franciscan Rule for Women.* University Park, PA: Penn State University Press, 2006.

Muessig, Carolyn, ed. *Preacher, Sermon and Audience in the Middle Ages.* Boston: Brill, 2002.

———. "Sermon, Preacher and Society in the Middle Ages." *Journal of Medieval History* 28 (2002): 74–91.

Mulchahey, M. Michèle. *"First the Bow Is Bent in Study . . .": Dominican Education Before 1350.* Toronto: Pontifical Institute of Medieval Studies, 1998.

Müller, Wolfgang P. *Huguccio: The Life, Works, and Thought of a Twelfth-Century Jurist* Washington, DC: Catholic University Press, 1994.

Murray, Alexander. "Piety and Impiety in Thirteenth-Century Italy." *Studies in Church History* 8 (1972): 83–106.

———. *Suicide in the Middle Ages.* Oxford: Oxford University Press, 1998.

Nash, David. *Blasphemy in the Christian World: A History.* Oxford: Oxford University Press, 2010.

Newhauser, Richard. "Jesus as the First Dominican? Reflections on a Sub-Theme in the Exemplary Literature of Some Thirteenth-Century Preachers." In *Christ among the Medieval Dominicans: Representations of Christ in the Texts and*

Images of the Order of Preachers, edited by Kent Emery Jr., and Joseph Wawrykow, 238–55. Notre Dame, IN: University of Notre Dame Press.

Newman, Barbara. "The Heretic Saint: Guglielma of Bohemia, Milan, and Brunate." *Church History* 74, no. 1 (March 2005): 1–38.

Nold, Patrick. *Pope John XXII and His Franciscan Cardinal: Bertrand De La Tour and the Apostolic Poverty Controversy.* Oxford: Oxford University Press, 2003.

Nyberg, Tore. "The Canonization Process of St. Birgitta of Sweden." In *Procès de canonisation au moyen âge—Medieval Canonization Processes*, edited by Gábor Klaniczay, 67–85. Collection de l'école Française de Rome, 340. Rome: École Française de Rome, 2004.

Orioli, Raniero. *Venit perfidus heresiarca: Il movimento apostolico-dolciniano dal 1260 al 1307.* Rome: Istituto storico italiano per il Medio Evo, 1988.

Paciocco, Roberto. *Canonizzazioni e culto dei santi nella "Christianitas" (1198–1302).* Medioevo Francescano, Saggi 11. Assisi: Edizioni Porziuncola, 2006.

———. "Innocenzo IV e la santità, in Martire per la fede. San Pietro da Verona martire e inquisitore." In *Atti del Convegno storico nel 750o anniversario della morte (1252–2002), Milano, 24–26 ottobre 2002*, edited by Gianni Festa, 248–75. Bologna: Edizioni Studio Domenicano, 2007.

———. "Miracles and Canonized Sanctity in the 'First Life of St. Francis.'" *Greyfriars Review* 5, no. 2 (1991): 251–74.

———. "Perfette imperfezioni: Santità e rivendicazioni papali nell'Italia centrale intorno al 1252." *Studi medievali* 49 (2008): 711–27.

———. "Processi e canonizzazioni nel Duecento: Documenti e riflessioni a proposito di Filippo de Bourges." *Archivum Historiae Pontificiae* 40 (2003): 85–174.

———. "'Sine papae licentia non licet aliquem venerari pro sancto.'" La santità medievale tra processo romano-canonico e diplomatica pontificia. *Collectanea franciscana* 77 (2007): 265–311.

———. *"Sublimia Negotia" Le canonizzazioni dei santi nella curia papale e il nuovo Ordine dei frati Minori.* Padua: Centro Studi Antoniani, 1996.

———."'Virtus morum' e 'virtus signorum': La teoria della santità nelle lettere di canonizzazione di Innocenzo III." *Nuova rivista storica* 70 (1986): 597–610.

Paolini, Lorenzo. "Italian Catharism and Written Culture." In *Heresy and Literacy, 1000–1530*, edited by Peter Biller and Anne Hudson, 83–103. Cambridge Studies in Medieval Literature 23. Cambridge: Cambridge University Press, 1994.

———. *L'Eresia a Bologna fra XIII e XIV secolo.* 2 vols. Rome: Istituto storico Italiano per il medio evo, 1975.

Patschovsky, Alexander. "Heresy and Society: On the Political Function of Heresy in the Medieval World." In *Texts and the Repression of Medieval Heresy*, edited by Caterina Bruschi and Peter Biller, 23–41. York Studies in Medieval Theology 4. York: York Medieval Press, 2003.

———. "Konrad von Marburg und die Ketzer seiner Zeit." In *Sankt Elisabeth. Fürstin, Dienerin, Heilige. Aufsätze, Dokumentation, Katalog*, 70–77. Sigmaringen: Jan Thorbecke Verlag, 1981.

Pegg, Mark Gregory. *The Corruption of Angels: The Great Inquisition of 1245–1246.* Princeton, NJ: Princeton University Press, 2001.

———. *A Most Holy War: The Albigensian Crusade and the Battle for Christendom.* Oxford: Oxford University Press, 2008.

———. "On Cathars, Albigenses and Good Men of Languedoc." *Journal of Medieval History* 27, no. 2 (2001): 181–95.

Pellegrini, Letizia. *I Manoscritti dei predicatori.* Dissertationes Historicae 26, Institutum Historicum Fratrum Praedicatorum. Rome: Istituto storico Domenicano, 1999.

———. "Negotium imperfectum. Il processo per la canonizzazione di Ambrogio da Massa." *Societá e storia* 64 (1994): 253–78.

Pennington, Kenneth. *Popes, Canonists and Texts: 1150–1550.* Aldershot: Ashgate, 1993.

Peters, Edward. *Heresy and Authority in Medieval Europe: Documents in Translation.* Philadelphia: University of Pennsylvania Press, 1980.

Petersohn, Jürgen. "Die Litterae Papst Innocenz III zur Heiligsprechung der Kaiserin Kunigunde (1200)." *Jahrbuch für fränkische Landesforschung* 37 (1977): 1–25.

———. "Die päpstliche Kanonisationsdelegation des 11. Und 12. Jahrhunderts und die Heiligschrechung Karls der Grossen." In *Proceedings of the Fourth International Congress of Medieval Canon Law: Toronto, 21–25 August 1972,* edited by S. Kuttner, 163–206. Rome: Biblioteca Apostolica Vaticana, 1979.

———, ed. *Politik und Heiligenverehrung im Hochmittelalter.* Vorträge und Forschungen 42. Sigmaringen: Thorbecke, 1994.

Peterson, Janine Larmon. *Contested Sanctity: Disputed Saints, Inquisitors, and Communal Identity in Northern Italy, 1250–1400.* PhD diss., University of Indiana, 2006.

———. "Holy Heretics in Later Medieval Italy." *Past and Present* 204 (2009): 3–31.

Peyer, Hans Conrad. *Stadt und Stadtpatron im mittelalterlichen Italien.* Florence: Le Lettere, 1998.

Piacentini, Ernesto. "L'infallibilità papale nella canonizatione dei santi." *Miscellanea Franciscana* 91 (1991): 187–225.

———. *Santa Rosa da Viterbo: Culto liturgico e popolare, teologia, diritto, prassi canonica, devotione.* Viterbo: Biblioteca Archivio Monastero S. Rosa, 1999.

Platelle, Henri. "Crime et châtiment à Marchiennes: Etude sur la conception et le fonctionnement de la justice d'après les miracles de sainte Rictrude (XIIIe s.)." *Sacris Erudiri* 24 (1978–79): 156–202.

Praeger, Wilhelm. "Der Traktat des David von Augsburg über der Waldesier im Mittelalter." *Abhandlungen der Historischen Classe der Königlich Bayerischen Akademie der Wissenschaften* XIII (1877): 181–235.

Prinz, Friedrich. "Hagiographische Texte über Kult- und Wallfahrtsorte: Auftragsarbeit für kultpropaganda, persönliche Motivation, Rolle der Mönche." *Hagiographica* 1 (1994): 17–42.

Prudlo, Donald. "The Friars Preachers: The First Hundred Years of the Dominican Order." *History Compass* 8 (2010): 1275–90.

———. "The Living Rule: Monastic Exemplarity in Mendicant Hagiography." Forthcoming in an edition from Brepols, edited by Krijn Pansters.

——. *The Martyred Inquistior: The Life and Cult of Peter of Verona (†1252)*. Aldershot: Ashgate, 2008.

——. "Martyrs on the Move: The Spread of the Cults of Thomas of Canterbury and Peter of Verona." *Peregrinations* 3, no. 2 (Summer 2011): 32–62.

——. "Women, Wives, and Mystics: The Unexpected Patronage of a Dominican Martyr." Edited by Margaret Cormack. *Journal of the History of Sexuality* 21, no. 3 (May 2012): 313–24.

Pulignani, M. Faloci. "Il B. Simone da Collazzone e il suo processo." *Miscellanea Francescana* 12 (1910): 97–132.

Racine, Pierre. "Saint patron et religion civique en Italie: L'exemple Milanais." *Le moyen âge: Revue d'histoire et de philologie* 105, no. 2 (1999): 475–79.

Randolph, Daniel E. "The Desire for Martyrdom: A Leitmotif of St. Bonaventure." *Franciscan Studies* 10, no. 32 (1972): 74–87.

Rashdall, Hastings. *The Universities of Europe in the Middle Ages*. London: Oxford University Press, 1958.

Ratzinger, Joseph. "Der Einfluss des Bettelordensstreites auf die Entwicklung der Lehre vom päpstlichen Universalprimat, unter besonderer Berücksichtigung des heiligen Bonaventura." In *Theologie in Geschichte und Gegenwart*, edited by J. Auer and H. Volk, 697–724. Munich: K. Zink, 1957.

Reames, Sherry. *The Legenda Aurea: A Reexamination of Its Paradoxical History*. Madison: University of Wisconsin Press, 1985.

Reeves, Marjorie. *The Influence of Prophecy in the Later Middle Ages*. Oxford: Clarendon, 1969.

Regesta Pontificum Romanorum Inde ab a. post Christum Natum MCXCVIII ad a. MCCCIV. 2 vols. Ed. Augustus Potthast. Berlin: prostat in aedibus Rudolphi de Decker, 1875.

Reinburg, Virginia. "Praying to Saints in the Late Middle Ages." In *Saints: Studies in Hagiography*, edited by Sandro Sticca, 269–82. Medieval and Renaissance Texts and Studies 141. Binghamton, NY: Medieval and Renaissance Texts and Studies, 1996.

Rener, Monika. *Die Vita der heiligen Elisabeth des Dietrich von Apolda*. Marburg: Elwert Verlag, 1993.

Renna, Thomas. "St. Francis as Prophet in Celano and Bonaventure." *Michigan Academician: Papers of the Michigan Academy of Science, Arts, and Letters* 33, no. 4 (2002): 321–32.

Rézeau, Pierre. *Les prières aux saints en français à la fin du moyen âge*. Geneva: Librairie Droz, 1983.

Richards, Lily. "San Ranieri of Pisa: A Civic Cult and Its Expression in Text and Image." In *Art, Politics and Civic Religion in Central Italy, 1261–1352: Essays by Postgraduate Students at the Courtauld Institute of Art*, edited by Joanna Cannon and Beth Williamson, 179–235. Courtauld Research Papers 1. Aldershot: Ashgate, 2000.

Richter, Michael. "Procedural Aspects of the Canonization of Lorcán Ús Tuathail." In *Procès de canonisation au moyen âge—Medieval Canonization Processes*, edited by Gábor Klaniczay, 53–65. Collection de l'école Française de Rome, 340. Rome: École Française de Rome, 2004.

Rigon, Antonio. "Dévotion et patriotisme communal dans la genèse et la diffusion d'un culte: Le bienheureux Antoine de Padoue sournommé le 'Pellegrino' (†1267)." In *Faire croire: Modalités de la diffusion et de la réception des messages religieux du XII au XV siècle*, 259–78. Collection de l'École française de Rome, 51. Rome: École Français de Rome, 1981.

Rinaldi, Odorico. *Annalium Ecclesiasticorum Caesaris Baronii, Sacrae Romanae Ecclesiae Cardinalis, Continuatione Odorici Raynaldi*. Lucca: Typis Leonardi Venturini, 1740.

Ristori, Giovanni Battista. *I Paterini in Firenze nella prima metà del secolo XIII*. Rome: Libreria editrice Francesco Ferrari, 1905.

Roberts, Phyllis B. "Thomas Becket: The Construction and Deconstruction of a Saint from the Middle Ages to the Reformation." In *Models of Holiness in Medieval Sermons: Proceedings of the International Symposium (Kalamazoo, 4–7 May 1995)*, edited by Beverly Mayne Kienzle, 1–22. Textes et études du moyen âge 5. Louvain-la-Neuve: Fédération international des instituts d'études médiévales, 1996.

Robinson, Ian S. *The Papacy, 1073–1198: Continuity and Innovation*. Cambridge Medieval Textbooks. Cambridge: Cambridge University Press, 1991.

Robson, Michael. "Saint Bonaventure." In *The Medieval Theologians*, edited by G. R. Evans, 187–200. Oxford: Blackwell, 2001.

Rosser, Gervase. "The Miraculous Image in Medieval Italy: Religious Cult and Source of Social Justice." *Zeszyty Naukowe Uniwersytetu Jagielloñskiego: Prace Historyczne* 128 (2000): 7–18.

Rottenwöhrer, Gerhard. *Der Katharismus*. 4 vols. in 6. Bad Honnef: Bock + Herchen, 1982.

Rousseau, Ludovicus. *De Ecclesiastico Officio Fratrum Praedicatorum Secundum Ordinationem Humberti de Romanis*. Rome: A. Manuzio, 1927.

Rubin, Miri. "Choosing Death? Experiences of Martyrdom in Late Medieval Europe." *Studies in Church History* 30 (1993): 153–83.

——. *Corpus Christi: The Eucharist in Late Medieval Culture*. Cambridge: Cambridge University Press, 1991.

——. "Fraternities and Lay Piety in the Later Middle Ages." In *Einungen und Bruderschaften in der spätmittelalterlichen Stadt*, edited by Peter Johanek, 185–98. Städteforschung: Veröffentlichungen des Instituts für vergleichende Städtegeschichte in Münster, Reihe A: Darstellungen 32. Cologne: Böhlau, 1993.

Russo, Daniel. "Des saints et des stigmates: A propos de saint François d'Assise et de saint Pierre de Vérone, martyr: Iconographie et projet de Chrétienté au XIIe siècle." *Les Cahiers de l'Herne* 75 (2001): 55–70.

Ryan, James D. "Missionary Saints of the High Middle Ages: Martyrdom, Popular Veneration, and Canonization." *Catholic Historical Review* 90, no. 1 (January 2004): 1–28.

Sackville, Lucy J. *Heresy and Heretics in the Thirteenth Century: The Textual Representations*. Heresy and Inquisition in the Middle Ages 1. York: York Medieval Press, 2011.

Sankt Elisabeth: Fürstin, Dienerin, Heilige: Aufsätze, Dokumentation, Katalog. Sigmaringen: Thorbecke, 1981.

Schatz, Klaus. *Papal Primacy: From Its Origins to the Present.* Collegeville, MN: Liturgical Press, 1996.

Schenk, Max. *Die Unfehlbarkeit des Papstes in der Heiligsprechung: Ein Beitrag zur Erhellung der theologiegeschichtlichen Seite der Frage.* Freiburg, Switzerland: Paulusverlag, 1965.

Schimmelpfennig, Bernhard. "Die Berücksichtigung von Kanonisationen in den kurialen Zeremonienbüchern des 14. Und 15. Jarhhunderts." In *Procès de canonisation au moyen âge—Medieval Canonization Processes,* edited by Gábor Klaniczay, 245–57. Collection de l'école Française de Rome, 340. Rome: École Française de Rome, 2004.

———. *The Papacy.* New York: Columbia University Press, 1992.

———. *Die Zeremonialbücher der römischen Kurie im Mittelalter.* Tübingen: M. Niemeyer, 1973.

Schlafke, Jacob. *De competentia in causis sanctorum decernendi a primis post Christum natum saeculis usque ad annum 1234.* Rome: Officium Libri Catholici, 1961.

Schmitt, Jean-Claude. "De bon usage du 'Credo.'" In *Faire croire: Modalités de la diffusion et de la réception des messages religieux du XIIIe au XVe siècle,* 337–61. Rome: École Français de Rome, 1981.

———. *The Holy Greyhound: Guinefort, Healer of Children since the Thirteenth Century.* Cambridge: Cambridge University Press, 1983; 2009.

———. "Les Reliques et les images." In *Les Reliques: Objets, cultes, symbols; Actes du colloque international de l'Université du Littoral-Côte d'Opale (Boulogne-sur-Mer) 4–6 septembre 1997,* edited by Edina Bozóky and Anne-Marie Helvétius, 145–67. Hagiologia: Études sur la sainteté en occident / Studies on Western Sainthood 1. Turnhout: Brepols, 1999.

Schmucki, Octavian. *The Stigmata of St. Francis of Assisi: A Critical Investigation in the Light of Thirteenth-Century Sources.* Translated by Canisius F. Connors. St. Bonaventure, NY: Franciscan Institute, 1991.

Schneyer, Johannes Baptist. *Repertorium der lateinischen Sermones des Mittelalters für die Zeit von 1150–1350.* 13 vols. Munster-Westfalen: Aschendorffsche, 1969–1990.

Scholz, Bernard W. "The Canonization of Edward the Confessor." *Speculum* 36, no. 1 (January 1961): 38–60.

Schürer, Markus. "Die Findung des Heiligen. Dominikus von Guzmán und Petrus Martyr als Figuren zwischen Topik und Singularität." In *Das Eigene und das Ganze. Zum Individuellen im mittelalterlichen Religiosentum,* edited by Gert Melville and Markus Schürer, 339–77. Münster: Lit, 2002.

Schwerhoff, Gerd. *Zungen wie Schwerter: Blasphemie in alteuropäischen Gesellschaften 1200–1650.* Konstanz: UVK, 2005.

Sharpe, Richard and Alan Thacker. *Local Saints and Local Churches in the Early Medieval West.* Oxford: Oxford University Press, 2002.

Siegel, Arthur. "Italian Society and the Origins of Eleventh-Century Western Heresy." In *Heresy and the Persecuting Society in the Middle Ages,* edited by Michael Frassetto, 43–73. Leiden: Brill, 2006.

Sieger, Marcus. *Die Heiligsprechung: Geschichte und heutige Rechtslage.* Wurzburg: Echter, 1995.

Sigal, Pierre-André. *L'Homme et le miracle dans la France médiévale*. Paris: Cerf, 1985.

——. *Les Marcheurs de dieu, pèlerinages et pèlerins au moyen âge*. Paris: A. Colin, 1974.

——. "Naissance et premier développement d'un vinage exceptionnel: L'eau de saint Thomas." *Cahiers de civilisation médiévale, Xe–XIIe siècles* 44, no. 1 (2001): 35–44.

——. "Un aspect du culte des saints: le châtiment divin aux XIe et XIIe siècles, d'après la littérature hagiographique du Midi du France." In *La religion populaire en Languedoc du XIIIe à la moitié du XIVe siècle*, edited by M.-H. Vicaire, 49–59. Toulouse: Cahiers du Fanjeaux 11, 1976.

Smith, Damian J. "Saint Rosendo, Cardinal Hyacinth, and the Almohads." *Journal of Medieval Iberian Studies* 1, no. 1 (January 2009): 53–67.

Smoller, Laura A. "Miracle, Memory, and Meaning in the Canonization of Vincent Ferrer, 1453–1454." *Speculum* 73, no. 2 (1998): 429–54.

——. "Northern and Southern Sanctity in the Canonization of Vincent Ferrer: The Effects of Procedural Differences on the Image of the Saint." In *Procès de canonisation au moyen âge—Medieval Canonization Processes*, edited by Gábor Klaniczay, 289–308. Collection de l'école Française de Rome, 340. Rome: École Française de Rome, 2004.

Snoek, Godefridus. *Medieval Piety from Relics to the Eucharist: A Process of Mutual Interaction*. New York: Brill, 1995.

Spedalieri, Franciscus. *De Ecclesia Infallibilitate in Canonizatione Sanctorum: Quaestiones Selectae*. Rome: Officium Catholici Libri, 1949.

Stancliffe, Clare E. "Red, White and Blue Martyrdom." In *Ireland in Early Mediaeval Europe: Studies in Memory of Kathleen Hughes*, edited by Dorothy Whitelock, Rosamond McKitterick, and David Dumville, 21–46. Cambridge: Cambridge University Press, 1982.

Straw, Carole. "Martyrdom and Christian Identity: Gregory the Great, Augustine and Tradition." In *The Limits of Ancient Christianity: Essays on Late Antique Thought and Culture in Honor of R.A. Markus*, edited by William E. Klingshirn and Mark Vessey, 250–66. Recentiores: Later Latin Texts and Contexts. Ann Arbor: University of Michigan Press, 1999.

Sumption, Jonathan. *Pilgrimage: An Image of Medieval Religion*. London: Rowman and Littlefield, 1975.

Tanner, Norman, and Sethina Watson. "Least of the Laity: The Minimum Requirements for a Medieval Christian." *Journal of Medieval History* 32, no. 4 (December 2006): 395–423.

Taylor, Claire. *Heresy in Medieval France: Dualism in Aquitaine and the Agenais, 1000–1249*. London: Boydell and Brewer, 2005.

——. "The Letter of Héribert of Périgord as a Source for Dualist Heresy in the Society of Early Eleventh-Century Aquitaine." *Journal of Medieval History* 26 (2000): 313–49.

Thacker, Alan, and Richard Sharpe, eds. *Local Saints and Local Churches in the Middle Ages*. Oxford: Oxford University Press, 2002.

Thompson, Augustine, O.P. *Cities of God: The Religion of the Italian Communes, 1125–1325*. University Park, PA: Penn State University Press, 2005.

——. *Francis of Assisi: A New Biography*. Ithaca, NY: Cornell University Press, 2012.

——. *Revival Preachers and Politics in Thirteenth-Century Italy: The Great Devotion of 1233*. Oxford: Clarendon, 1992.

Thomson, Williell R. "The Earliest Cardinal-Protectors of the Franciscan Order: A Study in Administrative History, 1210–1261." *Studies in Medieval and Renaissance History* 9 (1972): 21–80.

——. *Friars in the Cathedral: The First Franciscan Bishops 1226–1261*. Toronto: Pontifical Institute of Mediaeval Studies, 1998.

Tierney, Brian. [Untitled Exchange with Alfons Stickler] *Catholic Historical Review* 60 (1974): 427–41; and *Catholic Historical Review* 61 (1975): 265–79.

——. *Origins of Papal Infallibility, 1150–1350: A Study on the Concepts of Infallibility, Sovereignty and Tradition in the Middle Ages*. Leiden: Brill, 1972.

Tillman, Helene. *Pope Innocent III*. Translated by Walter Sax. New York: North-Holland, 1980.

Tocco, Felice. *Quel che non c'è nella divina commedia o Dante e l'eresia*. Bologna: Nicola Zanichelli, 1899.

Töpfer, Berhard. "The Cult of Relics and Pilgrimage in Burgundy and Aquitaine at the Time of the Monastic Reform." In *The Peace of God: Social Violence and Religious Response in France Around the Year 1000*, edited by Thomas Head and Richard Landes, 41–57. Ithaca, NY: Cornell University Press, 1992.

Torrell, Jean-Pierre, O.P. *Saint Thomas Aquinas*. Translated by Robert Royal. Washington, DC: Catholic University of America Press, 1996.

Touron, Anthony, O.P. *The First Disciples of Saint Dominic*. Translated by Victor F. O'Daniel, O.P. Somerset, OH: Rosary Press, 1928.

Toynbee, Margaret. *Saint Louis of Toulouse and the Process of Canonization in the Fourteenth Century*. Manchester: Manchester University Press, 1929.

Traver, Andrew. "The Forging of an Intellectual Defense of Mendicancy in the Medieval University." In *The Origin, Development, and Refinement of Medieval Religious Mendicancies*, edited by Donald S. Prudlo, 157–96. Leiden: Brill, 2011.

Tugwell, Simon. "L'Evolution des Vitae Fratrum." *Cahiers de Fanjeaux* 36 (2001): 415–18.

——. *The Way of the Preacher*. London: Darton, Longman, and Todd, 1979.

Tunberg, M. Sven. "[Commentary]." *Analecta Bollandiana* 63 (1945): 273.

Turner, Victor. *The Ritual Process: Structure and Anti-Structure*. Ithaca, NY: Cornell University Press, 1982.

——, and Edith Turner. *Image and Pilgrimage in Christian Culture: Anthropological Perspectives*. New York: Columbia University Press, 1978.

Ullmann, Walter. *The Growth of Papal Government in the Middle Ages: A Study in the Ideological Relation of Clerical to Lay Power*. London: Methuen, 1970.

Urry, William. *Saint Anselm and His Cult at Canterbury*. Paris: J. Vrin, 1959.

d'Urso, Giacinto. *Beato Ambrogio Sansedoni*. Siena: Biblioteca cateriniana, 1986.

Van Engen, John. "The Christian Middle Ages as an Historigraphical Problem." *American Historical Review* 91 (1986): 519–52.

——. "Dominic and the Brothers: Vita as Life-Forming Exempla in the Order of Preachers." In *Christ among the Medieval Dominicans*, edited by Kent Emery

Jr., and Joseph Wawrykow, 7–25. Notre Dame, IN: Notre Dame University Press, 1993.

———. "Observations on *De Consecratione.*" *Proceedings of the Sixth International Congress of Medieval Canon Law* (1985): 309–20.

Vauchez, André. "La commune de Sienne, les ordres mendiants et le culte des saints: Histoire et enseignements d'une crise." *Mélanges d'archéologie et d'histoire publiés par l'école française de Rome* 89 (1977): 757–67.

———. "L'historiographie des hérésies médiévales." In *L'Ogre historien: Autour de Jacques Le Goff,* edited by Jacques Revel and Jean-Claude Schmitt, 243–58. Paris: Editions Gallimard, 1998.

———. "Jacques de Voragine et les saints du XII s. dans la Legende dorée." In *Legenda aurea: Sept siècles de diffusion,* edited by Brenda Dunn-Lardeau, 27–56. Montreal: Editions Bellarmin, 1983.

———. *The Laity in the Middle Ages.* Translated by Margery J. Schneider. Notre Dame, IN: University of Notre Dame Press, 1993.

———. *Omobono di Cremona (1197): Laico e santo, profilo storico.* Cremona: Nuova editrice cremonese, 2001.

———. *Sainthood in the Later Middle Ages.* Translated by Jean Birrell. Cambridge: Cambridge University Press, 1997.

———. "Saints admirables et saints imitables: Les fonctions de l'hagiographie ont-elles changés aux derniers siècles du Moyen Âge?." In *Les Fonctions des saints dans le monde occidental (IIIe–XIIIe siècle): Actes du colloque organisé par l'École française de Rome avec le concours de l'Université de Rome "La Sapienza," Rome, 27–29 octobre 1988,* 161–72. Collection de l'École française de Rome 149. Rome: École Française de Rome, 1991.

———. "The Stigmata of St. Francis and Its Medieval Detractors." *Greyfriars Review* 13, no. 1 (1999): 61–89.

———. "Une campagne de pacification en Lombardie autour de 1233." *Mélanges d'archéologie et d'histoire publiés par l'école française de Rome* 78 (1966): 519–49.

Vicaire, M. H. *Histoire de Saint Dominique.* 2 vols. Paris: Éditions du Cerf, 1957.

———. *Saint Dominic and His Times.* Translated by Kathleen Pond. New York: McGraw-Hill, 1964.

Villemagne, Augustin. *Bullaire du bienheureux Pierre de Castelnau: Martyr de la foi (16 février 1208).* Montpellier: Imprimerie de la Manuf de la Charité, 1917.

Wakefield, Walter L. "Burial of Heretics in the Middle Ages." *Heresis* 5 (December 1985): 29–32.

———. *Heresy, Crusade, and Inquisition in Southern France, 1100–1250.* Berkeley: University of California Press, 1974.

Wakefield, Walter L., and Austin P. Evans, trans. *Heresies of the High Middle Ages.* New York: Columbia University Press, 1991.

Walther, Helmut G. "Ziele und Mittel Papstlicher Ketzerpolitik in der Lombardei und im Kirchenstaat 1184–1252." In *Die Anfange der Inquisition im Mittelalter,* edited by Peter Segl, 103–30. Vienna: Bohlau Verlag, 1993. 103–30.

Walz, Angelus. *Compendium Historiae Ordinis Praedicatorum.* Rome: Herder, 1930.

Ward, Benedicta. *Miracles and the Medieval Mind: Theory, Record, and Event, 1000–1215.* Philadelphia: University of Pennsylvania Press, 1982.

Webb, Diana M. "Friends of the Family: Some Miracles for Children by Italian Friars." *Studies in Church History* 31 (1994): 183–95.

———. *Medieval European Pilgrimage, c. 700–c. 1500.* New York: Palgrave, 2002.

———. *Patrons and Defenders: The Saints in the Italian Cities.* London: Tauris, 1996.

Weinstein, Donald, and Rudolf Bell. *Saints and Society: The Two Worlds of Western Christendom: 1000–1700.* Chicago: University of Chicago Press, 1982.

Weitlauff, Manfred, ed. *Bischof Ulrich von Augsburg, 890–973: Seine Zeit- sein Leben- seine Verehrung; Festschrift aus Anlass des tausendjährigen Jubiläums seiner Kanonisation im Jahre 993.* Jarbuch des Vereins für Augsburger Bistumsge-schichte 26–27. Weissenhorn, Bavaria: A. H. Konrad, 1993.

Wetzstein, Thomas. "Audivimus (X 3.45.1) and the Double Failure of Raymundus de Peñafort." Edited by Uta-Renate Blumenthal, Kenneth Pennington, and Atria A. Larson. *Proceedings of the Twelfth International Congress of Medieval Canon Law: Washington, D.C. 1–7 August 2004.* Vatican City: Biblioteca Apostolica Vaticana, 2008.

———. *Heilige vor Gericht: Das Kanonisationsverfahren im europäischen Spätmittelalter.* Cologne: Böhlau Verlag, 2004.

———. " 'Iura novit curia' Zur Verfahrensnormierung der Kanonisationsprozesse sed späten Mittelalters." In *Procès de canonisation au moyen âge—Medieval Canoniza-tion Processes,* edited by Gábor Klaniczay, 259–87. Collection de l'école Française de Rome, 340. Rome: École Française de Rome, 2004.

Whalen, Brett Edward. *Dominion of God: Christendom and Apocalypse in the Middle Ages.* Cambridge, MA: Harvard University Press, 2009.

Wilken, Robert Louis. *The Spirit of Early Christian Thought.* New Haven, CT: Yale University Press, 2003.

Wilson, Stephen, ed. *Saints and Their Cults.* Cambridge: Cambridge University Press, 1984.

Winroth, Anders. *The Making of Gratian's Decretum.* Cambridge: Cambridge University Press, 2000.

Witkowska, Alexandra. "The Thirteenth-Century 'Miracula' of St. Stanislaus, Bishop of Krakow." In *Procès de canonisation au moyen âge—Medieval Canon-ization Processes,* edited by Gábor Klaniczay, 149–63. Collection de l'école Française de Rome, 340. Rome: École Française de Rome, 2004.

Wolf, Kenneth Baxter. *Life and Afterlife of Elizabeth of Hungary: Testimony from Her Canonization Hearings.* Oxford: Oxford University Press, 2010.

Zanella, Gabriele. *Itinerari ereticali: Patari e Catari tra Rimini e Verona.* Rome: Istituto storico italiano per il Medio Evo, 1986.

———. *Hereticalia: Temi e discussioni.* Spoleto: Centro di studi sull'Alto Medioevo, 1995.

☙ INDEX

CPSIA information can be obtained
at www.ICGtesting.com
Printed in the USA
LVOW08*2332050717
540365LV00006B/122/P